W9-BCV-499

EUROPE

The Superregions

N
W E
S

AND

RUSSIA

ki

allinn
ONIA

ga
VIA

UANIA
s

Moscow

Kiev

UKRAINE

Caspian Sea

MANIA

Bucharest

Black Sea

ASIA MINOR

EUROPE ADRIFT

EUROPE ADRIFT

John Newhouse

A Council on Foreign Relations Book

PANTHEON BOOKS NEW YORK

For Symmie

The Council on Foreign Relations, Inc., a nonprofit, nonpartisan national membership organization founded in 1921, is dedicated to promoting understanding of international affairs through the free and civil exchange of ideas. The Council's members are dedicated to the belief that America's peace and prosperity are firmly linked to that of the world. From this flows the mission of the Council: to foster America's understanding of its fellow members of the international community— their peoples, cultures, histories, hopes, quarrels, and ambitions—and thus to serve, protect, and advance America's own global interests through study and debate. The Council takes no institutional position on policy issues and has no affiliation with the United States government. All statements of fact and expressions of opinion contained in its publications are the sole responsibility of the author(s).

John Newhouse held the Council's Whitney H. Shepardson Fellowship in 1996.

Permissions acknowledgments are on the facing page.

A portion of Chapter II originally appeared in *Foreign Affairs*.

Library of Congress Cataloging-in-Publication Data
Newhouse, John.
Europe adrift / John Newhouse.
p. cm.
Includes bibliographical references and index.
ISBN 0-679-43370-8
1. Europe—Politics and government—1989– 2. Europe—Economic policy.
3. European Union. I. Title.
D2009.N5 1997
320.94—dc21   97-2943
CIP

Random House Web Address: http://www.randomhouse.com
Book design by Chris Welch
Printed in the United States of America
First Edition
2 4 6 8 9 7 5 3 1

PERMISSIONS ACKNOWLEDGMENTS

Grateful acknowledgment is made to the following for permission to reprint previously published material:

The Economist: Excerpts from "Return of the Habsburg" from the "Survey of Central Europe" (*The Economist*, 11/18/95, p. 5). Copyright © 1995 by The Economist Newspaper Group, Inc. Excerpts from "Launching Deutsche Telekom" (*The Economist*, 10/26/96, p. 73). Copyright © 1996 by The Economist Newspaper Group, Inc. Reprinted by permission of *The Economist*.

Foreign Affairs: Excerpt from "Powershift" by Jessica Matthews (*Foreign Affairs*, Jan./Feb. 1997). Copyright © 1997 by the Council on Foreign Relations, Inc. Reprinted by permission of *Foreign Affairs*.

The New York Times: Excerpts from "In a Search for Turkishness" by Celestine Bohlen (*The New York Times*, 5/18/96). Copyright © 1996 by the New York Times Co. Excerpts from "Reimagining Berlin" by Paul J. Goldberger (*The New York Times*, 2/5/95). Copyright © 1995 by The New York Times Co. Reprinted by permission of *The New York Times*.

Transaction Publishers: Excerpts from "Germany's Social and Political Culture" by Michael Mertens (*Daedalus*, Winter 1994). All rights reserved. Reprinted by permission of Transaction Publishers.

CONTENTS

Contents

PREFACE

For most of the first half of this century, Europe was enfeebled by the effects of two vastly destructive hot wars. The second half was, of course, dominated by the Cold War. The purpose of this book is to show how Europe is trying to find its way through the heavy wake of this singular experience: to describe the effects of German unification on Germany and its neighbors, starting with France; to explore the question of whether Russian weakness would become a bigger problem than Soviet power had presented; to determine whether rechristening the European Community as the European Union would rally the listless movement toward integration; and to discover the prospects for enlarging Europe's best club to include newly independent and democratic societies further east.

With the Cold War a memory, I wanted to see if Europe's dependence on America's leadership and military presence would diminish, and if the trio of key countries—Germany, France, and Britain—might be able to exercise some joint leadership; for example, whether these three and their partners could jointly arrange to settle, or neutralize, explosive problems in the Mediterranean, especially those that pit Turkey against Greece. I wanted to examine how governments were dealing with the streams of unwanted refugees who were provoking a political backlash in some countries. And I wanted to know if growing impatience with national governments and the European Union meant that regional and city governments in Europe were acquiring greater scope and authority. Briefly, I wanted to find out how Europe was reacting to the dramatic change in its affairs that the Cold War left behind.

When I took on the book, my point of view—uncomplicated and unremarkable—could be described as follows: The outbreak of World War I was the beginning of the end of Europe's dominance of the world's affairs. The arrival of American troops in 1917 put the handwriting on the wall. America and Europe lost the peace, but America became the pivotal force in world affairs during and after World War II. Although much of what lies ahead is obviously unclear, chances are that Europe will not again play a dominant role in world affairs; its influence will in the foreseeable future depend on the nature and quality of its relationship with the United States.

Writing is a learning experience, and I am indebted to the people who enriched my understanding of how Europeans are coping, or not coping, with the new era, one that bears some resemblance to the confusion of the post-Bismarckian era. Much of this book draws upon information obtained in innumerable interviews and conversations, and some of which were "on background" with people who therefore could not be identified.

A number of organizations and some individuals helped along the way, and I feel a deep sense of gratitude to the following: The Brookings Institution of which I have been a guest scholar over the past several years; the Alfred P. Sloan Foundation and especially Arthur Singer, its vice president emeritus, who arranged support for this book, as he did for my last one.

I owe a special debt to Nicholas Rizopoulos who nominated me for the Whitney H. Shepardson Fellowship at the Council on Foreign Relations in New York. This award allowed me—obliged me, actually—to present drafts of some chapters to a group of rigorous, knowledgeable critics. However, no one who participated in these exhaustive sessions exceeded the chairman—Nick himself—in knowledge and rigor in dealing with the issues.

I am equally grateful to Frank Loy who in his former capacity as president of the German Marshall Fund arranged grant support for the book. Additional support was provided by the Twentieth Century Fund. The Friedrich Ebert Stiftung covered the expenses of one of my numerous trips to Europe in connection with research for the book.

The people who have been named in the acknowledgments, along with those who took part in the Shepardson sessions, bear no responsibility for the book's point of view or its conclusions. That is mine alone.

A final note of thanks to Erroll McDonald, executive editor at Pantheon for his commitment to the book and his help. I also want to thank Altie Karper, the managing editor at Pantheon, for her help and her patience.

May 1997

EUROPE
ADRIFT

EUROPE REDEFINING ITSELF

W estern Europe had a good Cold War. Societies ravaged by hot war recovered their moorings and built a community aimed at overcoming centuries of strife and disunity, mainly by reconciling France and Germany. Indeed, West Germans, besides sinking sturdy democratic roots, developed a culture of truly Scandinavian passivity. The threat from the east obliged Western Europeans to huddle together and helped them break bad habits. America's military forces insulated them from the threat and, to a degree, from reality. For different reasons, two of the three key countries—Britain and Germany—came to feel as much like wards as allies, whereas the third, France, while no less reliant on American guarantees, rejected the role of junior partner and insisted on having what various among its leaders called, rather extravagantly, "free hands."

With the simple certitudes of the Cold War a swiftly fading memory, Europe is now redefining itself in ways that most Europeans don't recognize, partly because there exists no precedent for the hodgepodge that seems to be emerging. It isn't a Europe of self-contained, independent states, nor is it a cohesive European Union (EU). Power is shifting unevenly among national capitals, Brussels-based institutions of the EU, and, most conspicuously, regional centers. The trends are fairly clear, Europe's capacity for seriously affecting them increasingly feeble. Little political or moral leadership is being exercised in most capitals. In London, Prime Minister Tony Blair's government does have energy and some direction, not to mention a strong mandate. Still, there is no agreement, let alone a shared vision, on how Europe in its various parts should be organized. Briefly, what we have is a deeply transitional moment that bears no resemblance to earlier European watersheds.

The threat from Moscow has been replaced by more familiar uncertainties and traditional sources of instability—ethnic passions, territorial disputes, myopia, limp leadership. There is a surface similarity to the pre–World War I setting: an unstable, chaotic Russia; an increasingly dominant Germany; tension and instability in the Balkans; the inability of Europe's oldest nation-states—France and Britain—to act together on their own behalf. One is reminded of what was said about the Bourbon kings: "Nothing learned, nothing forgotten."

Put differently, Europeans appear to lack a purchase on events and in that sense are about where they were at the start of the century. One of the more apprehensive European notables, Václav Havel, observes that "Europe today lacks an ethos; it lacks imagination, it lacks generosity. . . . Europe does not appear to have achieved a genuine and profound sense of responsibiity for itself."[1]

While European societies were creating the world's highest living standards, economic growth trailed off and unemployment rose. To protect themselves politically and maintain social peace, governments went on expanding the social safety nets. Demographics drove up the costs of financing ultramunificent European welfare states, starting with pensions and medical care. Rising employment costs, driven by inflated social benefits, caused employers to substitute capital for labor. Governments added to the strain on pension systems by encouraging early retirement. Now serious long-term unemployment, along with middle-class job insecurity and increasingly heavy pressure on the plush social wage and safety net, threatens stability and has further eroded the confidence of Europe's leadership.

The message delivered by France's electorate to its president, Jacques Chirac, in the snap legislative elections of June 1997 wasn't lost on governments. Chirac wanted a fresh mandate so as to impose the belt tightening that French membership in a European monetary union (EMU) would require. But France's voters, most importantly the younger voters, chose to reject their government and protect their safety net. Like most other Continentals, they intend to prolong the twilight of the welfare state.

What matters most in Europe now is not so much what is happening as what isn't. The various governments of the EU feel themselves too weak either to take controversial steps or to expose differences between themselves and other members. Their preoccupation now is European monetary union, partly because there are no other joint projects being undertaken seriously. But monetary union may, ironically, create disunity in the form of a three-tiered structure: the handful of countries which, because they meet the entry requirements, become members; those which are turned away but feel as if they do meet the requirements or are close enough to be judged in compliance; the laggards who, for as far as the eye can see, will be unable to take part.

The quest for monetary union and a single currency is posing large risks, mainly because Bonn and Paris have established it as a make-or-break issue for a cohesive EU, and even for the special Franco-German relationship. Not much else is clear, except that

Europe is despondent and confused. We have been through periods of Europessimism and Euroweariness before—as recently as a decade ago, in fact. Europe may one day recover its poise and balance, although this time the process is sure to be more gradual and protracted and, unlike the more recent "down" cycles, only after serious change has occurred.

Few, if any, national frontiers will change, but the political landscape is being redrawn as countries and regions within them move, like iron filings, toward different magnets. "Europe" is no longer Western Europe, although its actual contours are as yet unclear. Not so long ago, members of the EU were consumed by an argument over whether it should deepen—that is, integrate—or widen itself. The argument is over. Most of Scandinavia has since entered the fold, and much of east-central Europe should eventually come in, although which countries and how soon is far from clear.

The borders of central and eastern Europe invite notice, because the societies there are recovering their pasts. The collapse of the Soviet empire repealed four decades of experience with Moscow's yoke and revived ethnic and nationality groups whose quarrels had set Europe on its self-destructive course early in the century. The past lies nearer the surface in eastern Europe than elsewhere. Progress may be measured against some better time—a moment of glory, however brief, a moment of humiliation, however distant, is not easily forgiven, let alone forgotten. But most of today's eastern Europeans regard themselves as belonging to Europe, not to a well-worn regional bloc. They tend to be absorbed by the present and unruffled by shadows of the past. Travelers are finding more optimism in Prague, Warsaw, and Budapest than in Paris, Brussels, and Berlin.

WITH THE EXTERNAL pressure of the Cold War gone, the role of central governments is diminishing. Europe's democratic societies are being fragmented and factionalized politically, culturally, and linguistically. Mainstream political parties are losing support and credibility. The institutions of government are under even heavier pressure. At varying speeds and in varying degrees, authority is drifting down from national capitals to provinces and cities. Regionalism, whether within or across national borders, appears to be Europe's current and perhaps future dynamic. Its sources vary, although in many places it is seen as a protest against the authority of national capitals by people who see themselves as belonging, historically and otherwise, more to "Europe" than to a nation-state of clouded origins and dubious boundaries.

Officials in some provincial cities see the growing regional sentiment as a reaction to burdensome regulations descending from EU headquarters in Brussels. Yet many regional leaders and officials are self-professed Europeans; they talk about bypassing national capitals and dealing directly with Brussels.

In a time of global trade and capital flows, not to mention information highways, local entities feel better placed to manage their affairs than distant bureaucracies, whether located in national capitals or Brussels. The German state of Baden-Württemberg, for example, is making its own foreign and trade policies; it has signed several hundred agreements with other regions and entities. In this more freewheeling environment, bankers and industrial planners have begun to regard Europe as much as a group of distinct economic regions as an assortment of nation-states.

Regions within several EU member countries are watching one another develop agendas for dealing with problems such as reconciliation of economic growth with regional environmental quality; the relationship among learning, technology, and competitiveness; the social consequences of immigration, ethnic diversity, AIDS, drugs, and organized crime.

Some regional figures cite inequities arising from the disparate sizes of EU members. They ask why Luxembourg, for example, should have the benefits of membership when it is so much smaller than any number of cities in other member countries. Some of these same figures envisage a large European free-trade area built around resurrected city-states. Various others see the future as a series of interconnected regional systems, including, say, a Hanseatic League built roughly around its original northern European membership. Another system would link a group of cities along and behind the Mediterranean littoral; it would stretch from Barcelona on the western fringe to Turin and Milan in the east.

With various regions acquiring, or trying to acquire, separate identities, another question is whether some of them will tilt against one another as in the past. Old ethnic lines are emerging and not just in historically troubled and volatile areas. Some Bavarians, for example, worry aloud about what they see as an increasingly ethnic cast to regionalism at home. But another and probably better way of thinking about regionalism is to recognize that in Western Europe the Cold War was accompanied by a vastly successful process of modernization that blurred regional cultures. The revival of these cultures and various old languages, which is now under way, is in part a protest against all that, albeit a benign protest in most places.

THE REACH, INFLUENCE, and confidence of all EU countries are declining, except in Germany, where it is rising. France is the biggest loser in Germany's reemergence as Europe's strongest power, simply because it had the most to lose. All members used to be equal except France; now it is Germany that is more equal than the others. "If you ask any European country to identify its most important relationship, the answer would be [with] Germany, although through clenched teeth in a few cases," says an experienced British diplomat.

Germany is now unlikely to concede bits of sovereignty to EU institutions solely in return for rehabilitation and a quiet time with

France and other members. For the first time in its history, Germany is surrounded by congenial neighbors and markets. With Austria and most of the Scandinavian societies adhering to the EU and with the Benelux countries already there, Germany lies at the center of interconnecting arcs that may become an informal but distinct regional group; Bonn would like to move the boundary of this bloc eastward so as to transmute the societies of central Europe into market democracies capable of taking on the responsibilities of EU membership, a status that would establish them as a reliable buffer zone to the east. "Germans want to look east and see west," as some bemused Europeans put it.

French leadership has tried on occasion to use the EU to tie down a united Germany while it is still led by Helmut Kohl, a Rhenish Catholic chancellor who governs in the tradition of Konrad Adenauer, the father figure for whom reconciliation with France was a sacred charge. Kohl has been willing to meet France at least halfway. Like Adenauer, he distrusts his fellow Germans and would like to make the EU's deepening process irreversible, thereby ensuring a Europeanized Germany. Kohl and like-minded Germans feel that by pushing in this direction their country is not just breaking with the past but for the first time is doing the right thing for Europe. Still, Kohl is one of many Germans, along with many non-Germans, who worry that he may be the last chancellor who will seek to create this kind of Europe. And anything much less, they fear, could and probably would lead gravitationally to a dominant Berlin Republic—a Germanized Europe, the reality or mere perception of which could produce anti-German coalitions and a pattern of behavior that would recall the more fractious Europe of the past. "We need the constraints of further integration so as to avoid terrifying the others," says a senior German official. "Our comfort level increases with more integration. We can hide behind the EU on, say, Middle East policy. We don't have one of our own and haven't needed one. We don't want a renationalization of foreign policy or security policy."

These are the views of true believers—the political class's "Europeans," whom dissenting members deride as "fundamentalists." The Europeanists tend to dismiss their critics as people who think Germany should aspire to be no more than "a big, rich Switzerland," as some of them put it. Until quite recently, Germans avoided discussing the so-called national interest. Now people are talking about the national interest and where it lies. The country's EU policy, for example, was always made within the cabinet and attracted little public interest. That's changed, and a change in policy is also in the air.

After debating a basic policy interest, Germans usually reach a consensus that covers most of the political spectrum, and the debate is over. The consensus doesn't normally erode—doesn't shift direction slowly—but, when it does change, changes swiftly, sometimes radically. The next major change in Germany's consensus will probably be a decline of support for a more cohesive EU. The signs of an impending change are visible. It may happen after Kohl has left the scene, although it could happen on his watch and hasten his departure.

As Germany goes, so goes Europe. That is the fashionable view, and it may be borne out. Besides being the largest, strongest, most productive, and most populous EU member, Germany is better adjusted than the others to various importunities of the post–Cold War environment. Because of its federal structure, Germany is better positioned than its partners to delegate authority and cope with pressure from its *Länder* (states) for control of local and regional affairs. But Germany is also an anomaly. Its foreign policy is economic policy; there is no vision other than a peaceful Federal Republic locked into a peaceful and enlarged EU and prospering in an expanding global economy. The Germans, who deploy one of Europe's two largest armies, have consistently shown the least willingness to match their economic reach with measures to maintain or promote stability in and beyond Europe.

Today's Germany doesn't fit any of the shorthand that has been used to characterize it. "Economic giant and political dwarf" had become a misleading coinage even before the end of the Cold War. The widely heard reflection that Germany is too small to be a world power and too big to be a regional power is probably clearer than the truth. Just what the scale and nature of Germany's role in Europe and the world will be at the turn of the century is far from clear. But the likelihood is that, East Asia aside, three capitals will by then matter a good deal more than the others: Washington, Moscow, and Berlin.

WITH THE CENTER of political gravity moving steadily eastward from Paris to Bonn-Berlin, France has a lot to think about. Much of what lay at the core of the singular Franco-German relationship, notably France's precedence on political matters, is gone. Not long ago, Paris could intimidate the German leadership by reproaching it for being insufficiently "European," that is, putting national interests ahead of the greater good. That tactic won't work any longer, least of all with Kohl in the uncontested role of best European.

German unification has obliged Paris to presume less and to lower its sights.

General Charles De Gaulle, when he was president, spoke of French nuclear weapons as being able to tear an arm from Russia, but their chief role lay in creating a lasting difference between France and Germany. Politically, Germany, a more dynamic and potentially stronger society than France, was to be kept subordinate and divided because, as de Gaulle saw things, only Germany threatened France. Hence, the European Community (as it was then called) would have to be French-led and shorn of federalist notions of the sort that could tempt a post–Adenauer Germany. De Gaulle had a sharper intuitive knowledge of the uses of power than any of his contemporaries, but he had a distinctly modest tolerance for the limits of power. The two men who rule Germany and France now see themselves as the political godsons of Adenauer and de Gaulle. The difference is that whereas Adenauer routinely deferred to de Gaulle, Franco-German relations no longer have that simple clarity; Kohl does what he can to meet the French halfway, partly because Germany needs France, partly to sustain the appearance of a partnership of equals. Kohl's successor will probably take a less accommodating line.

In theory, each party will decide for itself whether what remains unchanged is enough to sustain the special character of their relationship. The question is whether that decision is necessarily theirs to make. The steep decline in French morale and self-confidence, along with divergent Franco-German interests, may erode the special tie. Neither of the two is likely—not anytime soon—to consciously downgrade its link with the other, although both are edging toward more flexible positions. "Embrace Germany all the harder and look for new friends" is how a senior British diplomat describes France's resurrection of the more traditional diplomatic method. Even before the arrival of Jacques Chirac as France's president, Britain itself had become the first and foremost of France's new friends to be cultivated.

Whatever else the EU experience has contributed, it hasn't managed—not yet—to purge the interrelationships of the three key members of a heavy deposit of negatives. The Franco-German relationship, although close, politically crucial, and indeed systematic, is complicated by the difficulty the parties have in understanding each other. Their EU colleagues in Brussels spend a good deal of time explaining each side to the other—interpreting the French position to the Germans and vice versa. French and Germans are equally prone to complain about the others' inexplicable behavior—"We thought we had a deal" and so on.

The Anglo-French relationship, although improving, is obviously less close and less important, but it is also less complicated. The British and French understand each other, and their interests often converge; but they have rarely formalized agreement because their bilateral habit is one of mutual distrust.

These three countries should dominate the EU. In practice, of course, France and Germany have dominated it; only in special situations has Britain exercised as much influence as the other two. With the structure becoming larger and even less cohesive, a dominant inner circle would seem to be essential. Britain has been vaguely tempted by the idea of being part of an inner circle, but it has never been willing to give up much, if anything, to be there. A tridirectorate appearing to manage Europe's affairs has been judged undesirable by certain elements in Whitehall, who reckon that equally good progress can be made bilaterally without creating the risk of upsetting Italy and the smaller members of the EU. For many years, however, many diplomats (and some officials) in Paris and London saw the Anglo-French relationship as being potentially nearly as important as the close tie between those old enemies, France and Germany. In Europe, only Britain and France deploy large, modern navies and have nuclear weapons. Only they are permanent members of the U.N. Security Council, however anachronistic their presence at the top table strikes much of the world.

It was largely because of these and other attributes held in common that de Gaulle kept Britain out of the European Community in the sixties; he didn't want to share the leadership of Europe, which he sought for France alone, although he disguised his motives with repeated warnings that granting Britain membership would give America a Trojan horse inside the European edifice. Today Britain continues to be seen by many, if not most, continental Europeans as insular and joined at the hip to America. This isn't caricature, not altogether; granted, Britain played a leadership role in the 1980s on some critical issues, including the creation of the single market, and has probably complied with the vast body of EU rules and regulations with at least as much punctilio as—and probably more than—any other member. And the American connection has become steadily less pronounced. But the charge that Britain marginalized its role and influence within the EU during the eighteen years of the Conservative Party's reign is beyond dispute.

The irony is that Britain has for years been all but off the screen as a serious force, and thus has lost influence in Washington despite its putative dependence on a special relationship with America. The Conservative Party's leadership seemed not to understand, or to accept, that America is part of Europe and that Britain must be so too. Diplomats hope that the Blair government will be able to broker differences between other EU members and Washington and recover the traditional role of mediator between the north and south of Europe.

Paris aside, most European capitals have deeply regretted the absence of a full-blooded British role within the EU. None of them has wanted to see it dominated by France, Germany, or the two together. The need for a more Europeanized Britain is felt as keenly in Bonn as elsewhere despite the sometimes comic anti-German tendencies of prominent British Tories, including former prime minister Margaret Thatcher. But Bonn's expectations are low. "Britain lacks a fantasy," says a senior German diplomat who still feels that the continental societies, for different reasons in some cases, presume that a European union will eventually create the sane and stable order that none of them could achieve with traditional methods. "Britain may have good ideas for the EU, some would say the best ideas," he continues. "Take free trade. Whatever they say, the French are basically opposed to free trade. And the Germans, whatever they say, are split. Only the British are unreservedly for free trade. But you can't deploy much influence from the sidelines." He speaks for a multitude.

Still, it's not as if Britain is alone in resisting the creation of an embryo European government in Brussels. Even before Chirac's return to the national scene, France's attitude toward giving EU institutions more independent power paralleled Britain's bias, not Germany's. In neither Paris nor London do mainstream political forces want to grant more power to the European Parliament or the European Commission, the executive arm. Kohl's regime does but has been unable to do anything about it. Some say that as long as

Britain remains unsure and tentative about its role in the EU—and cannot create its own fantasy—Europe itself will remain incomplete and unfulfilled. Perhaps. It may already be too late for that kind of Europe; most members of the EU, starting with France and now Germany, have set about interring their own fantasies.

THE EUROPEAN MOVEMENT is a creature of crisis. It drew inspiration from the onset of the Cold War. The 1957 Treaty of Rome was concluded in the aftermath of the Suez fiasco. From then on, the enterprise achieved its greatest momentum under maximum pressure. The most recent example was the collapse of the Berlin Wall and Germany's unification. However exalted, these events generated serious concern in various EU capitals, notably Paris and London, which, like Moscow, had come to rely on Germany being divided indefinitely, if not permanently. Unlike Moscow, Paris and London, shocked and alarmed, reacted churlishly to unification and actually tried at first to discourage it. Failing that, France sought to restrain Germany by binding it more securely to the EU.

The upshot was a laborious negotiation that led to a meeting of the twelve leaders of the EU in the Dutch city of Maastricht in December 1991. There they amended the 1957 Treaty of Rome and the 1987 Single European Act. The aim was to create an economic and monetary union, including a common currency by 1997 and also a more or less common foreign policy. Since the club was expected to be enlarged to include all or most of the countries of northern and central Europe, its institutions would have to be changed accordingly, or so it seemed. Obtaining cohesion at the level of twelve had been difficult enough. Achieving it at some number between fifteen and twenty-seven would be futile unless, for example, decisions on important matters could be made by a majority rather than by consensus.

Shorthand for the dominant issues was "deepening" and "widening." The former meant greater self-integration of the EU. The latter meant enlargement. Britain was a major booster of widening, if only to discourage deepening. France wanted to deepen but not to widen, assuming reasonably enough that new EU members, whether Scandinavian or central European, would sooner or later become part of a German zone of influence. Germany pressed to both deepen and widen. Kohl was more than willing to accept further strings on Germany in return for agreement on enlargement and on reform of the institutions. More specifically, he wanted more power for the European Parliament and some workable arrangement for devising a common EU foreign policy.

Italy and the Benelux countries were very keen to deepen, being always ready for steps that might dilute the dominant roles of France and Germany. Also, convinced "Europeans" in all capitals favored deepening; their union, they believe, has to move forward at regular intervals or it will drift backward into something less—a big, loosely strung free-trade area. However, François Mitterrand and Britain's prime minister, John Major, were strongly opposed to granting further power to the EU's weak parliamentary arm, and they were at least as hostile to the notion of allowing a cluster of EU members to intrude upon the foreign policy processes of individual countries, least of all France and Britain, players still on the world stage. (Many advocates of a coherent European union envisage an inner core—a group of like-minded member states seeking to prosper as a unit roughly within the perimeter of Charlemagne's empire—a Carolingian Europe.)

Mitterrand was pressing instead for a European monetary union (EMU), a stratagem that could put France in a heads-I-win-tails-you-lose position vis-à-vis Germany; or so it seemed. EMU's single currency would oblige Bonn to surrender the living symbol of German renewal—a surpassing prosperity and economic strength rooted in monetary stability. The deutsche mark was already the world's most important reserve currency after the dollar, and its dominion would gradually extend over an area bigger than the Holy Roman Empire. Moreover, EMU would mean that Germany's central bank, the Deutsche Bundesbank in Frankfurt—the first and last line of resistance to the curse of inflation—would have to give way to a jointly controlled European central bank. Could the German people be expected to swap their own and Europe's most reliable source of stability for a venture into the unknown? If Germany said no, then or later on, Paris would be in a position to accuse it of being a "bad European"—of putting national interest ahead of the interests of the EU. There you go again, France's leadership could say, wandering between the two worlds of western and eastern Europe.

But if Germany accepted EMU, France would have a seat on the central bank's board of governors. And a single EU currency, although a presumed surrogate for Germany's—a D-mark by another name—would disguise an embarrassing reality: the French franc "shadowing" the D-mark, that is, being subordinate to the German currency. Was the D-mark's dominance a metaphor of Europe's political future? French leadership had to worry that matters would be seen that way.

Before Maastricht, the EU was called the European Community (EC). But the Maastricht Accord opens with a bold assertion: "By this Treaty, the High Contracting Parties establish among themselves a European Union." However, the agreement did little to vindicate the stirring language. The member states couldn't agree on reforming their joint institutions even though negotiations on enlarging the EU were supposed to begin. Instead, institutional reform was tossed into a future negotiation—the intergovernmental conference (IGC) that began life early in 1996.

Kohl returned from Maastricht empty-handed. The meeting did produce agreed-on rules on creating EMU, a major goal of Mitterrand but for Kohl a concession fraught with difficulty. But that was then. It isn't likely that a German chancellor will ever again be victimized by France, even in the name of Europe.

The affair at Maastricht was handled in the old way—as if the Cold War hadn't expired and governments were still licensed to make decisions on broad issues without consulting popular opinon. Hence, the treaty was widely seen as flawed by a "democratic deficit." Although all EU members eventually ratified it after two years of wrangling, the outcome was a near thing in some countries, and the accord was viewed harshly in many of them. Governments hadn't understood the extent to which they were now seen as the problem, and most of them still don't.

EUROPE NEEDS TO develop a global political role to match its economic outreach. That's not happening and isn't likely to, not soon. Shifting magnetic fields are causing France and Germany to define their interests in different ways. France has probably committed a major strategic error by conceding Mitteleuropa as a German sphere of influence. The French see the chief threat to their security as lying due south in North Africa; the Mediterranean separates what has probably become history's largest gap in living standards.* Germany worries about instability, or worse, in Russia, and does not exclude a potential threat from Russia, even though Poland, Ukraine, and Belarus are buffers. One hears French complaints of German indifference to the pressure on Europe from the Maghreb, along with German complaints about the absence of serious French involvement in central Europe and Russia.

Among the harsher uncertainties is America. If, in the aftermath of the Cold War, numerous Europeans saw little further need of America's abnormal role in their affairs, the serial horrors in Yugoslavia—the spectacle of the Balkans again behaving like the Balkans—proved them wrong, at least in principle. Europe still needs to have America playing a pivotal role in the management of its security.

Most European leaders worry far less about a renewal of pres-

---

* Daniel Hamilton in "Europe, the Walls Go Up Again," *Baltimore Sun,* May 22, 1991.

sure from Russia someday than about America's disengagement from Europe's affairs. In a time of rising uncertainty and volatility, Europe has no good alternative to America's military presence and leadership. The continued presence of U.S. forces in Germany will discourage the renationalizion of defense in western Europe and reassure central Europe about Germany and Russia. Yet, as seen from Washington, the European states have broken with a basic responsibility—providing security. Their defense budgets, now including even France's, seem to be in free fall. Washington mutters about whiplash—having to suffer the shrinking investment of its allies in joint security with the claims of some of them, notably France, to more of the command responsibility. The pressure on European governments to lower the costs of their social wage and safety net is enormous. The question is whether they can accept that Washington, too, feels overstretched, without concluding that America is shrinking its role.

New and unfamiliar tasks are soaking up the energies of the western capitals. And much of what they do and are likely to do will be in response to the issues pushed at them by the societies of central and eastern Europe. Informal agreement exists on two somewhat contesting priorities: fitting Russia into the world community and fitting the countries to the east of Germany, not including Russia, into the EU and NATO. Russia is too big for the EU, and NATO membership is ruled out, if only because member parliaments would never approve any such step. Apart from these and other difficulties, Russia isn't so much a country as a vast territorial mix of largely separate jurisdictions. Still, the task that has defied fertile minds lies in creating an instrument that will link the western system and Russia. The problem for Russia's neighbors and old enemies isn't Russia's latent strength, but rather Russia's weakness. It's a problem that won't go away soon and will affect the calculations of all parties in the period ahead.

Many of the societies in east-central and eastern Europe are seeking admission to both the EU and NATO. But the obstacles to joining either club, especially the EU, are formidable. Extending EU membership to the economically weaker societies lying east of Germany is a contentious but vital proposition. Extending NATO—how far? how fast?—in that direction is less complicated but equally contentious. The risks were always clear: the issue could be exploited by Russian nationalists at the expense of moderates. Russia could step up pressure on what it calls the "near abroad," including the Ukraine.

What Russia wants, perhaps above all, is a security tie with America, ideally inside NATO's tent. NATO matters to Russia, largely because America is there. If Russia cares little about whether the EU enlarges, it is partly because America isn't there and partly because the EU is chiefly concerned with economics, not with security. Russians are, of course, aware that once Poland, the Czech Republic, and others join the EU, they will fall within the penumbra of the western security system. Russia wants to resume being a player in the European security arena, as it was for three hundred years or so.

France would prefer to see Germany remain the eastern frontier of both the EU and NATO. Although Germany wants buffers and is the only serious advocate of enlarging the EU, it has been unable or unwilling to advance the cause. Germany may have cause to regret allowing its seemingly more urgent cause—monetary union—to crowd out consideration of other initiatives, notably those designed to develop a zone of stability in a part of Europe that is prone to instability and could drift regressively.

Serious irony may surface: if monetary union is postponed or has a hard landing, EU countries, above all Germany, are likely to need a project, since literally nothing else of importance may be going on. The obvious project would be EU enlargement. The risk, however, is that if the EU is unable to move on other fronts, the enlargement process could be stalled indefinitely.

The inability of Europeans, either as individual nations or as a community, to manage the tragic course of events in the former Yugoslavia was a heavy blow to confidence at all levels. EU members now confront a powerful political and moral obligation to offer membership to societies that are as European as France or Germany or Italy and that are as much a part of Europe's history. They must find a way of doing so, or they will have an acute sense of having failed the only serious post–Cold War tests they have faced.

CHAPTER II

POWER
TRICKLES
DOWN

"The states are too big to run everyday life but too small to run international affairs," says Pasqual Maragall, urban economist, mayor-emeritus of Barcelona, a potential prime minister of Spain, and one of Europe's most accomplished political figures. Maragall reflects the bias of many of Europe's regional and big-city leaders, who are themselves gaining influence and authority. European cities and regional governments are acquiring bigger budgets and developing more professional bureaucracies. National cultures are being squeezed between a broader popular culture and briskly reviving regional cultures. The nation-state is in most cases a relatively recent phenomenon, and the process of cobbling it together left a deposit of sour memorabilia in many places.

Europeans are finding their national interests hard to see, let alone define. The role of European governments is also less than clear. National leaders had an easier time during the Cold War, when, thanks to NATO, they could satisfy the essential need, military security. But in this transitional time, economic security is far more pressing and far more elusive. Another industrial revolution is causing serious social dislocations. Leadership's inability to keep unemployment at a tolerable level while maintaining the social safety net has accelerated Europe's growing devolution of authority.

With the external pressures of the Cold War gone, people are indifferent to whether Poland is admitted to NATO or whether Germany acquires a seat on the U.N. Security Council. Foreign policy has now to be concerned with immigration, drugs, crime fighting, and other issues that directly affect people, and local authorities feel as if they, not national governments, are better placed to manage these problems, even if they must struggle with the capitals for adequate funding.

Regionalism is much more than a purposeful return to roots and a distancing of society from the capital. It has as much to do with the creation of wealth as anything else. "The Europe of regions is a Europe of enterprises," says Robert Maury, director of the Association for the Development of the Lyon Area. He means enterprises that can compete within both the single European market and the global market.

As European governments lose or concede control of their nations' economies, their constituencies are turning to the markets for help, and parallel processes have emerged. One is regionalism, the other globalization. European regions are linking themselves directly to the global economy. Instead of working through national capitals, they are exploiting global trade patterns, the information highway, the free movement of capital, and the ease of high-speed travel. Baden-Württemberg, as noted earlier, has signed several hundred agreements with other regions and entities. And what, if any, control does Bonn exercise over this activity? In Stuttgart, the capital of Baden-Württemberg, a senior official in the office of foreign economics maintains that no agreements with foreign governments or entities are made without Bonn's blessing. "They have never vetoed one," he says. "They make an occasional comment of no importance. We issued a joint declaration with Russia about economic cooperation, and Bonn was nervous but did nothing." But according to a senior official at the ministry in Bonn, he and his colleagues hear nothing about such agreements until after they have been made.

"We are globalized," says Dr. Helmut Becker, the chief economist for BMW. "The importance of capitals is decreasing, and regional centers that are independent of borders are becoming more important. Munich will be closer to Italy than to Hamburg, even though we have different languages. Tensions will be created as some regions become more prosperous and others less well off."[1]

Creating jobs is the priority task for governments, but cities and regions believe themselves to be better equipped for it than national capitals are. Moreover, ordinary people have been made aware, at times painfully, that the financial markets can generate more capital than the total funds normally held by the central banks of EU member countries. The realization that the markets are capable of exerting greater influence than a nation's leadership and its Parliament sharpens the popular perception of unavailing governments and the need for more local self-reliance. It also contributes to the jingoism of the radical right, as represented by Europeans such as France's Jean-Marie Le Pen (and in America by Pat Buchanan).

With governments running out of money and the welfare state in distress, regionalism is also partly about infrastructure. Raising taxes to finance new projects is probably not an option for most EU governments; their revenues already average nearly half of gross domestic product (GDP), compared to roughly a third in the United States. Hence, much of the investment in large projects is being done at regional and local levels, often on a cooperative basis with neighboring and economically interactive regions.

Many and probably most of the wealthiest provinces of western Europe are interacting with one another (and in some cases with parts of central Europe) and together creating superregions—large economic zones that dissolve national boundaries. In various banking and business circles, these zones are called "bananas." The idea is that Europe's industrial and financial heartland is being divided into banana-shaped configurations. Jordi Pujol, the president of Catalonia, Spain's dominant political figure, and Europe's most conspicuous prophet of regionalism, draws a picture in his office in Barcelona of what he sees as the two most developed bananas. The first, which he describes as the most important of them, stretches from southeastern England through northern France and the Benelux countries and down the Rhine Valley into Switzerland. The second traces an arc from the Veneto in Italy, west through Lombardy and the Piedmont into the Rhône-Alpes, across France's Mediterranean coast and hinterland, and into Catalonia. Pujol describes this second banana as Europe's sun belt, noting that it is experiencing the kind of economic growth that transfigured America's sun belt many years ago. Regional figures in Lyon have officially labeled this same configuration "the southern arc," and they see it gradually extending as far east as Budapest.

Other superregions, more potential than actual, are seen as including an Atlantic arc stretching from Ireland through Wales and Brittany across the Bay of Biscay into Galicia and Portugal. Another would closely resemble the former Hanseatic League, built around its original Nordic and Baltic membership.

Pujol has been a brilliant success in Catalonia, as has Maragall in Barcelona. Although he doesn't quite say so, Pujol seems to envisage a European Union that one day will be made up primarily of regions, not nation-states. "Spain," he says, "was on the fringe of Europe for seven hundred years, while Catalonia was always part of it. We want to be the Netherlands of southern Europe."[2]

Among the most important of the convinced regionalists is Kurt Biedenkopf, minister-president of Saxony and, after Kohl, the most prestigious of Germany's Christian Democratic leaders. Biedenkopf is a friend and ally of Pujol's. He complains about the disparate sizes of of the members of the EU, asking, "Why should Luxembourg have the benefits of full membership in the EU, when it is smaller than some German cities?"[3] He could have added that the state of North Rhine–Westphalia's population, about 18 million, exceeds that of ten members of the EU.

Regionalism's hostility to distant bureaucracies seems to apply to the Brussels-based institutions of the EU as well as to ministries in national capitals. But it's not that simple. To take advantage of economies of scale and compete globally, the regions need a single market. Pujol and his allies believe the regions and the EU fraternity in Brussels have a common interest: weakening the nation-state. The regional movement, they feel, has been better accepted by EU institutions than by the national governments.

However, in Germany, France, much of Spain, and most of Italy, there is a curious, perhaps predictable, ambivalence toward the EU; people by and large favor it, but they reject the proposition that it should exercise control over their lives. Even in hotbeds of regionalism such as Catalonia, Brussels is seen as overly bureaucratic and technocratic. It doesn't offer what Europeans are thought to be looking for—something they can relate to emotionally. The Germans call it *Heimat,* and some say it is the true source of regionalism. In France's referendum on the Maastricht Accord, the 49 percent who voted no were judged to be in large part pro-Europe but anti-Brussels.

Various regionalists see their role as one of stemming what some of them call the "centralizing tide" from Brussels. They ask whether it is the EU's job to build a highway in Portugal, or to tell farmers how many pigs to slaughter and how big their apples can be, or to ordain a standardized tractor seat for all fifteen countries of the union. The system's defenders respond that instead of having to deal with fifteen different standards and regulations, the makers of tractor seats need not think about meeting more than one set of specs.[4]

"It is not for us to tell states how to organize themselves," says a senior official of the European Commission in Brussels. "We are a club of states. We support the states. It will be easier to build Europe with a handful of states than with sixty or so regions. But the states must accept the regions and the need of citizens to have a sense of identity."[5]

The agreement reached at Maastricht in 1991 did create a so-called Committee of the Regions. Its secretary-general is Dietrich Pause, a genial and reflective Bavarian whose mind moves with restless charm across a dazzling array of topics, each of which he somehow manages to relate to regionalism. It is, he says, "more of a feeling than a fact—a metaphysical idea arising from people's intuitive fear of losing their roots and being overcome by centralization."[6]

As for attitudes toward national capitals, Pause said, "For a long time, governments determined how much poorer regions could get." (The regions, he indicated, are now looking after themselves.) And what about the EU? "There is a lot of hostility here toward Brussels," he replied.

Still, popular feeling within the original membership of the EU, excepting France for the moment, is usually described now as being opposed to the nation-state, not anti-Brussels. If the nation-state is modernism and the EU postmodernism, regions constitute the pre-modern. They are also the most direct link to postmodern Brussels; first, because they weaken the nation-states, and second, because their aversion to unnatural borders has led them, with some exceptions, to support an integrated EU more strongly than its membership has. Also, postwar modernism laid a heavy hand on regional cultures, blurring them and contributing to the buildup of anti–nation-state sentiment. Briefly, the nation-state is being squeezed—pressed to transfer authority both upward and downward.

"MAASTRICHT SHOWED THAT we need to be closer to people, not just in the capital cities, but in the other cities, too," says a senior official of the European Commission. "We must erase borders and have one market."[7] That process is under way, and a symbiotic link between the regions and the EU will gradually develop; the single market abets the purposes of both by blurring frontiers, hence weakening the nation-states. And the regions are aware of their need to have a single market so as to prosper from the economics of scale and compete in the global market. A great many of them have opened offices in Brussels, mainly for lobbying. Perhaps the rather widespread impression of the EU as being an abstraction, but an intrusive one, will fade, if gradually.

Borders are losing their meaning; deeply rooted patterns of commercial and cultural interaction are again ascendent in regions that may have a lot more in common with places across national frontiers than with neighboring areas within their own countries. Baden-Württemberg, Alsace, and Basel have become one region for employment purposes; a heavy concentration of universities as well as industry is producing a regional identity. The state of Saxony in eastern Germany is slowly becoming the midpoint of a similar region reaching north toward Berlin, south into the Czech Republic, and east to Poland.

In France, there is concern that a piece of the southwest will again become part of the Catalan sphere of influence. Cities that were once the cultural centers of Catalonia are watching a lot of Catalan TV. The area around Toulouse is doing more business with Catalonia than with other regions in France.

The Rhône-Alpes is France's strongest region, and Lyon, its capital and France's second city, is a major international center; its commercial policy is to acquire independence and extend its European and global reach. Lyon's airport became the first in France to acquire a high-speed train link. (The same type of link to Paris's Charles de Gaulle Airport came afterward.) And part of the growth plan is to give the city a similar link with Turin by tunneling thirty-five miles through the Alps and cutting travel time between the cities to seventy minutes. The wealthy triangle that links Lyon,

Turin, and Geneva, which is known as the "Alpine Diamond" and will reach well beyond these cities, is thought to have vast potential.

High-speed rail transport will increasingly become a chief agent in exploiting this potential, and it will be another equalizer as regions and major cities further detach themselves from national capitals. So-called intermodal transport will move people and goods through a tight network of air, rail, and road transport, itself based on joint planning carried out by regional centers in sometimes two, sometimes four or more countries. The most costly component is the as-yet-incomplete high-speed rail network; it requires trains of the kind first introduced in France and now used extensively and known as TGVs (*trains à grande vitesse*), along with fully modern rail terminals colocated with airports. Germany, Italy, and Spain have emulated France and introduced their own similar versions of the TGV. Not surprisingly, the relentless pressure for creating the rail system is supplied mainly by cities, not by the regions or nation-states.

In 1988, the regions surrounding Stuttgart, Barcelona, Lyon, and Milan formed what they call the "Four Motors Association." The idea was that these four—Baden-Württemberg, Catalonia, the Rhône-Alpes, and Lombardy—would together become the engine for European growth. The idea originated with Lothar Spath, who was then minister-president of Baden-Württemberg and seen as a potential successor to Kohl. Spath worried that Europe was not adjusting to changes in the world economy, The prevailing attitude toward high technology especially troubled him; most of Europe seemed largely uninterested in the newer technologies that America and Japan were in the early stages of exploiting; in Germany there was open hostility to high technology, traceable in part to antinuclear feeling; the movement in Germany against nuclear weapons was under way.

Spath and those around him felt that Baden-Württemberg, although very strong, would benefit from links to other prospering regions. "We started with Catalonia," says Hans-Peter Mengele, who now directs European policy within Baden-Württemberg's office of foreign economics. "It was Spath and Pujol. We all thought that regions with high technology had something in common and should promote integration, not of the constitutional kind, but learning and shared experience and joint projects."[8]

Not much is clear about what the group has actually accomplished apart from managing to forge an alliance with the EU leadership in Brussels, but that in itself was important. None of the four members, of course, harbors a national capital. Some say the only function of the Four Motors is to coordinate regional policy with Brussels and work around the various disputes between EU members over so-called integration issues.

"We all wanted a lot of sharing of information on how to deal with Brussels," says a colleague of Mengele's who spoke on a not-for-attribution basis. "We wanted to make Brussels more sensitive to regional concerns, and that is the trend now—more regionalism and more sensitivity to it in Brussels. Bonn has no problem with the Four Motors, but Brussels was very critical at first. Why, they asked in Brussels, does this club have only rich members? So we Germans tried to add the central region of Portugal to the group. But this failed. The French and Catalans blocked it."[9]

Thus far, the group has not managed to build a sense of priority importance around knowledge-intensive industries, which seems to have been its early purpose. The most prosperous parts of the EU are still reluctant to interfere with the methods that have worked so well in the past, even if competing in the global market argues for changing course.

Questions arise: If regionalism in these four places, as well as some others, is more about wealth creation than a conscious return to roots, will the process drive politics in such regions to the right, especially as some become richer and others poorer? Who will protect the poor and disadvantaged? Nation-states? The EU? Will new and wider polarities be created? And to what extent is regionalism in some places corrupting local politics? Corruption is already a powerful and debilitating force in numerous European countries, notably France, Italy, and Spain. Increasing the number of decision makers and the money available to local governments also increases the opportunities for graft, as has been widely demonstrated.

A large and unexamined question is the effect of regionalism on Europe's security. Most European members of NATO are scaling back their spending on defense, and self-absorbed regions may in more than a few cases insist on smaller commitments of resources for this purpose. Germany is a conspicuous example. When the Berlin Wall came down, local *Land* leaders wanted in some cases to convert military bases into schools and to use them for other benign purposes. But mayors in some of these places argued for keeping the bases because of the jobs involved; in neither case, however, did officials see the bases as instruments of territorial defense, present or future. By and large, Europeans have lost the habit of thinking about providing for their security at the level of the nation-state. Instead, they appear to draw an existential sense of security from membership in both NATO and the EU. But European governments should understand that a diminishing commitment to their own security may weaken support for the North Atlantic Alliance within the United States, its leader and prop. Washington hasn't yet thought about the implications of western Europe's regional dynamic. Still, it can't fail to notice that in some countries—Germany is again a conspicuous example—the percentage of public outlays for cities and towns is increasing and the amount for spending at the national level declining.

Pondering the effect on security raises another question: To what extent is the mix of porous borders, weakened national governments, and weakened national police forces complicating efforts to combat drugs, organized crime, and hot money. The European Commission says it needs more authority to cope with organized crime syndicates operating across national boundaries.

"We are struck by the fact that there is more and more organized crime," says Anita Gradin, the responsible commissioner. She adds that the syndicates in most cases straddle borders and cannot be dealt with by national police forces.[10]

The revival of ethnicity is a concern, and not just in historically volatile areas. Still, the net effect on security may be positive, at least to the extent that regional power can allay local anxieties and neutralize potentially violent separatist groups. By doing so, the regions can relieve the pressure on national governments; it's not by chance that the growth of regional power has grown with the willing assent of various governments. However, it has grown in some places because national governments couldn't deter it by any acceptable means.

THE REGIONAL CURRENT is running strong in most parts of the EU, most conspicuously in Germany, Belgium, northern Italy, Spanish Catalonia, southwest France, and the Rhône-Alpes. The pattern varies. Only Pujol thinks about becoming a head of state, according to other regional leaders who know him; Pujol himself, however, disavows any such ambition. In Italy, a highly centralized state must cope with a highly decentralized economy and a regionalist north that wants a federal structure. With its even more centralized system, France will have the most trouble in coping with regional sentiments. Germany, thanks to its well-established federal structure, is better prepared than its partners. Also, German regionalism has the strongest root system partly because of history and tradition, partly because of the country's federal structure. Germany's brief but tumultuous history as a nation-state has strengthened the regional and tribal instincts of a people that suspects it has no vocation for doing business as a nation-state. Berlin as the seat of government was never a popular place, whereas Bonn as the capital has been regarded sympathetically. Bismarck imposed nationalism on a people that had not begun to develop a national identity,

let alone a national ego. Hitler was the *dernier cri* of German nationalism. Today's Germans exist comfortably within their federal
structure; many, if not most of them, feel as if they are living once
again as Thuringians, Bavarians, Westphalians, and so on. It's easier to say "I am a Swabian" or "I am a Saxon" than to say "I am a
German." Some (who can say how many?) would add, "I am also a
European."

Today's German federalism was not imposed by victorious allies
in 1948–1949, although they strongly supported it, but rather by
the founders of the new Federal Republic. They were convinced
that political life in West Germany should be built around reconsti-
tuted *Länder*. In East Germany, the Soviet occupation authorities
replaced the five eastern *Länder* with fourteen military districts.[11]
But when the Berlin Wall came down and unification became a reality, eastern Germans instantly reclaimed their regional identities.
Regional flags, not the national flag, were raised. The Communists
had banned the expression of these identities. We hear a lot about
how eastern and western Germans, although now rejoined into one
nation, remain divided economically and socially. But given how
little time has elapsed since they were living within polarized systems, it could hardly be otherwise.

German federalism is the model for regionalists elsewhere, but
it doesn't travel; it requires a large administrative capacity at the
state level, which the sixteen *Länder* possess but which does not
exist in most other places. The *Länder* governments dominate social policy, including education, and they have a voice in foreign
policy through the offices they maintain in both Bonn and Brussels. These offices are used to lobby members of the Bundestag
(the Parliament) and the diplomatic community, along with trade
and industry people. Parliamentarians, diplomats, and other lobbyists all agree that the *Länder* offices give the best parties in Bonn
(and more than hold their own in Brussels, too).

"We have so much power in Bonn that we can't see any sense in
a separatist movement," says Georg von Waldenfeis, Bavaria's fi-

nance minister.[12] However, the chief source of the *Länder's* power in Bonn lies not in their lobbying prowess but in their control of the Bundesrat, the upper house of Parliament, which represents the sixteen *Länder*. The Maastricht Accord was ratified only after the Bundesrat had bowed to pressure from *Land* leaders for more authority over EU policy. The Bundesrat must approve more than half of all bills, especially those that concern the financial and administrative affairs of the *Länder*. When the two houses don't agree, a committee is formed to mediate and work out a compromise.

Evidence of the decline of the German state is reflected in the diminished status of various ministries, including even the Finance Ministry. According to Herbert A. Henzler, chairman of McKinsey & Company in Germany, 40 percent of public spending there is federal in origin, 30 percent is by *Länder,* and 30 percent is by cities and towns. Federal spending is in a continuing decline, he says.[13]

Every regional capital in Germany, whether east or west, seems to have a map that illustrates in concentric circles its new role as the center—the beating heart—of a unified Germany in a now-undivided Europe. In Munich, Stuttgart, and Dresden, these maps are included in promotional kits. One encounters them as well in Berlin, the city that will be the sprawling center of the new Europe. Bavarians, for example, rejoice in having left the periphery, as they see it. "We are literally the center of Europe," says the director-general of the Bavarian State Ministry of Economy and Transport. "And we have nearly twelve million people. We are bigger than some members of the EU. Within Germany, we are only one of sixteen *Länder,* but we always have had a self-conscious position."[14]

"Self-conscious" in this case translates as nationalistic. "Bavaria has an historic identity," says Pause, a worldly European and non-nationalist. "It is always pulled between Hapsburgs and Bourbons. It resembles the Scots, Catalonians, and Basques." Pause sees the past as having "uprooted Germans," but in different ways. "Munich," he says, "became a hotbed of revolution. It harbored Lenin, the romantic poets without money, philosophers—mostly from the north. And, of course, the leadership of the Third Reich—Hitler, Himmler, Heydrich—all began their careers here."[15]

As they tell it, Bavaria's politicians and civil servants worked as hard as their Austrian counterparts to maneuver Austria's accession to the EU in 1995. "We have backed the entry of Austria with all our means," says one senior official of the state government. "We are its main partner in trade. For future development of the EU, Austria is our natural ally. And Austrians think their Bavarian tie can help them preserve their style, cultural and otherwise."[16]

Bavaria's historic ties with Austria and their shared ethnicity lie close to the center of the thinking of its leadership. "Austrians think of themselves as more Bavarian than Bavarians, because in Bavaria you also find Swabians and Franconians," says Hubertus Desloch, the chief of the Bavarian government's European office. "Both of them are different and speak different dialects. It all goes back to Friedrich Barbarossa in the twelfth century. He split Austria from Bavaria, but the close ethnic tie remains because the Bavarians came from Bohemia to the Alps and settled south of the Danube as far as Vienna. But Bavaria had become too powerful for the German kings, so Barbarossa split it [in 1180]" and gave the eastern part to an obscure dynasty that preceded the Hapsburgs.[17]

Talking to Bavarians, one wouldn't sense that a portion of its economic power is shifting to the north, mainly to Hamburg and environs. Bavaria sees itself as the strongest of the regions and declares its regional bias most strongly. "We Bavarians invented the idea of regionalism," says Desloch. "We wanted to stabilize regional autonomy. The economy requires networking and technological transfers. We are all globalizing. Regions are the cultural power stations," he added, shifting the focus. "Civil virtues develop within the regions. Our own identity dates to the fifth, sixth, and seventh centuries." Still, however deeply rooted the Bavarian identity, dialects vary from valley to valley and people living in villages just a few miles apart can barely understand one another.

Prussia is fooling itself in thinking that Berlin is the center of the action, say Bavarians, who claim a broader array of interests, starting with Austria, northern Italy, and Catalonia. They have little interest in the eastern *Länder* surrounding Berlin. They point to separate agreements they have reached with Ukraine, Quebec, and a province of China. Bavarians disavow seeking autonomy, carefully distinguishing themselves from separatist Tyrolians and Lombardians in Italy. They profess to feel closer to Spain's Catalans and Belgium's Walloons.

"Our policy is built on a Europe of regions," says Desloch, adding that creating the Committee of the Regions was a Bavarian idea and first proposed by Stoiber, its hard-driving, plainspoken minister-president. Stoiber's role model is the late Franz Josef Strauss, Bavaria's legendary strongman, from whom he is said to have acquired both his vigorous political style and his strenuous commitment to parity between nation-states and regions, starting with his own Bavaria. Bavaria also benefits from the presence in Bonn of Finance Minister Theodor Waigel, another ambitious high achiever against whom Stoiber had to struggle for the job of leader. Both are expected to be candidates for chancellor when Kohl leaves office.

Unlike Pujol and other regionalists who see the EU as an ally, Stoiber sees it as a threat to nation-states, just as the latter threaten regions such as Bavaria. On November 9, 1993, Stoiber sent a frisson through the EU by calling for a "Europe of the nations." Klaus Kinkel, the German foreign minister, called on Kohl to censure Stoiber. (At the time, Kinkel was leader of the Free Democrats, a small party and one of Kohl's two coalition partners. The other is Bavaria's Christian Socialist Union [CSU], which is led by Stoiber.) A month later, Stoiber called the chancellor a "European illusionist" and charged his party, the Christian Democratic Union (CDU), with ignoring the average German's concerns about the

EU. Stoiber has further said that Germany should give itself the right to secede from the EU. He intends for the Committee of the Regions, his supposed creation, to stem what he sees as a centralizing tide from Brussels and acquire an equal standing with the EU's Council of Ministers and Parliament. "Brussels wants to change our constitution," says Desloch. "We don't know where we stand."[18]

Like other German regions, Bavaria relies on its business community for leverage against Bonn. A big auto company such as BMW, which is Munich-based, can threaten to take jobs elsewhere—further east or across the sea to Puerto Rico or Asia, where costs are not oppressive. Companies of this kind—pacesetters and worldly—feel a need to be part of the corporate culture in parts of the global market where they must compete—areas such as North America and East Asia. This presence can't be obtained by deploying networks of dealers. It requires integration—establishing plant and training labor forces—as BMW and Daimler-Benz have both done in the southern United States. BMW is now a presence in Thailand, Malaysia, and Indonesia; it is planning a move into Korea. Japan is now the biggest importer of BMW cars.

It is politically correct to be involved with the so-called east, but investors in Munich are thus far less interested in the new *Länder* of eastern Germany than in the Czech Republic, Hungary, and other east-central European countries. Siemens, a Munich-based conglomerate and the third largest German company behind Daimler-Benz and Volkswagen, has a presence in every eastern European country, including Bosnia. Siemens reckons that its labor costs in these places are about 10 percent of those costs in Germany and that the productivity of its eastern operations is about 70 percent of what it is at home.

The Swabians of Baden-Württemberg, who share a long border with Bavaria, are equally strong regionalists and equally committed to the global market. Their region also shares with Bavaria a southern German aspect—forests, half-timbered houses, *Lederhosen,* and so on. Swabians, too, have a distinctive culture and their own dialect. And they consider themselves the most industrious of the Germans. But unlike Bavarians, Swabians are Protestants, and they are a solemn lot, often compared with the German Swiss. "We are a people who, it is said, do not to know how to laugh," says Stuttgart's popular mayor, Manfred Rommel, a son of Erwin Rommel, the legendary general. "We are the most industrialized region of a heavily industrialized country." Mayor Rommel, like his father, was born in Stuttgart; his mother was Prussian. He is very popular; in 1990, he was reelected to his third eight-year term, with 72 percent of the vote. (At the end of 1996, Rommel resigned as mayor to join the foreign ministry as coordinator of French–German relations.)

Rommel appears to bear little resemblance, either physical or stylistic, to his father. He is rumpled, rather plump, good-natured, low-key, and prone to irony. But while discussing a newspaper article that cited Stuttgart as having the highest quality of life of any city in Europe, Rommel commented soberly on the sharp rise in unemployment, adding that 25 percent of Stuttgart's population does not have German passports. He then said, "We have 450,000 jobs—cars, car parts, electronics, machine tools. We can survive only if the labor force increases productivity. That means employing fewer people." He then turned to labor costs, noting that "for the price of one German engineer, you can employ ten Polish engineers."

Rommel has no fondness for the EU but feels it may allow Europe to compete in the world market. "We live under the dictatorship of the global economy," he said. "There is no alternative to a united Europe," he added, sounding, however, as if he judged it a doubtful prospect. Asked what a united Europe meant, he said, "Monetary union would be useful. But it is very emotional [a comment on the opposition of ordinary Germans to swapping the deutsche mark for a common currency]. A common social policy is desirable, but very difficult. Germans wouldn't like it. Imagine trying to merge social policies here with Portugal's and the Visegrad countries." (He was referring to Poland, the Czech Republic, Hungary, and Slovakia, none of which is as yet a member of the EU.)

Rommel is a regionalist who, like Stoiber, doesn't mince words when talking about Brussels, which he sees as a nuisance. "We feel it," he said. "We have problems trying to understand all the rules and regulations." Then he began to ramble indignantly: "We Germans obey orders when we get them. We are not like the Italians. If Brussels tells us to improve our sewer systems so we can have even purer water, we do it. Here in Germany, we have the strongest local administrations, except for the Swiss, and they don't have to worry about Brussels. We complained to the chancellor about having to improve our sewer systems. We already had a superior system. He was sympathetic and leaning in our direction until he discovered that the initiative in Brussels was taken by a German. He then leaned in the other direction. In the end, it turned out be very costly as well as unnecessary. And we had to bear all the costs locally. We had to tax our people in order to pay for it."

Not surprisingly, Rommel is known to favor devolving more authority on those who manage local affairs. When asked whether the Europe of tomorrow would be built around regions, not nations, he said, "I've discussed this very often with Maragall." Then he dodged the next question—whether he shares the Barcelona mayor's putative vision of resurrected city-states. "Cities," he said, "do not want to be represented only by states."[19] Rommel then noted an unavoidable tension in city-state relations. He may have been thinking personally as well as generally. He and Lothar Spath, a dominant regional figure before moving into the private sector, were serious political rivals, just as Pujol and Maragall are strongly competitive personalities in Catalonia/Barcelona. However, Pujol and Maragall belong to different political parties, unlike Spath and Rommel, who are both members of the CDU.

Among the *Länder* of eastern Germany, Saxony is the pacesetter and Dresden the most influential capital city, thanks in part to its minister-president, Kurt Biedenkopf, who is at least as respected as any of the country's political figures and, aside from Kohl, widely regarded as the most resourceful of them.

Biedenkopf was born a Rhinelander and a Catholic. In 1990, as unification took shape, he began managing the affairs of Saxony, most of whose people are not Christians, strictly speaking, and are said to vote for "King Kurt," as they call him, not the leader of the Christian Democratic party. (Kings have ruled during most of Saxony's one thousand years of experience as a governed territory.) "We don't even call the party the CDU here," Biedenkopf says. Yet, thanks to Biedenkopf's achievements and immense popularity, Saxony is the only one of the new eastern *Länder* that is governed by the CDU; the others are led politically either by a coalition of left-of-center parties or by the Social Democratic Party (SPD), the chief opposition party.

Biedenkopf and Kohl have been political rivals since the mid-1970s. At that time, many handicappers saw Biedenkopf as the next leader of the CDU, but it was Kohl who took control and then kept Biedenkopf well away from the center of power. Biedenkopf was judged the stronger of the two intellectually and a better strategic thinker, but Kohl was the better operator within the CDU, and won most of the battles; in 1987, he helped displace Biedenkopf as leader of the most populous *Land,* North Rhine–Westphalia. With unification, Biedenkopf was able to refashion his political career in Saxony and become his party's principal advocate of promoting the recovery of the eastern part of a united Germany. Biedenkopf is still seen by some as the best of the potential successors to Kohl as leader of the CDU and the country, but the combination of his age (sixty-seven) and outright opposition to him within the party, starting with Kohl, would seem to rule out that notion.

Biedenkopf is a convinced regionalist, and not just, one suspects, because he is in charge of a region but because, like many others, he thinks about his country's brief but troubled history as a nation-state and its deeper experience as a patchwork of regions. He shares a fairly widespread concern that a dominant, centralized Berlin Republic would foster anti-German coalitions elsewhere. "We are in the center of things, with nine neighbors on our borders," he observes. "A centralized Germany of eighty million isn't acceptable to them. Our only option is to decentralize. And we must make it clear to others that Germany is highly decentralized."[20]

Biedenkopf has high hopes for Saxony, which, he says, had the highest gross national product (GNP) in Europe early in the century and was the country's industrial heartland. Saxony did once have a stronger industrial base than even the Ruhr, and it continues to have the strongest and most diverse economy of the eastern *Länder*. It also has nearly twice the population of any of them. "But I tell them the truth, that it will take us fifteen years to catch up," Biedenkopf says.

His administration is developing productive links with Bavaria and Baden-Württemberg, a task made easier by Biedenkopf's position as a major figure within the CDU. And there has been talk of Saxony becoming part of the Four Motors Association. Biedenkopf and Pujol meet at regular intervals, but the signs are that Saxony won't be judged ready for membership in this powerful elite until its redevelopment has gone considerably further.

Biedenkopf is promoting commercial ties further east, especially in the Czech Republic and Poland. He points to Saxony's 375-mile border with these countries. "They must develop confidence that they can raise their living standards," he says. "They must have access to our markets." That means being allowed to join the EU. "Otherwise nationalism will be rekindled," he says. "They will seek to regain their pride that way. It would be a catastrophe."

Biedenkopf worries about the dark side of freedom's abrupt arrival further east. "A new threat must be recognized," he says. "It is disorder, creeping disorder. The breakdown of the Soviet Union meant the end of tsarist tyranny." Borders have, of course, become more open, partly as a consequence of interregional transactions, partly because of the EU's single market. Germany, according to Biedenkopf, is especially vulnerable, not just because of its location but because, he says, "Germans assume a cultural environment stretching west to east. And that is an illusion. Germany doesn't understand its vulnerability." Saxony is, of course, a frontier state and especially vulnerable.

Biedenkopf and those around him are convinced that Germans will hold *Land* governments, not Bonn, responsible for solving their problems. His aides note that after the Wall fell, the *Länder* were re-created even before the two parts of the country were reunited. The two officials who manage Saxony's trade and external relations both felt that the *Länder* were gaining influence over federal policy. As for Brussels and the EU, both felt strongly that the attitude of the new—that is, eastern—*Länder* blended indifference with hostility.

"We are thirty years behind in the new states," said a colleague of his. "Brussels causes huge problems for us. We cannot afford to meet the standards of the EU. We cannot comply with the new directives Brussels keeps giving us. People in the new states think very little about Europe or the EU. We used to see it as something large and benign and set up to build a better world. Now we feel differently. No one here votes in the EU parliamentary elections." But this official is quick to add that what is really needed is a better division of labor among regions, national governments, and Brussels. "We still need central institutions and a commission in Brussels," he said. "We must have competence at levels where the issues are transnational."[21]

Biedenkopf agrees and is as eloquent as anyone in addressing the need for leadership. "The end of a plausible, visible threat from the east means that the cohesive force that held Europe together has gone," he said. "Cohesion is essential to the functioning of highly complex institutions," he continued. "We therefore need more, not less, leadership. There is no substitute for that, as Maastricht demonstrated. Maastricht relied on the external threat to provide cohesion. The people there didn't realize they were in a new era. The EU's leaders couldn't point to Moscow and obtain the ritual acquiescence from the people as in the past. They had instead—and for the first time—to explain what they were doing."[22]

The question is where and when the competent leadership will be exercised and who will supply it. Biedenkopf is not optimistic: "the end of a plausible, visible threat from the east," he says, "means that the cohesive force that held Europe together has gone."

CATALONIA TENDS TO think of itself as a nation, not a region. It's hard to disagree, even though Catalonia hasn't known political independence since the late seventeenth century. It was among the early European nations, actually a medieval imperium whose maritime power gave it control for a time of Sicily, Corsica, Sardinia, and the Balearic Islands. The Catalan language reached into Provence, and by the fourteenth century most of southwestern France was ruled from Barcelona.

Two hundred years later, Spain's Philip II tried and failed to commandeer the services of Catalan carpenters to help build royal galleys. At a time when the king liked to boast from his desk in the Escurial that he could "govern half the world with two inches of paper," the answer to his summons was: "The people of Catalonia, by the liberties they have been granted, are not like those of Toledo, where any constable can order carpenters to be brought by force. Here your Majesty is seen as an individual involved in a contract."[23]

Today's Catalans see themselves as charting their course on a similarly large canvas. "We have three dimensions—Spanish, Mediterranean, and European," says Joaquim Llimona, director of external relations for Pujol's government.[24] He means that Catalans not only consider Barcelona the first city of the Mediterranean, which it is, but regard themselves as constituting the north of the south and the south of the north. Pujol, as noted, sees the Netherlands as the model for Catalonia, notably because of its network of multinational enterprises, which thrive in an area possessing few natural resources. In a memorable speech delivered in Amsterdam on September 30, 1992, he traced "the idea of making Catalonia the Holland of the south" to the seventeenth century, a time he cited as "the beginning of modern Catalonia, which did not want to see itself submerged in the climate of Spanish decline."

Pujol reflects and promotes the dominant Catalan conceit: that it belongs to a community of northern European nations. In a speech in Aachen just after Spain's entry into the EU—"my great speech," he calls it—Pujol described Catalonia as the southern corner of Charlemagne's empire. He will refer to southwestern France as French Catalonia. "Barcelona, Perpignan, and Montpellier may now be considered as one big metropole," says Llimona. "The Perpignan region was historically part of Catalonia. Some of the people there can still speak Catalan."

Barcelona's web of traditional links with neighboring French cities deepens its northward thrust and its affinity with southwestern France. For example, several generations of the Catalan medical community have studied in Montpellier, a city with a strong and deep medical tradition. The duke of Montpellier hid the Jews during the time of medieval pogroms because they were judged the most skilled in medicine.

All that is needed to complete the commercial, if not cultural, fusion of Catalonia and at least a major part of southwestern France is a high-speed train, according to people in both the Catalan and city governments. The train is coming but won't be operating until early in the next century; the project requires the cooperation and approval of the governments of France and Spain, and they've been in no hurry to accommodate the interested parties.

It isn't unusual to hear about Barcelona businessmen who travel regularly to Lyon, Düsseldorf, and Amsterdam but who haven't been to Madrid. Carlos A. Gasoliba, the secretary-general of the Patronat Catala pro Europa, says he has been to Madrid only as a teenager—to see the Prado and other monuments. Otherwise, he says, "my family and I always went north."[25]

Catalonia used to be protectionist. Its market was the region and the rest of Spain. No longer. "Now we think of the EU as our market," says Llimona. "We are part of the European structure—with four hundred million consumers."

Pujol and most politically aware Catalans feel that by any standard measure, including economic stability, per capita income, population, cultural attributes, history, and outlook, they are a northern European nation, more so than a region of the less prosperous, less dynamic, more agrarian, and historically divergent mother country. It was Catalonia's entrepreneurial spirit, along with its location, that gave Spain access to the Industrial Revolution. Barcelona's cultured bourgeoisie acted as a magnetic field for sequential movements—Romanticism, Art Nouveau, and Surrealism. For the Barcelonese, the Castilian capital, Madrid, is a rather provincial city of limited interest. Pujol and his fellow nationalists like to emphasize Catalonia's Europeanness—how it played no part, for example, in the Islamization of Spain and was always oriented to the north and east. Among the long list of Catalan claims is that in 1359 the Kingdom of Catalonia became the world's first parliamentary government.

Pujol is a well-known personality in most of western Europe, partly because he is a fervent "European," meaning he supports the EU and its works. On some questions involving the EU, his intentions are clear; they are less so on some others. He clearly uses the EU to help him distance Catalonia from Madrid. EU institutions, he observes, are more sympathetic to the regions than the member states are. What isn't clear is whether he envisages an EU that will eventually be built mainly around historic regions, as distinct from nation-states. He has said that Catalonia is no less a nation than Slovenia, one of the first two states of the former Yugoslavia to split away from the federation. Still, whatever Pujol's long view may be, he clearly sees Catalonia as first and foremost a nation, only secondarily as a region of Europe.

Pujol is not a separatist, except perhaps in his heart; he knows Catalonia is and is likely to remain part of Spain. He says as much, but when asked about the limits on Catalan nationalism he does become cagey, noting, "Our home rule is not sufficient." And what do the Catalans want? "We are not asking for independence, only more autonomy." In fact, they already have a great deal of autonomy; along with the Basque country, they have more than any other region of Spain.

Pujol probably disguises his exact intentions because he presides over a society that harbors radical tendencies, some of which, composed mainly of the young, are frankly separatist. During the Olympic Summer Games held in Barcelona in 1992, for example, one of Pujol's sons joined a demonstration for an independent Catalonia. The games themselves were advertised internationally as the "Catalan Olympics." Some full-page newspaper ads proclaimed Barcelona the capital of the "country." Others displayed a map of Europe and asked where the Olympic Games were being held. Answer Barcelona. And where is Barcelona? In Catalonia.

Separatist sentiments in Catalonia are stronger than those in Italy's northern regions of Lombardy and the Veneto, where a frankly separatist political movement has gotten a lot of attention and has had some modest success at the polls but has probably attained its full growth. But Catalan separatism also has its limits, offset by various influences, including the region's banking and industrial elite, which won't risk rocking its own boat and reckons that Madrid will not surrender complete control of Spain's richest source of revenue and its gateway to Europe. With less than 14 percent of the population, Catalonia produces a quarter of Spain's exports, 40 percent of industrial exports; its renovated port handles

nearly a fourth of the entire Mediterranean shipping trade. Catalans share with northern Italians a resentment of their nation's capital, which they see as sponging up the wealth they create and
top-heavy with bureaucracy.

Among Pujol's weapons for distinguishing his putative nation
from Spain, none has been more effective than the Catalan language, which he uses to both sustain and extend the Catalan personality within the Spanish state. The language of instruction in
the schools is Catalan. Spanish is an elective, as are English and
French. In a court case involving a group of parents who sought to
insist that children of Spanish-speaking parents be taught in Spanish, the parents lost. Such people say bitterly that having a place in
Pujol's Catalonia obliges one to speak his language instead of the
mother tongue. Pujol's people argue that to do otherwise would
mean creating two communities, one opposing the other. The
Catalan language is the equalizer, they say, in a society of which
about 40 percent consists of Andalusians and other non-Catalan
people—"immigrants from Spain," as Pujol has called them. It all
goes down badly in Madrid, where during the 1996 elections his
critics chanted, "Pujol, you little man, speak Spanish if you can."[26]
Journalism is different, however. Barcelona's major outlets for both
print and broadcast journalism are divided roughly evenly between
the two languages.

One of Pujol's political opponents and most articulate critics is
Aleix Vidal-Quadros, who thinks that Pujol's nationalism collides
with Barcelona's interests. "The city must be open to diversity," he
says. "Great literary figures—Federico García Lorca, Mario Vargas
Llosa, and others—lived and published here. It was the center of
publishing in the Hispanic world. Not any more. Mexico and
Madrid have displaced Barcelona. Catalonia is too small for
Barcelona, which requires a bigger stage."[27]

Robert Hughes, in his splendid book *Barcelona*, makes the same
point, noting that Barcelona's two major Spanish-language dailies
publish cultural supplements—"reviews of books, art, theater,

movies—in Catalan, which suggests . . . that Catalan in Barcelona is mainly a language for the upscale, the university educated, the cultivated. But these are the very people who need to communicate with the rest of Europe, and nobody can do that in Catalan. The hope that a uniquely Europe-oriented culture could be created around a minority language like Catalan worked as long as Barcelona was a nucleus of liberal ferment, the one spearhead of an open society in an otherwise black, inward-turning, authoritarian Spain. That long moment lasted from the mid-1960s to Franco's death. It is gone."[28]

Pujol's claims for Catalonia, together with his somewhat imperious and didactic style, have created a rich lode of anecdote; one story that has wide acceptance despite a somewhat apocryphal ring recounts Pujol greeting King Juan Carlos, who was arriving for a visit. Pujol supposedly expressed the hope that his Majesty would feel at home in Barcelona, and the king supposedly replied, "I always feel at home when I am at home." A propos, when traveling abroad Pujol is said to expect to be treated as a visiting head of state. His allegedly lofty view of himself and his role has earned him derisive nicknames in the press, including "King Jordi" and "little de Gaulle."

Pujol, who was born in June 1970 and is a banker by training, was elected to his first term in 1980 and reelected to his fifth in 1995. Hughes describes Pujol as "a highly recognizable Catalan type of politician—the reincarnation of those Catalan burghers who ran Barcelona in the late nineteenth century on a platform of industrial expansion and local patriotism, preaching self-determination for the province while constantly negotiating with Madrid."[29] He is a Conservative but supported the government of Felipe González because Spain's Socialists take a more sympathetic view of regional autonomy than do its Conservatives, who belong to the tradition of Spanish centralism.

Pujol is a short, roundish man who is said to be very fit and inclined to vigorous exercise such as running up mountains. He talks forcefully and at length; he can do so fluently in any one of five languages, including, besides Catalan and Spanish, German, French, and English. It's generally agreed that Pujol is a poor listener but a born lecturer. The two great cultural influences of his youth, he says, were German and French. He attended a German school in Barcelona, taking his baccalaureate there. In 1995, he was the keynote speaker for the school's hundredth anniversary. He pays regular visits to various leaders of German *Länder,* especially Biedenkopf; Johannes Rau, minister-president of North Rhine–Westphalia; and Edmund Stoiber. He also sees Chancellor Kohl at regular intervals.

Whatever his admiration for French culture, Pujol takes a stern view of the centralized style of the French state and its hostility to regionalism. Only Germany, he feels, can move the EU in the right direction. Germany is the country Pujol most admires, not least its federal structure. However, he doesn't want to see federalism in Spain, acccording to close Pujol watchers, because, as one of them said, "it would put the rest of Spain on the same level as Catalonia. And that is unacceptable."

Pujol began to acquire standing in the 1950s, first by campaigning for Catalan autonomy and, in the bargain, opposing the caudillo, Francisco Franco, who disliked and distrusted the region's independent ways and Barcelona's cosmopolitan, seemingly un-Spanish style. Then, in 1959, Pujol founded Catalonia's independent banking system by creating the Banca Catalana, the first such institution and one that was followed by others. These meant that Catalan businessmen no longer had to seek loans from branches of Madrid banks. A year later, during one of Franco's visits to Barcelona, Pujol was arrested following a demonstration on behalf of Catalan nationalism. After serving three years of a seven-year sentence, he was released in 1963 and swiftly became the authentic voice of the movement.

Not surprisingly, Pujol identifies himself with Catalonia and its people. Over the years, he has characterized attacks on himself by official sources in Madrid as attacks on Catalonia. But such is his power that in recent years he has come to be regarded as co–prime minister of Spain. Through his bloc of deputies in Spain's Parliament, he held the balance of power in the Socialist government of Felipe González, which fell during the March 1996 elections. He used this leverage to extract numerous concessions for Catalonia. Today he runs his own health, education, prison, and police systems. According to one newspaper report, "He has created a state within a state, now employing 110,000 people."[30]

Pujol can lay claim to even more of the authority that he regards as Catalonia's rightful portion. But for him, José María Aznar, a Conservative who succeeded González, would not have been able to form a government. Doing so required eight tough weeks of bargaining, during which he and Pujol met three times in what some of the press called "summits." What Pujol got then included partial control of the authority for income taxing in Catalonia; more precisely, he arranged for a system of coresponsibility whereby Catalonia and Spain's sixteen other "autonomous communities" would (1) control a 30 percent share of the tax revenue paid by their constituencies and (2) have the authority to raise or lower the rates paid by their people. Briefly, Pujol and through him Catalonia are going from strength to strength. All this creates frustration among Madrid politicians; they complain through the press that although Pujol and his minions do not want to be part of Spain, they are nonetheless calling the shots.

Yet while Pujol can hold center stage in Spain, in Barcelona he had to share it with the mayor, Pasqual Maragall. It is tempting and probably not an overstatement to observe that in Pujol and Maragall, who resigned as mayor on September 21, 1997, the city of Barcelona has deployed two of Europe's most skillful, successful, and admired politicians. And in a region with a radical tradition that used to be known for the volatility of its politics, each belongs to the moderate mainstream. But inevitably, they have been keen rivals, and will probably remain so if Maragall stays in politics, as he very well may. Maragall belongs to the Socialist Party, although he is no more a socialist than Pujol; he is, at most, a social demo-crat whose striking popularity in Barcelona was unaffected by the scandals and stories of mismanagement that bedeviled the Social-ists at the national level. But much more interesting than Pujol and Maragall's different affiliations are their divergent visions of the fu-ture. Pujol's mystical attachment to Catalonia and his commitment to its European nationhood translates, many would say, into a vi-sion of an EU eventually composed of regions. Maragall, not sur-prisingly, believes in cities, not regions. And he is not much of a nationalist. In a speech at Oxford in 1986, he said, "A Catalan who claims . . . not [to] like nationalism finds himself in a somewhat difficult position. But it is my position."[31] The powerful ex-mayor and his confederates clearly have little interest in exchanging one central authority—in this case Madrid—for another, the Generali-tat, as the Catalan state government is known.

The Generalitat Palace and the Ajuntament, Barcelona's city hall, occupy fourteenth-century palaces that stand symbolically op-posite each other in the Plaça de Sant Jaume, just behind the cathedral in Barcelona's Old City. Pujol's visitors pass a lovely Gothic interior courtyard flush with orange trees on the way to his office. Liveried footmen serve coffee. The style within the less grand Ajuntament across the square is considerably more informal.

Maragall is said to envisage a resurrection of city-states, some of which, including Barcelona, would form a metropolitan system stretching across the Mediterranean littoral from Barcelona through southern France and into Italy. "We are not in the middle," he says. "We are the north of the south. All of southwestern France, except for Toulouse, was part of the Catalan empire."

Like Pujol, Maragall is a bit cagey and occasionally elliptical when asked what Barcelona's future position ideally should be. As for wanting to resurrect the city-states, he said, "That is a carica-ture of what I said." (That may be, but he often says something similar.) "Cities, not nations, will become the principal identity for most people in the world."[32] And again, "The cities will make alliances among themselves. We are being forced to unite and create an urban system."[33] Maragall's office displayed a satellite map of a huge urban agglomerate in an area covered by England, the Benelux countries, France, Germany, northern Italy, and Catalonia. It makes the point that within this mosaic, which happens to be the mainspring of European wealth and industry, most people live in cities, with the outlying areas seemingly inert and sparsely populated.

"Maragall is open, romantic, and imaginative," says Vidal-Quadros. "He wants a Mediterranean version of the Hanseatic League."[34] "He envisions a fusion of great cities," concurs an aide to Maragall. "The human resources available to the cities are the same as those available to the nation-states. Cities do not have the economic capacity [to finance] big projects, but they are better at launching projects. Cities occupy the space where cooperation between the public and private sectors is most effective. The trend now is for the public and private sectors to work together. This provides a framework in which the private sector helps in meeting the city's goals. This is happening in Barcelona." And what about the relationship between cities and regions? "That is too delicate for now," replied the aide. "City power is our objective. We think that in the future cities and regions will be on equal footing with central governments."[35]

Of the four tiers of local and national government that manage affairs in Spain, city and central government have the chief authority for taxation. States such as Catalonia are largely financed by block grants from Madrid (although Pujol may be able to change that), and cities manage their own budgets.

When asked about competing visions, Pujol spoke carefully. "Maragall has a Hanseatic concept," he observed. "He is strongly supported by local elements. The cities are strong and have existed longer than regions; at least, the forces promoting their fortunes have existed longer. What is important to them is the chief town

[Barcelona]. We think the chief town must not absorb the rest."[36] The term "chief town" seemed intended by Pujol to make the point that Catalonia is more than greater Barcelona and has other towns. "I have nine hundred forty-one municipalities, one of which is the city," he says.[37]

Maragall belongs to an old, upper-middle-class Barcelona family. Before he acquired political prominence, its best-known member was Joan Maragall, his grandfather and a major poet. For him, Barcelona was "the great enchantress." Ironically, the scene of the anti-Franco demonstration that led to Pujol's arrest and imprisonment was a concert given for Joan Maragall's centenary that included a musical rendering of one of his poems.[38]

After collecting an assortment of degrees, including one in urban land prices, Maragall entered politics. He became mayor of the city in 1982 and was elected to the job five times. People referred to him proudly as "our mayor."

Maragall thinks that a system of cities can function more smoothly and productively than a system of nation-states. "Cities," he's said, "have no frontiers, no armies, no customs, no immigration officials. Cities are places for invention, for creativity, for freedom."[39]

"Before Maragall, this was a hidden city," says a local journalist. "We are witnessing its transformation."[40] Maragall, some say, gave this once-neglected, laid-back city a Type A personality without surrendering any of the charm and beauty that distinguish it. In June 1995, the *Financial Times* cited a survey that ranked Barcelona seventh as a European business location—above Milan, Geneva, Munich, and Stockholm and three places higher than its ranking two years earlier.[41]

The author of Oxford University's Reith Lectures in 1995, Sir Richard Rogers, the architect, said, "Autonomy, vision, and strong leadership have totally transformed the city." He pointed to "the realization of a master plan, including the refurbishment of Barcelona's streets and squares and the construction of new housing and services." Rogers held up Barcelona as an example for London.[42]

Maragall's design for the city is far from complete, as he sees it. He envies Milan and says, "We must be able to sustain an international airport, serving New York and Tokyo nonstop." La Scala is another object of his envy. "We need and we can sustain one of the major opera houses here," he says. "It's a costly and highly sophisticated operation."[43] The high-speed train that will eventually connect Barcelona to Montpellier, Lyon, and northern Italy is also high on his list of musts. Even if he does become prime minister, there's little else Maragall can do in overcoming what he most envies about Milan—its mid-European location.

Barcelona's closely plotted renewal had been under way for several years when, in 1986, Maragall succeeded in pocketing the 1992 Olympic Games for Barcelona. The games did, of course, contribute to and considerably hasten Barcelona's reinvention of itself and its feeling that it had become the center of Mediterranean culture and enterprise; in leveraging the Olympic moment, the city is said to have accomplished in four years what otherwise would have taken twenty. In the bargain, it also vastly outperformed other Olympic venues, most recently Atlanta, in building parks, roads, and bridges, along with other public facilities, and generally enriching the city's aspect.

Pujol shares some of the credit for Barcelona being selected for the games. "Cooperation between Pujol and Maragall was essential," says a European diplomat who watched these events. "But after the games, they went back to the status quo ante. Normally they compete, and there isn't much cooperation. Each identifies the place and the region with himself."

Both want more authority, and both are well positioned to obtain more. Both are playing the European card to promote what they see as their constituent interests. Pujol, as noted, uses Brussels against Madrid, as did Maragall, who says there is "complicity between cities and the [European] Commission. Both see the Jacobin character of the nation-states."[44] Maragall argues that cities are in better touch with problems of air and noise pollution, along with other issues affecting quality of life, than are state or central governments. He professes to favor leaving other and broader issues to the EU. And Maragall showed that he, too, could play the regional game. In 1996, he became the chairman of the EU's Committee of the Regions.

Maragall is judged ambitious, but for what? So far, he hasn't shed much light on his goals for himself. His party fancies him as a potential national leader and prime minister, and he is clearly tempted to challenge Gonzales for the leadership of their party. He would also like to teach urban planning in the United States, possibly at the New School in New York. There has also been some talk that when Pujol's current term expires he might find himself challenged by Maragall, who is younger by more than a decade and probably more popular than his imperious rival. Whether Maragall became prime minister, or succeeded Pujol, he could be relied on to put Catalonia to the service of its chief city and a great enterprise: building his version of a Hanseatic League across the northern shore of the Mediterranean and beyond.

JUST ACROSS THE Catalan border, control of Perpignan still rests with Paris, but somewhat tenuously. The city is trying vigorously to expand its commercial ties to Barcelona and revive its Catalan affinities—ethnic, linguistic, and cultural. Perpignan was once the second city of Catalonia. For most of its residents, Barcelona remains the nerve center and Paris could be on the far side of the moon. They use Barcelona's airport and see the future as depending largely on the high-speed train that will connect Barcelona to Lyon and pass through Perpignan and Montpellier.

About two years ago, a few local officials in and around Perpignan proposed building a monument to be called "Les Portes de la Catalonia" (The Gateway to Catalonia); it was to be located at a

point astride the north-south autoroute where the more traditional
border between France and Catalonia is supposed to lie—about
thirty miles inside France. Word of this initiative reached Paris,
where it was promptly snuffed out.

Still, not everyone in Perpignan feels as if the city's future lies in
Barcelona. There is concern that the real Catalans, starting with
Pujol, will use their French cousins but otherwise treat them as
distant and undeserving.

The conflict between Paris and the major regional cities varies
in expression from place to place, although it usually stays just beneath the surface. Toulouse, which lies to the north and somewhat
east of Perpignan, has an anti-Paris tradition that dates to the sup-
pression of the Albigensian heresy in the early thirteenth century.
John Ardagh, in his book *A Tale of Five Cities,* describes how much
time is spent by "old" Toulousains in discussing local history. "Go to
a *bourgeois* dinner party," he writes, "and you may hear families
solemnly comparing the roles of their ancestors in the medieval
woad (blue dye) trade or the revolt against Richelieu. 'Did your
family fight in the First or the Second,' I heard one scion ask another. He was not referring to this country's World Wars, but to the
Crusades. Another Toulousain said to me, 'We are all deeply
marked here by the Roman Conquest, it makes us feel different
from Paris,' and then added, 'We're marked by the Nazi Occupation, too'—as if the two events were roughly contemporary."[45]

Geography contributes to Toulouse's sense of isolation from
Paris and separateness; it lies on the wrong side of the Massif Central. Moreover, within the small triangle that connects Toulouse
with Barcelona and Montpellier, a prosperous commercial partnership has developed; it combines Barcelona's port facilities with
Toulouse's engineering sweep and Montpellier's large capacity in
advanced technology.[46]

France is the world's consummate nation-state; its uniquely
centralized authority dates to 1792, when the country was divided
into eighty-eight *départements,* each run by a *préfet* appointed by

Paris. In 1964, the *départements* were grouped into twenty-one regions, all drawn in a way that avoided similarity to the culturally distinct provinces.[47] Everyone, they say in Paris, "still feels French," and to some degree that is probably true. But the freewheeling activity in cities and regions across France's borders with Germany, Spain, Italy, and Belgium has had a ripple effect. Most major French cities have acquired larger budgets and more authority than ever before. In 1982, the newly arrived regime of President François Mitterrand, who saw the *préfets* as a conservative Gaullist elite, granted fairly broad powers to regional councils; since then, the councils and the *préfets,* who are still appointed by Paris, have coexisted within a complex system of checks and balances.

A decade later, the glossiest of French institutions, the École Nationale d'Administration (ENA), a school that trains an ultraelite sifted from the elitist products of France's toniest undergraduate schools, was partially uprooted. Its trainees now divide their time between Paris and Strasbourg; although a seemingly small gesture, it was nevertheless a controversial step away from tradition.

More recently, the regional current has broadened and acquired momentum, enough so that in May 1996 the Paris daily *Le Figaro* ran a series of six articles on what it called "France's regionalist awakening."[48] In neighboring countries, some commentators saw the publication of these pieces as an event—as the first time a major French newspaper had dared to suggest that France might be other than a changeless nation-state, with everyone there being first and last French. A few weeks later, in early July of the year, the government disclosed plans to delegate more decision-making power from Paris to the regions. The minister in charge of the public sector cited "profound archaisms" in the management of the state, including water, which, he said, was being handled by six separate services in each government department. Ministries in Paris, he noted, would lose 70,000 jobs, and the number of headquarters functions in Paris would be cut by 30 percent.[49]

French regionalists, like those elsewhere in Europe, are left standing somewhere between awe and envy by the federalist model, which seems to work as well in a united Germany as it did during the Cold War. And some French regionalists have convinced themselves that because the elections in Spain in 1996 seemed to establish Pujol as the pivotal figure, the last defense against federalism there had fallen. (That perception is overdrawn.)

The chief threat to the Paris edifice and Bonapartist tradition lies in the biggest French region, the Rhône-Alpes, and most conspicuously in Lyon, its capital city and France's second largest. In economic strength and versatility, along with the depth of its cultural and educational institutions, Lyon is, again, second only to Paris. The city has nine universities with 110,000 students, along with a vast technological base. And the Rhône-Alpes is one of Europe's most potent regions; its territory stretches from the Rhône River in the north to the Savoie Mountains on the Swiss and Italian borders in the east to the rural Ardeche in the south. Other large cities within the region, starting with Grenoble, one of Europe's premier centers of advanced technology, and Saint-Étienne, are collateral sources of economic power and reach.

The senior officials and planners in Lyon convey the same sense of a region and hub city on the move as do their counterparts in Barcelona. Indeed, they compare their projects and goals with those of their colleagues there, whom they know well and consult regularly. The chief difference is that the Lyonnais make no claim to nationhood or cohesiveness. The Rhône-Alpes, they recognize, is an artificial construct—an assortment of dissimilar *départments* patched together by the state against which the region is beginning to turn. "This is not a historic region, and it has had to assert itself," says Jacques Moulinier, the deputy mayor and a planner who is among those who envisage what he calls a *"renaissance des grandes villes."* [50]

"We can't compare ourselves to the Catalans or the Lombards or Piedmontese," says Alain Merieux, president of Lyon's International Council and first vice president of the Regional Council of the Rhône-Alpes. "We are an administrative structure, not a nation."[51] The Lyonnais may not have the soaring ambition of the Catalan nationalists. But they have a similar sense of wanting to run their own show and being allowed to make the external commercial links that will help them compete effectively on both the European and world markets. And Lyon does have some confrontational history. It was once a center of French Protestantism and became the publishing center—both above and below ground—of the movement. The city was also, in the 1940s, the wartime headquarters of the French resistance and its greatest leader, Jean Moulin.

"Lyon's ambition is to become a European city like Barcelona," says Robert Maury, director of the Association for the Development of the Lyon Area.[52] However, another difference is that the Lyonnais, despite their growing sense of confidence in themselves and their autonomous development, profess to feel unambiguously French, even while also noting that ministers in national governments, including their own, are losing authority and the political bases they once had. They also sound like Catalans and Germans of whatever region when they talk about distancing themselves from the center and marching to the drumbeat of world competition. "The great risk in Europe is the secession of the regions," says Michel Foucher, director of the European Geopolitical Observatory and a principal planner for the Rhône-Alpes. "There is now permanent tension between the state and the regions," he adds. "Pujol's fantasy is to become a chief of state. Italy is a country with a highly centralized state, but a highly decentralized economy. The north is federalist and regionalist. Its people prefer working with outsiders to supporting the south."[53]

Among the principal "outsiders" is the Rhône-Alpes, which now does more business in Italy's Piedmont, just across the frontier, than with the Ile-de-France around Paris. Lyon likes to think of itself as having had a serious Italian experience, some of which stuck. For Italian silk merchants, Lyon was the center of their trade. An old section, *Vieux Lyon,* has an Italian Renaissance look and is alleged to contain Europe's largest concentration of sixteenth-century houses—about nine acres; a Mediterranean patina is dominant. Lyon also likes to think of its heritage, unlike that of Paris, as distinctly Latin; there is no shortage of reminders that it was the capital of Roman Gaul.

Lyon was always a town of merchants and possessed of a flair for business. It is unembarrassed by the Paris-made tag *"Lyon la bourgeoise"*; on the contrary. Lyonnais share with much of the northern Italian bourgeoisie strong feelings about the capital city, which they see as abounding with bureaucrats—an intrusive lot, they feel, who don't contribute to the economy but do burden it with taxes and regulations. Moreover, Lyonnais planners argue that the heavy—the disproportionate—concentration of French economic activity in the Paris region impairs growth within the regions, in part by sponging up too much of the labor market and by capturing the bulk of media attention. The Ile-de-France constitutes one half of the French economy, the Rhône-Alpes about 10 percent.

Paris is characterized as "a corrupt successor to Versailles" by Dominique Nouvellet, a prominent venture capitalist in Lyon, according to one newspaper report that went on to quote him as saying, "It's an administrative and political bureaucracy that kills off entrepreneurs, and that's why people are rebelling against capitals that exercise too much control over their lives."[54]

If France has become somewhat less centralized politically since the early 1980s, it has also, say the Lyonnais, become more centralized economically. "France has lost its taste for capitalism," says Merieux. "We have all the capacity in France, but we lack investment. The country needs confidence in itself and venture capital. It has all the other advantages."

Lyon has the confidence, not to mention the entrepreneurial ethos. Within the axis formed by Lyon and Grenoble, the region's main cities, lies a flourishing private sector of more than four thousand companies—exporters that, by and large, have created trade surpluses in most of the world in products as diverse as food and biotechnology.[55] Local people like to compare this aggregation with the huge but weakly performing state-owned companies that have dominated the French economy. The comparison, they feel, helps explain why the Rhône-Alpes began its recovery from the recession of the early 1990s before other regions did.

Because the Rhône-Alpes is the most freestanding French region, the sense of estrangement from Paris is probably stronger there than elsewhere in metropolitan France. "We don't want to be a province," says Michel Foucher. "We want strategic autonomy. We don't want to have to go to Paris two or three times a week. It is embarrassing not to have the same authority as colleagues in neighboring areas." Their biggest problem, say Lyon's planners, is the lack of coherent decision-making authority outside Paris. If, for example, the Rhône-Alpes wants to launch a joint project with a Swiss counterpart, it must work through the Paris-appointed *préfet,* whereas the Swiss canton is sovereign in such matters. The regional councils have assemblies, plus presidents and vice presidents. It is a maze of players and jurisdictions. "One never kills anything in France," they say in Lyon. "One just adds to the structure."

With the arrival of TGV service, Lyon seemed to become a virtual suburb of Paris; travel time was reduced to two hours, and a commuter from Lyon was presumed to have an easier time than someone driving from an outer suburb through the heavy congestion surrounding Paris. "The TGV was such a great success that economists and journalists in Paris were saying that Lyon no longer needed an airport," recalls Robert Maury. "But they missed the point. Lyon is a great European city, and Paris is further away from it than Turin is."

Lyon's Satolas Airport is now a large part of the rapidly expanding blueprint for regional development, although for a time it appeared that it, too, would become an instrument put to the service of greater Paris. Paris needs a third airport. At first, officials in the Rhône-Alpes pushed to have Lyon-Satolas designated. It made some sense; Lyon was building a TGV terminal at Satolas, which became operational in 1995 and provides high-speed rail service to Paris's Charles de Gaulle Airport. Then, rather abruptly, Lyon's planners were struck by what seemed a better idea: instead of having Paris's number three airport, Lyon would lay claim to being the number one airport in southern Europe. The city would become the capital of southern Europe, Satolas the hub airport.

Lyon's claim to the role of southern gateway is strong. Its location and other attributes, starting with a concentration of state-of-the-art transportation links, have attracted considerably more foreign businesses than any of France's other regions. Company executives, as they examine maps and charts, discover strong competitive advantages in colocating offices and warehouses with Satolas Airport, given its links to high-speed rail service and an expansive highway system.

The city sees itself as the center of what it calls the "southern arc"—a swath that ressembles the "banana" that Pujol likes to sketch. However, the Lyonnais version also includes Geneva and stretches across northern Italy to Venice, then later extending to the east to incorporate Vienna and Budapest. Also, planners and promoters say, Lyon is establishing the major north-south axis between Frankfurt and Barcelona and becoming the chief link between Europe's northeastern and southwestern quadrants."

The Rhône-Alpes is also stressing the Latin heritage as a tie that binds: "The regions located on the northern coast of the Mediterranean—in Spain, Italy, and France—have in common a Latin culture that ties them together," states an official publication.[56]

If the talk is not about the southern arc, it's about the so-called Alpine Diamond. "Our aces are Turin and Geneva," says Maury. And according to Jacques Moulinier, "There are few places in the world that offer the kind of synergy found in the Alpine Diamond. Right now we are setting up computer linkages and business part-

nerships. Later on we can think about the political ramifications."[57]
Asked what these might be, he replied, "The Alpine Diamond is
mainly about having greater independence from Paris."

Planners within the Alpine Diamond and contiguous areas are
preoccupied with the proposed rail tunnel through the Alps that
will carry people, freight, and containers between Lyon and Turin.
The project, when and if it goes forward, is expected to cost more
than the Channel Tunnel; the geological studies alone are very expensive, and the costs of harnessing the technologies are hard to
estimate but sure to be heavy. Lyonnais reckon that the chances of
obtaining the funding from a combination of public and private
sources are reasonably good, while conceding that the competition
for such funds in France, Italy, and the EU is stiff. In January
1995, the Lyonnais were disappointed by the French government's
decision to give a higher priority to another TGV project—one linking Paris to Strasbourg. And according to Foucher, the French state
supports Lyon's pet project in principle but has its own intra-
France regional strategy. Paris, Foucher says, insists on having
Lyon's help in linking a network of French cities; Lyon and Marseilles, for example, will be connected by TGV, as will Bordeaux
and Toulouse.

Foucher added that the Catalans are following the progress of
the new Alpine tunnel very carefully, because they, too, have a
strong economic involvement with northern Italy and expect to
have more. Going further, Alain Merieux says, "The great priority of
all southern Europe is the tunnel."

On November 14, 1995, Lyon's International Council assem-
bled the mayors of Turin, Geneva, Grenoble, and Saint-Étienne in
a meeting with Raymond Barre and numerous dignitaries—chief
executives of big companies such as Fiat, bankers, foundation
presidents, and representatives of other mayors, including Maragall. The Alpine Diamond was the conference's single subject.
Much of what was said stressed the links between the regions.
Paris was rarely mentioned, least of all approvingly. For Grenoble,

said its mayor, Michel Destot, "the common future" of the triad provided not just "the chance to break out of an enclosed geography and economy," but also "to break with overdependence on the Parisian capital—for Grenoble an economic, financial and political power far away and often suffocating."[58]

Given the difficulties of Alpine travel, transportation was a leit-motif. TGV service would be essential to creating the southern European arc and integrating Europe. And fully modern airports, linked to the service, would be essential to give the region the reach and distributive capacity the global market requires.

Among the regional advantages not mentioned but keenly felt by all conferees was the role of Raymond Barre, mayor of Lyon, deputy to the National Assembly, and president of Lyon's International Council. Barre is seventy-two, never wanted to be mayor, and agreed to run for the job only because his predecessor, Michel Noir, had been tried and convicted for corruption. (Corruption at the municipal level had become a serious matter; Alain Carignon, a former mayor of Grenoble, began serving a four-year sentence "for sleeze" in July 1996.) Few, if any, political figures in France are as respected as Barre. Besides having been prime minister for five years, he was and remains a greatly admired professor of economics; he has distinguished himself in numerous other roles, including finance minister of France and vice president of the European Commission. Barre enlarges Lyon's range of options and helps the entire region, if only because no one in Paris can accuse this states-manlike figure of promoting the interests of his city or region at the expense of the country's.

"Lyon is not very well known or recognized," Barre says. "I'm always struck by how impressed foreigners are when they visit the city. That is very important for the future. Lyon needs to be much more international."[59] Among Barre's first acts as mayor was to visit his fellow mayors of Grenoble and Saint-Étienne to suggest developing a common foreign policy for the region. Lyon itself now has nine foreign outposts in places as far off as Hong Kong and Montreal. These "embassies," as they are called by Bruno Chiaverini, director of international relations of the Rhône-Alpes, have created tensions with France's Foreign Ministry; so have some of the cross-border plans of the Rhône-Alpes.

As for the large question—will the Europe of the future be built mainly around regions?—Robert Maury, the chief planner for Lyon, says, "that will be the case with regard to business. The Europe of regions is a Europe of enterprises, and they must operate at the European level."

"The future lies in alliances between strong regions," Foucher says. The Four Motors Association, he notes, is "a club of the rich." And what about the poorer regions? "They will continue to be subsidized by Brussels," he says, "and their political power will have to help them at the national level." It may be a realistic evaluation, but it also sounds like *sauve qui peut,* and raises interesting questions about Europe's political future.

JUDGING BY THE press coverage and comment, northern Italy would seem to be the cauldron of so-called subnational regionalism. And it's true, of course, that in no other part of Europe, except possibly Corsica, is there more intense hostility toward the center, in this case Rome. In no other EU member state is there such an avowedly separatist movement or so much talk of a divided country. No other region harbors so shrill a secessionist or regionalist, or whatever Umberto Bossi, the chief of Italy's Northern League (Lega Nord), may be calling himself on any given day. But no part of northern Italy is likely to secede. As is usually the case in Italy, the raucous noises are deceptive, the situation more complicated than it appears.

Northern Italy is a medley of separate regions that have cultural and economic ties to neighboring countries. The Piedmont, Liguria, and Val d'Aosta lie within the French cultural orbit, Lombardy and the Veneto within the German. They are alike in their prosperity; the Veneto, the 7,000 square miles around Venice, probably has Europe's highest per capita income and lowest unemployment. All of northern Italy is also alike in its febrile hostility toward the central government, especially toward what are seen as an intrusive bureaucracy and punitive taxes. Over the past decade, taxes on business profits have jumped from 49 to 69 percent. These are regarded by those who pay them as tribute exacted from Rome to sustain the idle and feckless of the Mezzogiorno—the southern part of Italy, where in some areas unemployment hovers around 30 percent. "We used to say we can do without the state," says Piero Bassetti, the head of Milan's chamber of commerce, meaning that the state could be ignored. "We can now survive only if we get rid of the state or radically change it."[60]

Like the Catalans, northern Italians see themselves as belonging to northern Europe, less so to Italy. Unlike the Catalans, they lack political coherence, goals, and direction. The Catalans produce leaders such as Pujol and Maragall. The Rhône-Alpes can deploy a Raymond Barre to help legitimize its freewheeling behavior. Germany's pushy *Länder* are strongly led, many of them by baronial figures such as Stoiber, Biedenkopf, and Rau. In stark contrast, northern Italy's regional assertion is bound up with the random and volatile Bossi, one part rabble-rouser, one part screwball—"a certifiable loony," in the words of a prominent European ambassador who has observed him closely. He is given to odd locutions such as "Man is not a steak, and you can't treat him like one." He can pose as menacing, as when Milan magistrates began investigating Northern League officials for corruption. "They should know their lives are worth a bullet," Bossi warned.[61]

Bossi, a Lombardian, began political life in 1982 by launching a newspaper called *Lombardia Autonomista*. Two years later, he co-founded the League, of which his newspaper became an instrument. Bossi was not at first a secessionist but became one, demanding that Italy be divided into three republics. In the national elections of 1992, the Northern League emerged as a major political force in the north, with 23 percent of the vote. And in the elections of April 1996, which were won by a moderate center-left coalition led by Romano Prodi, the League outpolled other parties north of the Po. Nationally, it can claim a tenth of the electorate. It can tilt the balance in national elections, as Bossi showed when he joined with Silvio Berlusconi and his Forza Italia in the 1994 elections and when he withdrew his backing in 1996.

Bossi likes to say that his movement will be "the linchpin of the postwar order." Chances are, however, that the League and, above all, its leader have found the modest limits of their reach. Devoted support in a few cities in Lombardy and the Veneto—places such as Bergamo, Vicenza, and Treviso—will continue to go partway toward sustaining Bossi as a threat to a unitary Italian state, but not nearly far enough. His reliable support lies among the disaffected self-employed—shopkeepers, small-business men—who may be joined on occasion by upmarket elements of the entrepreneurial class. Treviso, a medieval city in the Veneto, provides an example. It has been a boomtown for thirty years, having become headquarters for ultrasuccessful ventures such as Benetton and the production center for a number of high-volume products. In 1995, Treviso exported products worth more than $7.5 billion. There is virtually no unemployment, and the Treviso district is carpeted with small businesses—one for every eight families.[62] The average annual income, about $20,000, is well above the national average. And yet feelings against the state in Treviso run so high that the League and its increasingly radical leader got 42 percent of the local vote in the 1996 elections.

In winning 10 percent of the national vote in the 1996 elections, the League lost some parliamentary seats. Two months later, its mayoral candidates in three northern Italian cities—Mantua, Lodi, and Pavia—failed to make it past the first round, finishing third behind those of the center-right and center-left alliances.[63]

Bossi's inflammatory rhetoric has become a drag on his movement, as have the memories evoked by green-shirted militants who surround him. He tells the faithful to stop paying taxes, and he has been pressing for a referendum on secession; on June 2, 1996, the fiftieth anniversary of the Italian Republic, he led tens of thousands of people in Lombardy in an oath of allegiance to Padania, a new state that would be composed of the breakaway northern provinces, Italy's economic heartland.[64] "It's time to choose the Czechoslovakian way," he said. "Let us divide up the country." Bossi then proceeded to select a ten-member "shadow government," step one toward creating Padania. He has since talked about creating a human chain that would demarcate the border between Padania and Italy, which itself would be divided: its center would become a republic called Etruria, the south another, as-yet-nameless one.

Otherwise, Bossi has no federalist plan or program, and neither does the League's less immoderate four-member brain trust. Asked to spell out their precise intentions during an interview, they fell back on the U.S. Constitution and talked of using it as a model after "delegating some powers to Brussels and spelling out the roles of the cities and regions and starting from the grass roots."[65] But Bossi's colleagues do not share the leader's secessionist bias. Depending on the audience, Bossi, too, sometimes disavows secession. Politically, the ambiguity is essential, since most of those who vote for the League don't favor secession. "Bossi needs this ambiguity," says Lucio Caracciolo, editor of the quarterly journal, *Limes*. "But it's dangerous. If we actually did confront secession, it would not be nice, as when the Czechs and Slovaks separated."[66]

While campaigning in 1996, Prodi promised to overhaul the tax system and grant more power to town halls; he's made no secret of his admiration for Germany's federal structure and social market economy. However, if his campaign utterances were also intended as an overture to Bossi and the League, they failed. Bossi doubtless feared that a reformist left-of-center government could marginalize him.

After arriving in office, Prodi found federalism a daunting and, at best, distant prospect—more an ideal than an attainable goal. Italy has well-developed administrative structures at the municipal level, but at its provincial level, bureaucracies are very weak. Moreover, when municipal authorities were granted some of the taxing authority they had been crying for some years ago, they subsequently complained; they didn't like the added responsibility. Creating a federal system would also mean trying to dismantle a vast, well-entrenched state bureaucracy.

In any case, federalism can't work in a country as divided as Italy is between the Mezzogiorno and the other regions. Of Italy's fifty richest towns, not one is in the south, although all of the fifty poorest are there.[67] During his successful campaign, Prodi talked of southern Italy becoming "Europe's Florida." The south, he said, "must take on Andalusia"—must become "the winter headquarters for elderly northern Europeans."[68] The south has all the natural advantages, but other attributes—major crime, primitive transport, dubious medical facilities—would seem to exclude the advent of tourism on the Florida scale.

The rich, disaffected northern regions take for granted a robust internal market and equate the future with their ties to the other side of the Alps. Several Piedmontese firms are moving into the Rhône-Alpes, where they consider the infrastructure better and the bureaucracy more responsive. Milan and the rest of Lombardy, once an outpost of the Austro-Hungarian Empire, feel a strong sense of belonging to Mitteleuropa. Milan's architecture matches its attitude. It was the Austrian Empress Maria Teresa who pushed for building La Scala, the opera house that Maragall so envies. A Milanese planner sees two arcs of prosperity—one stretching from Barcelona to the Danube Valley and enfolding northern Italy, Trieste, Bavaria, and Austria; the other extending from southwest England through the Rhine Valley to northern Italy. He sees Milan, the region's business and cultural hub, as the axis of the first arc and vital to the second.

As COMPETITION WITHIN the global market gathers force, so does the regional trend. The title of a book by Kenichi Ohmae, a prominent and widely respected counselor to major international corporations, conveys a sweeping forecast: *The End of the Nation State—The Rise of Regional Economies.*

Ohmae sees global markets as steadily diminishing the role of governments, which, he seems to think, can best help competitive enterprises by getting out of the way. Russia's twenty-one republics and forty-nine provinces, for instance, have held Boris Yeltsin to his 1990 declaration that Russian regions should take "as much sovereignty as they can swallow."[69] Eight of the republics have made special treaties with Moscow, and many of the provinces have reached agreements allowing them to keep a portion of tax revenue. Foreign companies are in some cases bypassing Moscow, the business hub, and investing in regions like Samara. Tatar President Mintimer Shaimiyev hired a consulting firm in Cambridge, Massachusetts, to develop a foreign investment strategy for his state; he also sent emissaries to the World Economic Forum in Davos, Switzerland, to make contacts with major players, and he has created trade offices in Washington and Paris.[70] In allowing authority to devolve and regional power centers to develop, Yeltsin probably helped himself get reelected in the June 1996 elections.

The question many Europeans are asking is whether regions are gradually supplanting central states as sources of political authority and custodians of public policy. The answer is unclear; the signs point in different directions. For a variety of reasons, European governments no longer seem capable of fulfilling the terms of the social contract they entered into—ensuring jobs and prosperity, not to mention absolute security from want, hardship, and inconvenience. Or, put differently, absolute security—too much welfare and so on—leads to weak and insecure governments that are unwilling to take risks and unable to accomplish much of anything. But if governments can't fulfill the social contract, on what basis will they govern? Will they be able to maintain social peace in large cities? Will they guarantee law and order? Will they espouse the exclusion of foreigners and other populist causes?

Regions and cities can and probably will assume responsibilities

that have belonged to central governments. Still, whatever happens, regions are in most cases unlikely to assume responsibility for
the social contract, least of all the burden of providing social security. Equally unlikely is the prospect of a European Union built
mainly of numerous regions, large and small. So far, the significance of the regions is a good deal more economic than political;
the heaviest impact is being made by the superregions and lesser
transnational communities, not least on the global economy. The
nation-state isn't going anywhere, not anytime soon. Its writ will
continue to cover taxation and defense. And it remains the only
proven instrument for protecting justice, tolerance, and other
human values. That said, the signs point to regionalism, not the
European Union, as constituting the larger threat to the authority
of the nation-state.

CHAPTER III

A COLLECTIVE NERVOUS BREAKDOWN

Compared to the unhurried years of the Cold War, the 1990s have for Europeans been a volatile and occasionally tumultuous time. A snapshot of the relations among the key EU capitals taken at any time in this new era would have looked dated, even quaint, within a year or so. Looking back, the fortunes of the EU, or the EC, as it was then known, appear to have crested in mid-1989. Communism was in disorderly retreat, and Europe's postwar order had begun to crumble. The EC's twelve members were moving on schedule toward becoming a single market in 1992; with 350 million consumers, the EC would become the industrial world's largest market, and there was talk of monetary union. Many serious Europeans openly looked forward to toasting the arrival of the year 2000 with champagne bought with a newly minted common currency issued by a European central bank.

Less than a year later, the good news—warm peace supplanting cold war—was being obscured by the general confusion of most governments. With no compass, the various helmsmen were relying on flash judgments and, in some cases, the biases of yesteryear. Moreover, the ripple effect of Saddam Hussein's *coup de main* in Kuwait, besides transforming the Middle East and much of world politics, made the start of the post–Cold War era even murkier. The year 1989 had belonged to Eastern Europe, and many diplomats in Europe and elsewhere reckoned that the focus in 1990— and perhaps even the entire decade of the 1990s—would shift to a prospering EC as it adapted to a more preeminent German role and a reduced American presence.

Again, less than a year earlier, the prospect of a unified Germany hadn't turned up on any government's horizon, including Bonn's. To the contrary: officials everywhere had convinced themselves that the issue of unification lay far ahead, well into the next millennium. Most Germans, after all, would oppose putting at risk the prosperity that had been gained westward in the EC, or the security provided by NATO, for the risks and uncertainties of union with East Germany. Even if East Germany should be willing to become an appendage of the Federal Republic, West Germans believed, it would be unable to switch from a command economy to a market economy. West Germany's allies had supported unification rhetorically, but the continued division of Germany was tacitly embedded in the policies of all of them. And in any case, Moscow could be counted on to veto unification. Or so it seemed.

The breach in the Berlin Wall was expected at the time to produce elections and political reform in East Germany—nothing more. And precisely because unification wasn't supposed to happen, various officials could glibly endorse it, as NATO's leaders did at the end of a summit meeting in May 1989; as French President François Mitterrand did in a newspaper interview that July; as he did again on November 3, a week before the Wall became a target of souvenir hunters. "I am not afraid of reunification," he said.

"I think the desire for reunification is legitimate for the Germans. What counts above all is the determination and will of the people."[1]

By mid-1989, it also seemed as though the policy apparatus of incoming president George Bush was going in circles and getting nowhere with the issues that now preoccupied America's European allies. "Status quo plus," whatever that meant in Washington, didn't resonate beyond the Potomac. Sardonic but plainly worried, observers in some European capitals asked, "Has America fallen off the planet?" A few months later, however, only Washington caught the political tide released by the Wall's collapse by actively and visibly supporting German unification. Paris and London struggled briefly against the tide before having to give way.

To have British Prime Minister Margaret Thatcher take—or try to take—an obstructionist line was interesting but not surprising; her fierce anti-German phobia lay unconcealed. Several newspapers quoted her as saying that unification was not on the agenda. But she was relying on Mitterrand, Chancellor Kohl's closest and most important European partner, to do the heavy lifting. And early in December, the same man who had pronounced himself unafraid of unification just a week before the Wall's collapse turned up in Kiev, where he held private talks with Soviet President Mikhail Gorbachev and in a joint press conference publicly warned West Germany against pursuing unification with East Germany.

Two weeks later, Mitterrand was in Leipzig and East Berlin, cautioning East Germans against quick moves toward unification and discussing cooperation between France's Socialist Party and the East German Communist Party. All that was bad enough, but more serious still was Mitterrand's refusal while in Berlin of Kohl's invitation to join in the ceremonial opening of the Brandenburg Gate. Worse perhaps, he tried to maneuver a meeting with the East German prime minister, Modrow, before Kohl himself had a chance to confer with him; Kohl got wind of this ill-advised gambit and got to Modrow one day ahead of Mitterrand, who a few days before had sent his foreign minister, Roland Dumas, to see East Germany's leader and urge him to keep his country separate and independent.

Mitterrand should have recognized that Gorbachev, who in his relationship with the Germans was the petitioner—he needed their help—would not interfere with unification. He actually told Kohl's foreign minister, Hans-Dietrich Genscher, about Mitterrand's request for help in blocking unification. Also, East Germans were already forcing events with their feet. School gymnasiums in West German towns and cities were filling up with refugees from the East.

Mitterrand, who was usually as ingenious as he was crafty, could have—should have—seized the moment. It was the end of one era, the start of another—one that France should have lost no time in starting to influence. But his maneuvering, apart from being futile and embarrassing, had a troublesome ripple effect that was strongly felt then, is still being felt, and will continue to be felt for some time to come. First, France's leader, the EU's other statesman and pivotal figure, was seen to have lost his edge. Second, the Germans felt betrayed; France, the partner and neighbor to which they had been bonded, was not there for them at this crucial moment and had even turned hostile. Third, Mitterrand's unavailing gambit marked, if not dramatized, what seemed a turning point in Franco-German relations and Europe's power balance before anything had actually happened.

The special Franco-German relationship survived the moment because it had to; all Europe depended on it. Moreover, the relationship could prosper only if the link between the two leaders could be restored and sustained, as in this case it was. When Mitterrand died in January 1996, the *Frankfurter Allgemeine Zeitung* described his twelve years in power as "the most fruitful era of cooperation" between France and Germany.[2] "Almost like a biblical patriarch from a far-off time," said the *Stuttgarter Zeitung*.[3] What did not survive, however, was the dream of European union in some advanced form. The shock of Germany's impending unification alarmed Mitterrand and clouded his vision. A unified Germany, he reckoned, would have to be bound over to a cohesive European Community and made its creature. Otherwise, Europe would be Germanized. "The new German equilibrium to which the Germans aspire must be part of a European equilibrium," Mitterrand declared in December 1989. "That is why the [European] Community needs to be strengthened."[4]

Questions arose: Just how cohesive—unified—should the EC become? How great a derogation of sovereignty would France, Europe's oldest and proudest nation-state, make to Brussels and its bureaucrats?

Mitterrand confronted a seemingly no-win proposititition. The center of political gravity would soon begin moving from the banks of the Seine to those of the Rhine. Within a more cohesive EC, Germany would displace France as the dominant member. Yet without more self-integration by the EC, France would be either tied to or isolated from a German-dominated regional bloc covering most of western and northern Europe. Put differently, the prospect of Germany drifting away from the EC and plotting its own course was unacceptable and would have gone down badly in all of France. But a Germanized EC looked to be almost as bad.

What Mitterrand did have working to his presumed advantage was Helmut Kohl's strong feeling about the sanctity of both the Franco-German partnership and a unified European Community. Yes, Kohl could unify the German nation, but could he keep it on the path of virtue, which meant putting the EC first and steering Germany away from its historic tendency to freewheel? Simply put, Kohl could not afford to let Paris reproach Bonn for using unification as a device for pursuing a less "European" and more independent German diplomacy. Already, German politicians and diplomats were making no bones about east-central and eastern Europe having become their priority concern.

They could hardly do otherwise. The newly delivered societies to the east were unstable and generating a heavy emigrant flow to Germany. The failed attempt in mid-August by eight old Soviet hard-liners to topple Gorbachev alarmed Germans, who were still equating the prospects for stability and progress in the east with his policies and person. Any alternative, they feared, would be accompanied by chaos that would quickly spread beyond the USSR's borders and provoke mass migration from East to West, with the larger part of the exodus halting in Germany. The speedy collapse of the attempted coup was reassuring but not enough to alleviate the Germans' concerns.

The Botched Meeting

By then, the members of the EC were preparing to meet at the Dutch town Maastricht, in December, in order to update and strengthen the Treaty of Rome. Heading an overcrowded agenda was the creation of economic and monetary union, including a single currency. A common foreign and security policy was another declared goal. Some streamlining and alteration of the institutions were in order, given the pressure to enlarge the EC by adding members from northern and eastern Europe; a larger club would clearly be less cohesive and more difficult to manage.

At bottom, however, Maastricht was mainly about Germany, having been conceived by Mitterrand as a means of anchoring a united German nation to a more closely knit EC—one that would continue to turn on a Franco-German axis. He and Kohl had precooked a deal, or at least Kohl thought so. France would get EMU (European monetary union); Germany would get serious progress toward political union. France wanted EMU because it would disguise the awkward realities: France's monetary policy was in fact controlled by Germany's Bundesbank; most of the EU had become a de facto D-mark zone. In any European central bank, the balance of power would probably be held by the Germans; still, having

France's central bank sitting at the same table as the Bundesbank and taking part in the decision-making process would for the French constitute an improvement over the status quo—that is, the president of their central bank being informed electronically every other Thursday about interest rate decisions taken in Frankfurt on that day—decisions that would then be applied to other European currencies, including the French franc.

Germany wanted progress toward political union, because it made sense. It was what the European movement was supposed to be about. Could members move toward a common foreign and security policy without acquiring both the habit and institutional means of making decisions jointly? Security matters were off the EC's agenda during the Cold War; then, as now, the membership lacked a decision-making culture, let alone a form of leadership that could deal with issues affecting war and peace. Authority is divided among the member governments, represented by the Council of Ministers, the Secretariat, and the Commission. None of them can take charge alone. The European Commission, in which the member states have vested some elements of supranational authority, makes proposals and implements the Council of Ministers' decisions. The Commission presidency is rotated among the members, each of whom acquires it for six months (or once every eight years, given the present membership of fifteen, which is, however, supposed to grow). Invariably, the leader of whichever country takes the chair comes determined to make an impact; in the process, problems can arise that may or may not be solved on a successor's watch.

Many EU members, starting with Britain and France, have become steadily more unhappy with their executive arm, the Commission, and its tendency, as they judge matters, to presume too much. Hence, advocates of a larger role for the Commission are making no headway. It does negotiate trade in goods but was turned down in September 1996, when it tried extending its authority to cover services and intellectual property.

The real power within the cluster of EU institutions in Brussels lies with member government surrogates that form an ultra-low-profile body known by the acronym "Coreper," which stands for "Committee of Permanent Representatives." It consists of elite senior diplomats who as individuals are chosen by capitals because they combine versatility, discretion, and negotiating ability with endless patience and an equally great capacity for working long hours. Besides being a bridge between national governments, Coreper has decision-making powers; indeed, it is the key decision-making authority. "One of the best-kept secrets in Brussels is that 90 percent of EU decisions are resolved in Coreper before they even reach ministers," according to a piece in the *Financial Times* that lifted the veil on Coreper, describing it as "an exclusive male club with an accent on classical diplomacy and intimate deal making, usually over lunch. 'If you want smooth decision making in Europe,' concludes a Coreper veteran, with no trace of irony, 'you must keep it away from the politicians.' "5 The Commission, by comparison, has considerable power of initiative but none for making decisions.

As seen from Bonn, monetary union also required a heavy infusion of political union, including more power for the Commission and especially for the European Parliament, whose role is largely consultative. Adding a single currency and a central bank to the single market would constitute a lot of integration. Inflation, budget deficits, and even unemployment would become Community-wide problems and would have to be dealt with accordingly, presumably by some central political authority.

Money is power, and the prospect of launching a European central bank that would be unaccountable to any such authority seemed then—still seems—bizarre at the least. The bank would control a single currency without being able to impose middle- and long-term economic goals. It would offer no protection against what economists call "asymmetric shocks." In the United States, Washington can offer relief in various forms to troubled regions in times of economic downturn. But in Europe, France, say, might go into shock during a recession, but not Germany, in which case a central bank would be powerless to help France. Instead, playing by the agreed-upon rules, the bank might well deny France the right to help itself if that meant enlarging its budget deficit. Briefly, creating EMU without first creating a parallel political authority appeared to be putting the cart before the horse. Or, to change the metaphor, a monetary union unaccompanied by political union of some sort would begin life with a serious birth defect.

It happened that way, however. EMU fell into place, but France and Britain denied Germany serious movement toward institutional reform or a common foreign and security policy or progress toward adding new members. British policy was being heavily influenced by the so-called Euroskeptics of the Conservative Party— hard-liners who referred to their adversaries, the advocates of European union, as "federastes." But France, still the EU's *primus inter pares,* bore a heavier responsibility for the mess created at Maastricht. The initiative for the blended proposal put forward there was Mitterrand's. Kohl had merely gone along with it. Mitterrand, he knew, had been describing Germans as a people who didn't know where their frontiers were. Mitterrand and company, like the British, were reluctant to surrender political authority to Brussels yet wanted to "Gulliverize" Germany. Having matters both ways wasn't possible. Paris couldn't bring itself to accept that France would be able to deploy more influence as a still-pivotal member of a more unified EU than as an appendage of an expansive German-led regional bloc, one that would gradually include most of northern and east-central Europe. France was still ignoring the substance of power and keeping faith with its shadow.

Stepping back, one sees that the meeting at Maastricht in December 1991 was not what it seemed but instead became a low point—perhaps *the* low point—in the fortunes of the EU. The high point had been the early years—the late 1950s and early 1960s— when the EC had created a vigor and direction that Europe hadn't

known since the Age of Exploration. But over the fifteen years preceding Maastricht, progress toward integration had been so slow as
to mock the goals of the Treaty of Rome and the movement's illus-
trious pioneers. The spirit and sense of adventure that had kindled
hopes for a federation of states capable one day of acting in concert
all but disappeared, despite the agreement on a single market. At
Maastricht, a major moment was missed. The EU members could
have used it to catch the new tide in Europe's affairs; they could
and should have taken political steps to adapt their Community to
the new era. Instead, they made a mess.

The mess included an addendum that linked the business of the
meeting—EMU, and so on—to the warfare then beginning in what
had been Yugoslavia. Five days after the meeting, the foreign ministers of EU members met in Brussels, in part to deal with pressure
from Germany to extend recognition to Croatia and Slovenia. Another serious mess was made. Until then, the members had made
little serious effort to settle the conflict, although all of them saw it
as a European problem and one to be solved by the EC. But what
to do about the disaster beginning to happen on their doorstep was
a question for which Europeans had no good, or even partial, answers. Germany, which is separated from Croatia and Slovenia only
by Austria, has old ties to the region that are very different from
those of Britain and especially of France. And Maastricht, besides
distracting Community leaders, especially Mitterrand and Kohl,
was accorded priority importance; nothing, including the sight of
the Balkans again behaving like the Balkans, would be allowed to
interfere. Differences among leaders, starting with Mitterrand and
Kohl, over what to do about Yugoslavia would not be allowed to
menace a meeting that would solemnize France's reconciliation
with a united Germany.

There was near paralysis in France's decision-making process;
the French had been able to deal with Maastricht but not much
more. There was also France's traditional ties to Serbia, Croatia's
enemy. In June 1991, Croatia and Slovenia declared indepen-

dence. Western governments then confronted the question of whether to recognize them as independent states. The leaders of Bosnia-Herzegovina leaders pleaded with the western capitals to withhold recognition, fearing that if it was granted the Serbs and Croats would instantly fall upon Bosnia. Their safety, they said, lay in being part of a multinational state. The western capitals were well aware of the stakes; the only way to contain the fighting, they knew, was to keep it from spreading to Bosnia. Western diplomats argued that recognition should be withheld unless or until the Serbs and Croats stopped fighting and agreed to leave Bosnia alone. Recognition was a card that could be played just once, and playing it early would only worsen things, most diplomats and officials felt. They knew that Serb and Croat officials had already met with maps to pin down their separate shares of Bosnia.

Germany's leadership felt some pressure to extend recognition. Mitterrand had Kohl agree that any such gesture could be taken only by the EC members acting in concert. But Kohl's foreign minister, Hans-Dietrich Genscher, had become a strenuous advocate of unilateral recognition. Genscher was an artful, stubbornly independent operator who often had his own agenda. Shortly before Maastricht, Kohl warned Mitterrand that it was becoming difficult to restrain Genscher on recognition. By December, Mitterrand and British Prime Minister John Major had maneuvered Kohl into a seriously high-risk position. He was being asked to give up Germany's largest and most symbolic postwar achievement, the strong and stable deutsche mark: it would be blended into a common currency that, in principle, would be controlled not by the German Bundesbank but by a European central bank. Yet Kohl's—and Germany's—objectives at Maastricht were not acceptable to either France or Britain. Quite clearly, Kohl and Genscher needed to bring home something that would play well in the German press and the Bundestag and help to soften the impact of surrendering the D-mark.

What Genscher got—seized, actually—at the post–Maastricht

meeting in Brussels was a deal on Croatia and Slovenia. He didn't link the deal to German acceptance of the Maastricht Accord. He didn't have to. The EC members agreed to recognize both republics the following month. But Germany did so just two days later.

Independence for Croatia and Slovenia confronted the Bosnians with the bleak choice that they had hoped to avoid. Trying for recognition themselves was likely to bring on civil war; not trying would mean becoming part of a Serbian rump state, with "ethnic cleansing" and the expulsion of Muslims. Bosnia held—or tried to hold—a referendum on independence in February. The Muslims and Croats chose freedom, but the Serbs boycotted the referendum, having already voted separately to be part of the rump Serbian-controlled state that had been proclaimed in April. The fighting—and with it Europe's worst atrocities since the Second World War—then began. Among the early casualties was the illusion, or myth, of European unity.

Monetary Union

Besides missing a rare opportunity at Maastricht, the EU governments found themselves being rebuked by the public, which felt left out of important decisions affecting their lives; for example, giving up national currencies—countries' badges of sovereignty—would be a vastly more important step than any other yet contemplated by the members. But parliamentary committees had not been involved in the process. Indeed, the EU members' leaders had left most matters, large and small, to be managed by their bureaucrats and were then surprised by much of what the experts had agreed to.

Since the ill-fated conference, the EU has been hobbled by the passivity and confusion of the key players, Germany and France, and the self-marginalization of Britain. The only project that has developed energy and focus is EMU. The model is Germany's Bundesbank, which, like the U.S. Federal Reserve System, operates independently of government control. But unlike the U.S. analogue, which operates in accordance with goals set by Congress, a Euro-Fed would have no such constraints and, in effect, would become the world's most independent central bank. At Maastricht, Kohl was obliged to make certain that any European central bank would lie outside the control of member governments. He couldn't put at risk the low rate of inflation and the economic stability for which the Bundesbank's policies are given most of the credit. Both Karl Otto Pohl, its president at the time, and his successor, Hans Tietmeyer, have insisted on the so-called Euro-Fed becoming a copy of their own iconic institution. Inevitably, the Euro-Fed's constitution as laid down in Maastricht went further in bolstering anti-inflationary policy than even the Bundesbank's. The Euro-Fed, for example, is obliged to maintain "price stability," tougher language than the equivalent Bundesbank obligation of "safeguarding the currency."[6]

A set of five highly restrictive rules governing eligibility for the new club was drawn up under the watchful eye—and indeed controlling hand—of the Bundesbank. These rules, which determine who will be eligible for the new and elite club, are known as the "convergence criteria." The most important—and for most of the key countries the most difficult—rule is that the budget deficit of any member or aspirant member must not exceed 3 percent of GDP, a technical term for national output. Another brake on heavy spending is that a country's public debt must not exceed 60 percent of GDP.*

---

* The three other criteria are as follows: (1) The country's annual rate of inflation must not exceed that of the three best-performing member nations by more than 1.5%. (2) The country's long-term interest rates must not exceed those of the three nations with the best inflation performance by more than 2 percentage points. (3) The country's exchange rate has to be kept within the normal bands of Europe's Exchange Rate Mechanism (ERM).

Monetary union has a clear logic and may one day be the right step, but not now. It is in fact a flawed project: first, because it has been pushed for the wrong reasons; second, because the timing couldn't be worse. Its purpose is not economic but strictly political. In early 1996, Douglas Hurd, who represented Britain at Maastricht and is no admirer of EMU, says it was devised "as the [EU's] next political leap forward." Then as now, advocates of EMU argued that a single market cannot operate properly without a single currency. But, as Hurd also observed, "It was not seriously argued on economic terms at the time of Maastricht that a single market required a single currency."[7]

Most economists insist that a single currency makes sense only if the members have roughly comparable economies and labor forces have cross-border mobility. That is not the case in Europe. Europeans lack the American habit of moving freely toward opportunity. They are tethered by linguistic, social, and cultural differences. Of the people inhabiting the EU, fewer than 1 percent are estimated to live outside their country of origin.[8] Moreover, the single market is not yet a reality; many EU members, starting with Germany, continue to throw up obstacles to neighborly trade. In 1995, Germany was the target of a fifth of the complaints about barriers to trade within the EU.[9]

Advocates of EMU argue that a single currency would benefit those who trade in the global market by reducing exchange costs. That argument, economists say, is heavily outweighed by a country's loss of control of its monetary and, eventually, fiscal policies.

Blending a common currency with a Euro-Fed may be a project worth pursuing down the road. But it is irrelevant to the problems and priorities challenging Europe in the 1990s—creating jobs, shrinking the system of social benefits to some more sustainable level, and extending the EU's zone of comfort and stability eastward by increasing its membership. EMU can't help with these tasks but could interfere with efforts to deal with them, not just because it is a massive distraction but because its importance has been greatly overstated; its advocates, starting with the leaders of France and Germany, have said that EMU and EMU alone can bring about a unified Europe—healthy, wealthy, and peaceful.

That is the line. Never mind that the only unifying force in Europe now is unemployment. The European Commission periodically calls on member governments to do something about it, along with the extravagant costs of social security. In December 1993, two years after Maastricht, the Commission offered a plan for creating 15 million jobs by the year 2000. It proposed doing so by lowering minimum wages and cutting nonwage labor costs such as social security payments. Unemployment benefits that year mounted to about $226 billion—about as much as Belgium's entire GNP. Five million jobs had been lost in the previous three years.[10] Moreover, the long-term unemployed accounted for more than one third of people without work in six EU countries: Belgium, France, Italy, Ireland, Greece, and Spain.[11] One-half of the members of Italian unions are pensioners. By February 1997, unemployment in Germany had risen to a level last seen in 1933, the year Hitler came to power.

The safety nets in many, if not most, EU countries were initially intended to protect the elderly, weak, and poor. But it wasn't long until the gap between what, say, a middle-class white-collar full-time worker with two children took home after taxes was little more than what an unemployed counterpart could obtain by relying on the full range of government benefits. Furthermore, this second person, by putting himself onto the black labor market, could bring home a larger income than his opposite number while paying a good deal less in taxes.

The social security programs also interfere with efforts to restructure European industry. In highly prosperous areas such as northern Italy and western Germany—areas on which large economies rely and which must be able to compete in the global market—the corporate cultures lag behind America's and Japan's. According to business leaders, their efforts to adapt—to restructure—have been undercut by the unions and by their own governments. More surprising is the continued reluctance in such centers of industrial strength and creativity to keep pace with America and Japan in exploiting knowledge-intensive industries.

Europe's job market doesn't stand comparison with America's, where, writes Robert Samuelson, "the private sector remains the prime engine of employment. Between 1970 and 1991, roughly six private jobs were created for every new government job. Europe's feeble job growth consisted of almost two government jobs for every private job, according to the Organization for Economic Co-operation and Development (OECD)."[12] By the start of 1995, the EU members were organizing themselves for Maastricht II—an intergovernmental conference, or IGC, ordained by Maastricht I and scheduled to begin early in 1996. The IGC was supposed to produce agreement on fulfilling the goals of Maastricht, including institutional reform, along with meaningful progress toward a common foreign and security policy. However, the planning went forward in a vacuum. Weak member governments were fearful of revealing the sharp divisions between them and reluctant to confront hard choices. Discussion of most issues was described by one Brussels insider as "naval gazing." The issue of how many commissioners an enlarging union should have was discussed acrimoniously but to no avail. Indeed, throughout the year nothing was taken up with a sense of urgency or assigned priority importance, with the important exception of EMU, which, although not a conference agenda item, was the sole topic being discussed seriously. And the discussion swiftly evolved into a debate more fundamental and divisive than any the organization had experienced in decades.

Questions arose: With the social compact under pressure, would the belt-tightening required to meet the EMU criteria generate more unemployment and social pain? Would the social pain threaten social peace in France and perhaps elsewhere? Advocates of EMU said that the criteria would make the restructuring of economies more manageable. But instead, would the combination of a Euro-Fed and a centralized currency deny nations the freedom, or the scope, to make the fundamental decisions affecting their own economies? And what about discipline? Or, as Douglas Hurd asked, "After convergence, what? Nothing in the treaty defines the morning after."[13] Suppose Country A managed to meet the criteria and enter the system; what would happen if hard times arrived and Country A decided it could no longer obey the rules?

The less complicated but most pondered question was whether societies, starting with Germany's, would agree to replace their currencies with some still-nameless European surrogate that various German politicians were already calling "Esperanto money." Inevitably, those who saw only disaster lying ahead began comparing EMU to the Australian emu—a bird that runs fast but can't fly.

One question—a persistent irritant—was whether Germans could or should allow EMU to go forward without a parallel move toward political union. In April 1995 Hans Tietmeyer said, "After a certain point, economic integration cannot realistically be expected to advance further without the prospect of further progress in the field of politics. The transfer of an elementary sovereign right such as monetary policy to a European central bank is likely to mark that point."[14] Tietmeyer repeatedly said that monetary union without political union would be untenable and that an institution would be needed to ensure the permanence of noninflationary policies—that is, prevent backsliding.

Quite clearly, the Bundesbank was hoping that EMU would go away or be put back onto the shelf. But the decision would be made in Bonn, not in Frankfurt. The Bundesbank could dictate strict adherence to the Maastricht criteria, but EMU was a political matter, and whether to push on with it or step back was up to Kohl. Whatever his calculation, he was betting heavily on a long shot.

In an important and dramatic sense, Kohl was alone. He had been one of three strong figures committed to building Europe. Mitterrand's term of office would expire in May 1995, and Kohl's other confederate, Jacques Delors, the EU's singularly strong, resourceful, and respected president, had stepped down at the end of 1994. Delors was replaced by an amiable nonentity: Jacques

Santer, former prime minister of Luxembourg. Mitterrand was succeeded by Jacques Chirac, whose presidency began inauspiciously, to say the least. Chirac's freewheeling style, especially his tendency to make decisions affecting France's partners without consulting any of them, including its special partner, was disruptive and caused consternation in Bonn. For the first six months or so of Chirac's tenure, France seemed free-floating, with no one at home in Paris for Germans to talk with. It was a shock and, for Kohl, a serious problem. Without strong and reliable help, especially from France, he would not succeed in binding Germany to Europe. More exactly, it was unlikely that he alone could impose EMU on Germany and its partners.

At home, the polls showed little support and great resistance to giving up the D-mark, the creation of which had provoked the division of Germany in 1948 and the establishment of the Federal Republic. One newspaper poll taken early in 1996 showed that 84 percent of the Germans interviewed felt that EMU should not start on time: 41 percent thought EMU should be postponed and 43 percent favored scrapping it altogether. Germans feel about the D-mark much the same as Britons feel about Westminster and the French about their national sovereignty. Giving it up in the name of Europe carried at least some risk of turning a large part of the nation against the idea of a common European purpose and identity. Fear of a single currency showed up in some drifting of D-marks toward Swiss francs. Briefly, Kohl, as Germany's leader, had to consider EMU's effects not just on his continued ability to rule the country but also on the cause for which he was struggling: a united Europe.

By the fall of 1995, Kohl's dilemma had become more acute. A few of the people around him were taking a relaxed view; experience, they argued, showed that Kohl could usually shift public opinion, however weighted against him, to his point of view. And he was in remarkably good shape politically, up ten points from where he had been just before his reelection as federal chancellor one year before. But at least some of his advisers worried that on EMU, Kohl was overreaching—equating struggles he had waged successfully on other issues, notably those involving deployment of major weapons, with the issue of giving up the D-mark, which seemed very different. On this one, Kohl would be tilting not against students and pacifists but against old-age pensioners and, according to some, every German with a bank account. Critics, including some within his government, felt that Kohl was also misplaying the hand he had dealt himself. Instead of portraying EMU as a device for spreading sound German monetary principles, he had set off a debate over swapping the D-mark for what what was being called "Esperanto" money.

Another problem was Kohl's method of maneuvering public opinion by first taking a controversial matter offstage and quietly selling it to elite groups. Only then would he confront popular opinion. But EMU was already out of the bag and had been since the debate over ratification of the Maastricht Accord. Actually, Kohl had been reluctant to start selling EMU because he hadn't wanted to open the debate. But the debate had begun anyway. The question was whether Kohl could control it. "We have approached it too cautiously," a senior official of the government told me in Bonn in early November. "We won't convince the people if we are seen as not convinced ourselves."[15] Various political adversaries had begun buzzing around Kohl, criticizing EMU. Members of the Social Democratic Party (SPD) began saying they had voted to approve the Maastricht Accord in the hope that it would unite Europe. But here was Kohl pushing EMU, a project that was dividing Europe.

In mid-October, Kohl told a party congress in Karlsruhe that EMU was essential and indeed could spell the difference between war and peace in the twenty-first century. He seemed to mean that without the unifying quality of EMU, Europe would drift back to its bad old ways. It was not a useful comment. Germans don't like hearing that kind of language. But it did excite Germanophobes in

London, who chose to regard EMU as surrogate Panzer tanks in a German drive to take control of Europe. One of them—Lord Tebbit, a prominent Thatcherite and former secretary of the Conservative Party, gleefully told readers of *The Sun,* a tabloid, that in Karlsruhe, Kohl had been threatening the rest of Europe with war.[16]

Otherwise, Kohl seemed to be holding himself in reserve and deploying his finance minister, Theo Waigel, to reassure Germans by insisting on an even more rigorous EMU system than called for in the Maastricht Accord. But why, asked some interested parties, had the problem of how to enforce budgetary discipline within the EMU system not been taken up a lot sooner and more methodically? No one in Bonn had a good answer, but talk about the need for self-enforcing punishment of potential backsliders abruptly surfaced.

Quite late in the day, Waigel, it seemed, was devising what Douglas Hurd described as "a fitness club which would keep everyone underweight for ever. This club is not in the treaty. Its underlying thought would be widely and deeply unpopular in practice."[17]

The bar to EMU membership was already set high—too high, in fact, for most EU governments. In fact, Waigel announced on January 9, 1996, that in the preceding twelve months Germany itself had not met the Maastricht criteria. Specifically, he said that the year-end data would show the country's public deficit as having exceeded the limit of 3 percent of GDP. He blamed the bad news on "high deficits for states and muncipalities and above all for the social security system."[18]

Actually, the only EU member capable of meeting the criteria just then was Luxembourg, as an editorial in the *Financial Times* began by observing: "If EMU were to start on the basis of a strict application of the Maastricht treaty . . . its sole result would be to end the monetary union between Luxembourg and Belgium. The grand duchy would manage the European Central Bank and enjoy the Euro [the single currency unit], all in splendid isolation. This fact does more than provide excellent material for farce. It indicates how difficult it will be to launch EMU—the European Union's flagship."[19]

Germans wouldn't budge an inch on the criteria, and the most unyielding of them was Waigel, Europe's senior finance minister and, like his fellow Bavarian, Edmund Stoiber, an aspirant successor to Kohl. In making Waigel his point man on EMU, Kohl had granted him broad discretionary power, which Waigel was exploiting in an effort to become Germany's second most powerful politician and a player on the European scene. In the spirited competition to name the new currency, for example, Waigel's favorite, euro, beat out other entries, including ECU (European currency unit) and Monnet.

More important, Waigel set about tightening still further the rules for members of the fitness club—"stability pact" was his term—including punishment for recidivists. He told the Bundestag that EMU members should agree to hold their budget deficits to an average of 1 percent, as distinct from the 3 percent ceiling set by the accord. He was also talking about how with EMU in place fiscal policies at the national level would be a thing of the past.

Although the French responded with some affirmative sounds, they were far from committed to the rigorous self-denial Waigel was pressing. They weren't ready for the debate, partly because of serious internal stresses and partly because they knew that the price for membership in EMU might be too high. Defending the franc by aligning France's monetary policy with Germany's had obliged France to accept much higher real interest rates than its partner had to. The high rates, in turn, were pushing up both unemployment and the deficit even more; all that was happening in a society whose workers were enduring the highest taxes in its history, higher than those of France's partners. Finally, making France's economy competitive with Germany's was going to require a lot of deregulation, more than the country and its elites were ready for.

By mid-1996, France was confronting a deficit in its social security spending program of nearly $10 billion, three times higher than
had been estimated; the rising pressure was due mainly to still-
rising unemployment that has hovered at between 12 percent and
13 percent. Meanwhile, Bonn had produced a more rigorous budget that added to the pressure on Chirac and his government.

Still, partisans of EMU in Paris argued that everyone who mattered—the mainstream political parties and so forth—favored it;
only the extremists on the right and left were said to oppose the
scheme. As for Chirac, the argument ran, he could afford to pay
the price for EMU because his mandate would keep him in the
Élysée Palace for seven years anyway. Advocates also alleged,
rightly or wrongly, that public opinion in France recognized the
value of having France's central bank at the same table as the Bundesbank and taking part in decisions.

Without France, nothing would happen. EMU would not go
forward unless France managed to squeeze its economy into the
German mold. A failure by France to do so would not just
bury hopes for a single currency but probably provoke accusations
in Bonn of reneging on commitments; that in turn could lead
to rival political blocs, a northern bloc led by Germany and a
French-led "Club Med" bloc farther south. Moreover, France's
failure could and probably would provoke wild currency gyrations
and a round of devaluations in some countries. One had to start
wondering whether the quest for monetary union and a single currency would drive the EU membership to a collective nervous
breakdown.

Over the latter part of 1995 and early 1996, Kohl and Chirac
had to decide what to do. Membership in EMU would be decided
early in 1998, based on the economic performance numbers of
1997. Those countries that were judged to meet the criteria in February or March 1998 would become part of the new club that
would begin life in 1999. Kohl and Chirac had to weigh the uncertain but perhaps heavy costs of going forward with the costs of

going backward, that is, postponing EMU, whether temporarily or indefinitely. They decided to go forward, feeling there was no alternative. "The single currency has become the symbol of success or failure," a senior and highly responsible French official told me in early November 1995. "We go back to zero if it fails." He meant that the EU's economic cohesion would disappear, and also that the special Franco-German relationship probably wouldn't survive the failure to create the euro.

That was the line, expressed in all seriousness and, indeed, with conviction. Senior figures on both sides, along with prominent personalities of past French and German governments, echoed it. Still, a heavy deposit of skepticism remained. Although France's economy was basically strong, investment was down, as was consumer confidence. Chirac had campaigned on a promise to solve unemployment. Going forward with the euro and maintaining the strong franc (*franc fort*) would probably make nonsense of the pledge and inflict serious political damage. Toward the end of 1995, a wave of strikes, led by railroad and Paris Métro workers, paralyzed the capital and eventually the country; they were supported by a majority of the public.[20]

But the feeling about EMU in France, at least among the political elite, has been more favorable than in Germany. Apart from recapturing some authority over monetary policy, EMU is seen by such people as a means of sustaining a period of low inflation that has lasted about a decade and was made possible by a strong franc shadowing the German mark.

Any conversation anywhere about EMU during this period reverted to Britain's position or absence of one. As on so many of Europe's basic issues, the British attitude toward EMU was deeply ambivalent. The City of London (the financial center) strongly favored being inside this club, if only to avoid being outside. But Whitehall, in its uncertainty, noted that if EMU collapsed, it would be worse to be inside than outside. Kenneth Clarke, the outspoken Europhile chancellor of the exchequer in John Major's government, characterized this cautionary view as "pathetic." British diplomats worried about Britain doing its usual thing—remaining apart from other members for a time and then joining them. Awaiting the next bus in this case would mean being outside a single currency, causing some parts of the financial and business communities in Britain to lose out.

The penalty for waiting, argued Eurocrats in Brussels, would be heavy indeed; whereas other EU institutions had evolved slowly, they pointed out, EMU would have to take shape quickly because the Bundesbank had insisted that monetary policy making become indivisible—fast. For Britain, not being there would mean not having its people in place to influence the shape of the institution and how it might work. For Britain's partners, the absence from EMU of Europe's most important financial services center would be worse than anomalous. The role expected of Britain—offsetting or at least diluting the overpowering weight of Germany and France—cannot be played from Europe's fringe. Inevitably, the unending discussions of Britain's detached style in the EU capitals had a waiting-for-Tony (Blair) aspect. Now Blair is prime minister, and starting to shorten the distance between Britain and its EU partners; but they will have to wait a bit longer to see just how much more "European" its new leader can afford to be.

In opposition, Blair did little to flutter his own party's covey of Euroskeptics. Less than six months before the election, Gordon Brown, who is now chancellor of the exchequer and the most Europhile figure on the front bench, said that Labour would hold a referendum before taking Britain into EMU.[21] Blair himself had already told an elite Japanese business group in Tokyo that the British people weren't yet ready for a single currency.

Germany's business community has been divided on EMU between a sizable segment of advocates and the rest—skeptics, mostly, who like the status quo and see the interests of their own companies, along with the country's commercial interests, as extending far beyond the EU and indeed as being global. Our leaders in Bonn, they say, have tried and failed to create political union in Europe. So far, their argument continues, the presence of several currencies has not impeded economic growth in Europe. Nor, they argue, is it the absence of a single currency that is preventing political union or denying Europe a world role. Let each EU member, and above all Germany, control its own monetary and fiscal policies, they say feelingly.

The advocates within this community are self-proclaimed Europeans who concede the risks of EMU but feel that larger interests argue strongly for it. Kurt Lauck, a member of the management board of Daimler-Benz and president of its utility vehicles division, says, "We need EMU to protect Germany from itself—from its history. If Germany isn't tied to the EU, it will be pushed into a balancing position between east and west." Lauck also feels that Europe cannot compete unless the welfare system is reformed and that EMU is needed to accomplish that. "The Maastricht criteria," he says, "are the best weapon against the welfare system." Lauck concedes the risks and some downside. "With a single currency there will be upheavals," he says, "along with negative consequences that will take five or ten years to overcome. Monetary union should be compared with German unification. If we do not do it, we lose a momentum that will take one or two generations to regain."[22] Lauck spends a good deal of time in France and feels that the business community there is as divided as Germany's.

Skeptics concede the force of the momentum argument and the need for reform. But the timing, they think, is critical, and a leap into the unknown at a time of low growth and high unemployment strikes them as unwise and too risky. In both Germany and France, political leaders and the business communities worry constantly about currency fluctuations. Both the franc and the D-mark, especially the latter, have risen in recent years against other currencies, notably Italy's lira and Spain's peseta. The British pound has been another problem. Between 1992 and 1995, the lira, peseta, and pound slid against the D-mark by 33 percent, 25 percent, and 21 percent, respectively.[23]

One of Chirac's first gestures as French president was to reproach his Italian and Spanish colleagues harshly for this performance, which, of course, had had the effect of making French and German exports more expensive, hence less competitive. The reproach was misguided. Countries do not usually devalue their currencies if they have a better alternative. The fiscal crisis that triggered the lira's slide hurt Italy itself more than the devaluation hurt any other country, as an editorial in the *Financial Times* observed.[24]

Nonetheless, as gaps develop between the D-mark and, say, the lira and peseta, so do German suspicions of so-called competitive devaluations. Over the past thirty years, Germany and Italy have been Europe's leaders in the design and sales of machine tools. But the weaker lira has given Italy a competitive edge. And with the franc having held its own against the D-mark in recent years, the French establishment is equally aggrieved. Germans and French both complain about EU countries that, while enjoying the benefits of free trade inside a single market, do not practice monetary self-discipline.

Bargain hunters in both countries have for some time been taking their D-marks and francs across the Italian or Spansh frontiers to save on purchases large and small. An Austrian or German can drive through the Brenner Pass into northern Italy and buy a two-door Volkswagen for $1,250.00 less than it would cost at home. The savings on a four-door luxury Mercedes-Benz sedan would be roughly $6,000.00.[25] In southwestern France, people who live near the Spanish border routinely cross it to fill their cars with cheaper gas, buy cheaper cigarettes, and so on.

Disparities of this sort will cause large sections of northern Europe's industry to be displaced by southern Europe's, some business leaders have warned. "Whether you're for the single currency or not, something has to be done in the period leading up to it, or the system is going to implode," said Jacques Calvet, chairman of the French automaker PSA Peugeot-Citroën S.A. And just before stepping down from a long tenure as chairman of Daimler-Benz, Edzard Reuter said that the strong D-mark would oblige much of German industry to move its production abroad.[26] His successor, Jurgen Schrempp, warned in April 1996 that the D-mark's increasing strength might force German companies with high technology components to shift their manufacturing.[27]

An apparent merit of a single EU currency is that fluctuations would belong to the past. The euro would reflect the composite financial strength of its combined membership. No longer would Germans have to worry about their D-mark being overvalued, their big exporters endlessly penalized—at least not in theory.

German and French businessmen remain skeptical. The euro won't necessarily banish disarray, first of all because differences will develop over just how strong it should be in relation to other currencies, such as the dollar. German pensioners need to be assured that they will lose nothing from the currency swap. The euro, as they see it, must be as strong as the D-mark so as to protect them from inflation, the ravages of which have a central place in the German memory. Germany's government will, of course, insist on a strong euro for the same reason, although not so strong as to discourage economic growth and job creation. However, a large part of the business community will complain loudly about a euro that may be strong enough to make German exports less competitive.

The Kohl-Chirac commitment to press ahead with EMU bore the mark of a solemn oath, even though opinion within and beyond their own entourages as to the likely outcomes has been divided. Something would have to give, according to most of the rapt gallery. The problems have argued for either postponing the project or lowering the entry bar. But postponement would be a disaster, argue the advocates: first, because the budgetary discipline being generated in many places by the EMU criteria would evaporate and probably couldn't be revived; second, because the effect could be a massive flight of member currencies to the D-mark, which would become abusively overvalued, thereby causing Germany's, and in turn Europe's, economy to suffer.

Lowering the bar was just as unlikely, if only because the Bundesbank is strongly opposed. Persuading Germans to give up the D-mark would be hard enough; trying to do that while facing down the Bundesbank would be political folly, even for Kohl. "Each of these criteria is so important and must be fulfilled in its substance if the monetary union isn't to be built on sand," said Hans Tietmeyer on May 4, 1996.[28]

A few months earlier, Germany's Council of Economic Experts, widely known as the "Five Wise Men," recommended postponing EMU if only a few members could qualify. The costs and risks of a mini-EMU exceed the advantages, they said, adding that it would jeopardize European unification, since key member states such as Italy might not be there. And fulfillment of the criteria, said the report, had to be given absolute priority over the timetable.

The report broke the taboo in Germany on discussing postponement of EMU. Kohl could have used it to help maneuver himself off the high wire on which he was perched. He didn't. Others among EMU's patrons and prominent supporters—people with voices that carried—then began to counsel delay. One was Jacques Delors. "The news from France and Germany isn't reassuring," he told the French newspaper *Sud-Ouest* in January 1996. "It will be difficult to achieve economic and monetary union within the agreed timetable."[29]

Over the next few weeks, backsliding swam into fashion. "The clock should be stopped" to enable all big countries to join, said Spain's highly regarded foreign minister, Carlos Westendorp. Jean-Marc Venot, the head of Société Générale, France's largest private bank, cited France's chances of meeting the criteria as "minimal," and he urged the parties to postpone and renegotiate. Other notables, including Valéry Giscard d'Estaing, France's former president and cofounder of the European Monetary System (EMS), argued for relaxing the criteria. Some said that Britain would have to be there from the start; others agreed but added Italy to the "must" list.

A voice to which careful attention is normally paid belongs to Ralf Dahrendorf, a German former European commissioner and now head of an Oxford college. He went further than the others, saying, "EMU is a great mistake, a misguided goal which divides Europe rather than unites it."[30] Others warned that if the electorate didn't punish governments for playing the EMU fame, the financial markets would.

These admonitory sounds coincided with efforts to decide what to do about EMU members who failed to keep their deficits below 3 percent. Waigel and his French opposite number, Jean Arthuis, announced at one point in the autumn of 1996 that they had moved "very far" toward agreement on a stability pact, but it turned out that the issue of sanctions—how to keep backsliders in line— was not even close to being settled. A *Financial Times* editorial likened fines being discussed to nuclear bombs. Forcing a country to pay the fines, it said, "would lead to direct collision between the domestic politics behind the deficit and the EU. The latter could easily lose."[31]

A basic question was gathering force. If states were unable to borrow money from themselves or from the Euro-Fed, where would they get it? If denied the right to create deficits, how could they manage threats to stability and social peace?

France's draft budget for 1997 caused a stir when it appeared because it barely cut the central government deficit, but was accompanied by a forecast that the next year's overall deficit would shrink to 3 percent of national output, as ordained. But the target was within reach only because a big company (France Telecom) was making a onetime payment to the government of $7.3 billion to cover future pension liabilities. Talk of "creative accountancy" filled the air, as Italy and Belgium swiftly made the French tactic their own. "If the French can get away with it, we can show them a trick or two, Romano Prodi, Italy's prime minister was quoted as saying. Tietmeyer, Germany's arbiter of budgetary rigor, said point-edly, "It is important in the selection that the member countries do not just reach the criteria through a breathless short-term effort with one-off results quickly cobbled together."

Within days, Italy and Spain put other members on notice that they, too, were planning to join EMU and would slim down enough to squeeze into its snug charter. Germany's banking community flinched, aware that the books kept by candidate-members are not likely to be properly audited by the Commission, which Germans see as subject to French manipulation. By the end of 1996, France was said by troubled Germans to want Italy, Spain, and perhaps Portugal inside the central bank so as to have three more players at the table who could be relied on to take a more relaxed view of monetary matters than their German colleagues.

By then, the differences between France and Germany over how to enforce fiscal discipline among members were widening. Indeed, among aspirant members, only the Dutch fully supported the German insistence on a stability pact that would penalize those who strayed from the path marked out by the Bundesbank.

Kohl and Chirac were still shouder to shoulder, and neither flinched, not publicly at least. Hortatory comment from EMU's boosters is still heard. A few *jusqu'au boutistes* around Kohl have actually equated a failure to press ahead with a failure of nuclear deterrence during the Cold War. Compliant German banks were busily preparing for the euro. Businesses were planning to adapt. And so was the federal government. As they left the country, Ger-man vacationers on charter jets were receiving a seventy-one-page illustrated booklet called "The Euro: Strong as the Mark," pub-lished by their Finance Ministry; it told them why they would soon be swapping their D-marks for equally solid euros. Newspaper ads told readers that "Europe is the future"; that the euro will be a guarantor of peace, freedom, economic stability, and job security.[32]

Only Helmut Kohl—virtuoso and one-man band—could have maneuvered monetary union to a gradually increasing and possibly adequate level of acceptance in Germany and beyond. If he isn't widely popular, he is widely trusted. Only he has a strategy for Europe, his people say. But what Kohl has is a vision, not a strategy, and he has allowed it to be badly skewed by EMU and its euro. Monetary union, if it isn't shelved or deferred to a more auspicious time, may well confront Germany with an awful dilemma: either bend the rules to accommodate sorely pressed members and thereby risk a violent reaction from a society that has given up the D-mark, or refuse to bend the rules and invite the prospect of economic chaos in Europe.

The trap was largely of Kohl's making. He cannot afford to allow speculations against weaker currencies to drive up the D-mark's value, and he probably cannot make EMU happen without allowing some fudging of some members' numbers, probably including Germany's, or appearing to fudge the criteria. The treaty may allow some fudging by suggesting that a country within range of the target and moving in the right direction could qualify for membership. And Kohl may have become just a little less willing to bend the rules than had been assumed. His position, as of the spring of 1997, wasn't easy to read. At a meeting of EU finance ministers at this time, Waigel surprised colleagues and many others by saying, "I have never nailed myself to the cross of three percent," an allusion to the limit on budget deficits. Back in Bonn, the line was that nothing had changed. However, the controlling question is how much fudge Helmut Kohl thinks he can eat in an election year. Or, put differently, can he risk losing his job in the '98 elections by swapping the D-mark for a weaker currency—one allegedly "to be built on sand," in the admonitory words of Tietmeyer cited before.

Most of the leaders of EU governments are caught in the trap. The feeling in Rome and Madrid is that not being part of EMU, if it goes forward, would mean being left out of Europe's hard core and thereby having no voice in the key political councils.

A highly suspicious EU Commission forecast released in late April 1997 predicted that thirteen of the fifteen members would be able to meet the criteria and qualify for membership. Only Italy and Greece were judged unlikely to pass muster. Most dubious was the prediction that the final figures for five of the thirteen members would show deficits of precisely three percent of GDP—the magic number for opening the gate. Independent forecasts were a lot less rosy. "Miraculous" was how the Dutch finance minister described the Commission's forecast.

Prodi and Aznar have both said they would resign if their bids were rejected. Although Spain seems to have done a little better than Italy in preparing for EMU, hard questions arose: Can Spain be admitted and not Italy, a founding member of the EU, Europe's third largest exporter and tied with Britain as the world's fifth largest economy? But should Spain be excluded just because Italy is? Can you have one without the other? A prominent board member of Germany's Dresdner, Ernst-Moritz Lipp, spoke out EMU in February 1997. "Spain can make it, Italy probably not," he said. He described the prospect of launching a single currency as a sword of Damocles hanging over financial markets."[33] Briefly, the net effect of this leap in the dark will almost certainly be divisive.

Governments had become obsessive about monetary union and the single currency. The British elections which brought Labour to power were preceded by a campaign during which the Conservative Party tore itself apart over the issue of Europe in general and monetary union in particular. Kohl's announcement in April 1997 that he would seek a fifth term in the federal elections the following year was timed to show his determination to complete EMU on his watch; he strongly mistrusts the resolve of those who may come after him. A few days later came Chirac's ill-advised decision to move up France's parliamentary elections by one year; he clearly felt a need for greater political leverage before imposing more economic pain on French society. But the voters, by tossing out Chirac's government and voting in the left, said no to more pain and yes to more of the same. Europe's most highly taxed people chose to sustain the continent's largest payroll and, apparently, to endorse Lionel Jospin's pledge to create 700,000 new jobs, half of them in the public sector. Jospin, now prime minister, was also proposing to cut the work week from 39 to 35 hours without a loss in pay, and to halt France's privatization program.[34]

This comforting line collided with the new government's declaratory commitment to monetary union, which, in principle, will require more, not less, austerity and deregulation of the French economy. The voters, according to Jospin, were not rejecting plans for a closer European union. But he also urged a more flexible approach to the club's admission rules. "We don't want to renegotiate the treaty, we want to renegotiate the application of the treaty," said a spokesman.[35]

German bankers, watching France with horrified fascination, reacted by predicting that EMU would go forward on schedule. "Financial markets overwhelmingly assume a 'fudge-or-death' scenario," reported *The Financial Times* a few days after the elections.[36] What most worried the bankers was the fudge—the prospect of softer membership rules creating soft monetary policy and a soft Euro. Among other effects, softer criteria would probably rule out blackballing Italy, as Germans, not very privately, had threatened to do.

The irony of France's political lurch is not lost on any of those who follow EMU's twists and turns every day: France called forth the project as a means of containing a unified Germany, and then French voters, to Bonn's consternation, put a dark cloud over it. And if France's Socialist government does try to live up to its campaign promises, it will push up interests rates and weaken the economy.

There is an unavoidably crushing agenda in 1998, a charged moment for which the members did not prepare and one they will have trouble winging or trying to muddle through. The decisions as to who the EMU's founding members will be are supposed to be made in February or March (unless the project is shelved). Negotiations between NATO and its new members from east-central Europe either will begin or will have started. Most difficult may be renegotiating the EU budget for another five-year period, starting in 1998; Germans will insist that their share, which they see as much too large, be slashed. In principle, the EU will also be negotiating terms for taking members of the former Soviet empire into the club, a process that requires decisions on hot-button issues such as reforming the Common Agricultural Policy (CAP) and arranging a redistribution of financial assistance to poorer members. Against the background of all this, Germany will have federal elections in the fall of '98. The question before the house is whether all this stressful activity will drive the EU face to face with itself. The signs suggest that it will not.

Enlargement

"Enlargement is both a political necessity and a unique opportunity," said the leaders of the EU at their summit meeting in Madrid in December 1995.[37] Although it's true, the burden of opinion in most EU capitals is that enlargement of the club is unlikely in the foreseeable future or will involve transition periods stretching to the Greek calends. Germany is the only member country that strongly favors expanding the EU eastward.* Germany, Kohl has said repeatedly, cannot indefinitely remain Europe's eastern boundary. He's also said that he won't leave power until Germany is securely integrated into an integrated Europe. But Germany, its eastern neighbors say, mainly wants buffers, not partners, and talks a good but disingenuous game about EU enlargement. Its neighbors, starting with the Czechs, accuse the Germans of dragging their feet on enlargement—of fearing competition from places where labor costs are much lower and thus create the prospect of higher unemployment in Germany.

Germans by and large know what they want—to be in the cen-

---

* Denmark, Finland, and Sweden strongly favor bringing in the Baltic states.

ter of Europe, not on the frontier of the EU. Otherwise, they haven't thought through the ins and outs of enlargement. Some of them cite France and Poland as being the closest of their European allies. Kohl is said to feel that just as Adenauer had the historic task of reconciling Germany with France, he himself must do the same with Poland. He has even announced that Poland should be the EU's next new member.

In Bonn, some officials hint that the problem with EU enlargement is foot-dragging in Paris. The French don't hide their reservations; some officials concede privately that however laudable enlargement may be, France just cannot afford the cost; EMU, of course, makes enlargement even less affordable. But the French also observe that the Germans, despite all their brave talk about enlargement, are no more prepared than they themselves are to invest funds to that purpose. The French do not, of course, have any interest in helping Germany extend its sphere of influence, feeling that the recent entries into the EU—Austria, Sweden, and Finland—have contributed more than enough to that end. Almost any among the new members who are envisaged will further dilute France's influence and add to Germany's.

Just talking about enlargement makes everyone unhappy, says one senior French official. It does seem to make many European officials uncomfortable, doubtless because they know it is the thing they should be making happen.

Britain should help with the cause of EU enlargement. Conservative Party governments supported the idea of extending the EU eastward, as distinct from actually doing so. Put differently, as seen from London, rhetorical support for widening the EU just might have helped to head off deepening it with more integration. But once enlarged, the EU would in fact require some remodeling, for example, tightening of the institutions and decision-making procedures. Britain's Tories opposed remodeling of that kind, even though the alternative would be a looser, even more unmanageable structure. The Blair government, as it tries to establish itself as a serious player within the EU, could make a project of enlargement; it could begin by seriously upgrading Britain's relations with Germany and taking a bilateral initiative that France might even want to join.

Thanks to the primitive politics of the Mediterranean, the EU got itself committed to having accession talks with Cyprus and Malta within six months of the end of the IGC. And there is support, mostly declaratory and mostly German, for the proposition that more plausible and deserving aspirants, starting with a few from east-central Europe, should be able to do the same. Kohl, typically, has pressed his partners to fold Poland, the Czech Republic, and Hungary into the same initial round of enlargement talks that will include Cyprus and Malta. He is reflecting a sentiment, shared in Washington, that the EU members and the United States must extend the zone of stability and prosperity in western Europe, starting with countries in east-central Europe that are politically and economically compatible.

In principle, all the states in east-central and eastern Europe are eligible for memberhip in the EU. In practice, the list of those considered ready for accession talks is a short one, as Kohl suggests. Bonn wants Poland inside the clubs Germany belongs to, whatever its problems with agriculture. Some aspirants will be excluded indefinitely by political criteria involving human rights and border disputes. EU members will want to avoid being saddled with the kind of tensions that Greece is capable of generating with its neighbors; its flare-up with Turkey in early 1996 over a tiny, uninhabited slab of rock in the Aegean Sea is a reminder.

Estonia, which could be a candidate in the first wave of talks, claims that it will be prepared to meet the EU's membership criteria by 1999 or 2000. The claim may be exaggerated, but probably not by much. Estonia is well ahead of the other two Baltic states and, except for the Czechs and Slovenes, is probably ahead of the other aspirants. But besides having the longest border with Russia, it has had the edgiest relations with Moscow. Thus, none of the

EU members, aside from the Scandinavians, is likely to lend support to Estonia, or to either of the other two Baltic states; this blend of indifference and overcaution is symptomatic of what ails the EU and, if unchanged, will eventually add to its own sense of having let down Europe's cause and treated some of its societies shabbily.

Ukraine provides another example. Ukraine, like its neighbors, would like to join the EU, but is too poor and underdeveloped to qualify. The EU is doing very little to help, according to Anders Aslund, an economic adviser to the Ukranian government, who says that while the country's economy is beginning to stabilize, "it is amazing how little the European Union has contributed to this process . . . Western European protectionism is probably the greatest threat to the success of Ukraine's economic reforms. . . ." Yet Helmut Kohl has often said privately that Ukraine is one of Europe's three most important countries (after Germany and Russia).

The good news is that relations between Poland and Ukraine are improving as Kiev tries to stress legacies other than Ukraine's history with Russia, including moments of close ties to Poland. And Poland's leadership, unlike the EU's, is sensitive to Ukraine's need for alternatives to its unbreakable connection with Russia. Alexsander Kwasniewski, the smooth ex-Communist who replaced Lech Walesa as Poland's president, has managed to give relations with Kiev a high priority without antagonizing Moscow. In edging partway out of Russia's shadow, Ukraine is trying to join a group comprising the central European free-trade area. Kwasniewski has pledged Polish support for the bid. And his government has also lobbied for Ukrainian membership in institutions like the Council of Europe, which are located even farther west.

The importance of EU membership to the countries on Kohl's shortlist, along with others such as Slovenia and the Baltic states, is obvious. Aside from gaining reliable access to the single market, membership would amount not to joining but to rejoining Europe; these societies feel as European as any EU member and have a need, political as well as economic, to be part of the structure. However, other EU capitals as well as Paris must deal with the prospect of all or most of the new members, aside from Cyprus and Malta, becoming part of the German sphere.

Enlarging the EU is more difficult than expanding NATO, first because it appears to require sacrifices by members at a time when their governments feel too weak to take risks or to expose the differences between themselves and other EU countries. The risks appear to include, first, having to amend the EU's system for supporting agricultural prices, the notorious CAP, a move that, however salutary, would enrage farmers, especially in in parts of France and Germany. Moreover, in most parts of France there exists a romantic, if not mystical, attachment to the land. Over half of the deputies in the National Assembly are mayors of small towns. And, according to *The Economist,* a third of the thirty-two ministers in the Juppé government are either mayors or involved in running regional affairs.[38] Then there are all those city dwellers, especially in Paris, with their *maisons secondaires* and their parents, still living close to their provincial roots.

The German problem is different and concentrated in Bavaria, the land of Stoiber, Waigel, and their party, the Christian Socialist Union, a deeply conservative but essential segment of Kohl's governing coalition. Bavarian farmers are less competitive vis-à-vis the world market than other German farmers and are strongly opposed to giving up the protection they get from the CAP.

The other risk, as seen by EU members, would be having to provide financial assistance to some aspirant members who could not otherwise function within the EU's single market or live by its various legal codes. Few, if any, of the EU governments are prepared to provide much of this aid beyond what is already being granted to poorer members such as Portugal, Spain, and Greece. This threesome takes a dim view of being asked to share the funds with newcomers from the northeast. And it's worth recalling that enlargement must be approved by fifteen parliaments.

In pronouncing Poland the EU's next new member, Kohl instantly raised the awful question of agriculture. Roughly half of the EU budget is absorbed by the CAP. And a third or so of the Polish population is involved in agriculture, although not as productively as most of the EU farming community. Fitting Poland into the EU system would be financially ruinous and hence not acceptable to members, at least not anytime soon. And the most resistant members are those who put more into the EU budget than they take out of it: Germany, France, Britain, and the Netherlands.

No one who isn't a farmer disputes the proposition that the CAP is the European Union's albatross—irrational, divisive, and abusively expensive—"the most costly system of price support yet invented," according to a harsh but not unjust critique of the system by Noel Malcolm printed in *Foreign Affairs*. It's worth pausing to see what experts say about the CAP. "By the time [it] was established in 1967," says Mr. Malcolm, "the EEC farm prices had been driven up to 175 percent of world prices for beef, 185 percent for wheat, 400 percent for butter, and 440 percent for sugar. . . . It dominates the EU's external trade policy, distorting the world market and seriously undermining the ability of poorer countries elsewhere to export their own agricultural produce. . . . Even the European Commission, which administers the scheme, has admitted that 'farmers' do not seem to have benefited from the increasing support which they have received."[39]

A World Bank study conducted in 1994 concluded that the EU's banana import policy was costing consumers $2.3 billion annually by keeping prices far above world levels. And, the study said, most of the money went to marketers and middlemen in Europe. The sum estimated as reaching the poor countries in Africa, the Caribbean, and the Pacific where the bananas are grown was only $300 million.

There isn't any mystery about how to fix the policy: first, the support prices for most products should be reduced to roughly world market levels; second, subsidies should be divorced from production, and member governments made responsible for protecting their own farmers. Briefly, income subsidies should replace price supports. The best way to admit Poland to the EU would be to open negotiations and drag them out, far out. Poland would eventually be granted full membership after an exceptionally long transition period, during which time the dwindling cohort of EU farmers who cannot compete on the world market would have to find their protection at home.

"The goal of enlargement to the east cannot reside in killing off the common agricultural policy," said Franz Fischler, the EU's commissioner for agriculture in mid-1995.[40] Given the importance of the subject, his job used to be a highly coveted plum. No longer. It was vacant for some time, and Fischler, an Austrian, took it because his country and the other new members had to take whatever jobs were available. His pronouncement was seen as a reply to Kohl, who had just promised, quite extravagantly, to bring Poland and a few of its neighbors into the EU by 2000.

But scarcely a year after stoutly defending the CAP, Fischler called for a radical change. "We will have to move toward more direct income support," he said, adding that EU aid for farmers should be redirected to supporting other activities in rural areas.[41]

Kohl is no more willing than other EU leaders to take on his farmers. Their number may be small, but at 3 to 5 percent of the electorate they could, it's argued, constitute the difference between winning and losing an election. And he is just as loath to commit regional aid funds to candidate members of the EU, given his constituents' unhappiness with the costs of both unification and the EU budget.

Chances are the CAP will be reformed—though gradually and contentiously—over a period of at least eight to ten years. As for regional aid for new members, the Czechs say they neither need nor want this kind of help; Slovenia doesn't need it either. Poland and other aspirants would need help, although some Eurocrats in Brussels argue that these mutating societies farther east won't need much of it; that they are well ahead of backward southern members, possessing, for example, the education, training, and infrastructure that are lacking in regions such as Italy's Mezzogiorno plus parts of Spain and Portugal, not to mention Greece.

The pessimism and declining confidence of EU members conspire to make the obstacles to enlarging the club seem larger than they are. Historically, the EU's genius lay in setting deadlines for overcoming obstacles. If the deadline was about to slip by unmet, members would simply ignore the clock and work around it to reach agreement. Enlargement could be dealt with in the same way.

A risk on all sides is that if the EU enlargement process continues to stagnate, central Europeans, starting with the Czechs and Poles, would probably lose interest. A vital, historically unstable region of Europe could drift regressively and hold back efforts to create a durable zone of stability. Some German officials are already expressing concern about this region's prospective disillusionment with the EU, combined with the potential reluctance of governments there to swallow the *acquis communautaire*—the body of rules and legal codes that govern members' behavior. Washington is aware that growing disillusion with the EU would cause these countries to feel that much more dependent on the United States for political support.

America's motive in supporting enlargement of the EU is not fully understood, or even trusted, in many member capitals. They tend to see it as reflecting Washington's preference—one normally shared by Britain—for a large, loosely connected community, instead of a structure capable of greater cohesion. But the EU members should by now understand that America's vital interest in Europe lies well beyond the degree of coherence within the EU. Washington remains sympathetic to the idea of European integration but doesn't expect to see much more of it. As for the single currency, Washington must worry that if EMU founders, the U.S. will confront a weaker and more factionalized Europe.

Washington is unlikely to worry aloud; doing so would invite accusations of American attempts to keep Europe divided. But EU members should consider the concern being expressed aloud in Washington—in both the executive branch and Congress—about whether they will help their neighbors to the east sink roots in parliamentary democracy and market economy by bringing some of them into the EU. The political commitment to do so converges with self-interest; the cognoscenti understand that. A great many thoughtful but uneasy Europeans know intuitively that enlargement, not EMU, is the priority task.

CHAPTER IV

GERMANY ADRIFT

Germanized Europe or a Europeanized Germany? Thomas Mann's famous question may have lost its point. Europe could become a fusion of both, with Germany in the role of strongest power while remaining the most exemplary European—the strongest advocate of a politically cohesive EU. For many Europeans with a sense of history, that is the course with the strongest appeal and the one to be encouraged. At least as many other thinking Europeans, while echoing the hope for such a trend line, don't like its chances of finding the main current. Briefly, the dominant strands of opinion belong to essentially like-minded people: the undeflected Europhiles and their lapsed and skeptical brethren.

Chancellor Kohl is Europe's strongest leader, perhaps its only strong leader, as well as the most "European" and experienced. As such, he has emerged, however involuntarily, as a kind of *grand solitaire.* Until the winter of 1996–97, very little in German politics was clear except for what had been clear for some time, that is, Helmut Kohl's Olympian dominance of the scene. Nothing had been allowed to grow or flourish in his shade during a period in which he outlasted four U.S. presidential terms. He intends to fight and win the federal elections in the autumn of 1998. But unemployment and financial squeezes have reduced him to more human size. And if German newspaper articles bearing headlines such as "Twilight of the Chancellor" and "The Beginning of the End" are to be taken seriously, another political era may have begun. Even if Kohl does stand again and win, his authority will be less.

Inevitably, German politics in the post–Kohl era has become one of Europe's critical uncertainties, with all sides wondering how Germany will manage its power; the relative strength of the economy, along with rising political influence, raises questions for Germans as well their partners. Will Germany's power be used to sustain the European Union and help create more integration? Or will the heirs to Chancellor Kohl, together with an influential segment of the business community, elect to put global commercial interests ahead of the EU and its single market, deciding, in effect, that the cause of integrating Europe doesn't justify any greater investment of resources or more self-denying ordinances?

According to the Europhile faithful, the logic of the situation arises from both their country's history and its requirements. Ordinary Germans, the argument runs, know that they are not loved by their neighbors. They also know that every third mark is earned by foreign trade—that Germany needs an open trade policy; that the single market may not be sustainable unless there is more integration; that a refusal to proceed with more integration carries the risk of some member countries renationalizing their policies. "Germans know instinctively that the European Union must go forward and must never go backward or even pause for very long," says a senior German diplomat.

Doing the right thing for Europe, perhaps for the first time, amounts to promoting our own higher interest, say the Europhiles, who, like many other Germans, are ever alert to the risk of anti-German coalitions forming. In commenting on this pervasive anxiety, the product of their history and geography, Germans are prone to use the stronger French phrase, *"cauchemar des coalitions"* (nightmare of coalitions). Bismarck's phrase was *"Kaunitzsche Politik,"* a reflection on the formidable coalition that confronted King Frederick II in the Seven Years' War.

Another among the foremost German worries is the reappearance of the Weimar-style politics. The danger lies in the weaknesses of the country's major parties, a problem impartially confronting most of Europe's democracies; but in Germany, where gloom and worst-case thinking come naturally, it is underlined by the past. In the 1920s, the country became disillusioned and even bored with the major parties and took a fancy to minority parties; the rest we know.

Germany lacks the tradition of unity that characterizes France and Britain; it never molded a national identity or ego. German nationalism materialized in Bismarck's time, partly in reaction to hostile coalitions and partly because such sentiment was in fashion in Europe. So let's bury the century-old German question once and for all by anchoring the country to Europe, the Europhiles say, and in the bargain bonding permanently with France.

Most skeptics regard themselves as equally good Europeans. The EU and its single market are in place and working, which, they say, is just as it should be. But Germany's interests extend well beyond the EU, skeptics observe; Germany, they add, must be able to compete in the world market with the new tigers of Asia and the Pacific, along with other newly industrialized areas where labor costs are not oppressive. "Most of our politicians say the EU is our first priority," says an official close to Kohl. "But it isn't true." And a member of Kohl's entourage—a skeptic as well as a Europhile— says, "When we were a divided country, the EU was a means to an end—rehabilitation. People were ready to yield sovereignty. That has changed."

Now, abruptly, Germans are citing and discussing national interests, and many of them, while disavowing any intention of turning away from Europe, want to behave as "normally" as other Europeans do. These Germans wonder how long they should be expected to do more in the name of Europe than others are willing to do. Should they surrender the ineffable D-mark while their partners surrender so little? There are no gains, only pain, from the EU's activities, they are saying, and they point to monetary union and the Maastricht criteria as Exhibit A. Also, a rising number of Germans simply feel exploited; besides paying the federal taxes they can relate to and accept, they feel as if they are being obliged to sacrifice far too much for the eastern Germans, starting with the 7.5 percent solidarity tax (a surcharge on individual income tax), while also providing an unfairly large share of the EU's budget.

Kohl and most of his senior people continue to pronounce in favor of a Europeanized Germany. But by and large the dispassionate gallery reckons that Germany after Kohl, whenever that is, will almost certainly be more assertive and less European. Inevitably, the passage of a generation has begun to blur the Europhile creed. "Younger Germans are asking whether we need the EU," says one of them who himself is a convinced Europhile. "They say, 'Let's concentrate on unifying our country and strengthening ties to eastern Europe and working out improved trade relationships with America and Asia.' Kohl can no longer offer them convincing arguments. The case lacks credibility. It seems complicated and abstract." Finally, some Germans feel strongly that they are outperforming their partners in the ways that matter and hence will prevail. The rest of Europe, they reckon, will follow them, because their economy will globalize—and as the German economy goes, so goes Europe.

The generation gap bears on the Kohl succession, even supposing he does win another election and remains in power until the year 2002. Kohl's potential successors—a short list—are younger men, all in their fifties. Two of them are Bavarians: Edmund Stoiber, the minister-president of Bavaria, and Theo Waigel, the finance minister; both are members of the CDU's smaller sibling, the CSU. Neither is a Europhile. Stoiber has publicly called for a "Europe of the nations." He has attacked Kohl as a European "illusionist." And he has charged the CDU, Kohl's party and the major component of the governing coalition, with ignoring the average German's concerns about the Brussels bureaucracy and its long arm. Kohl has been advised by at least one member of his government to censure Stoiber; but he declined to censure a leading member of his coalition. Stoiber professes to favor sustaining the EU, but he also says that Germany must have the right to secede if national interest and EU interest collide. Stoiber exudes strength.

Waigel, Stoiber's rival for preeminence in both Bavaria and the Federal Republic, cannot afford, as a senior government figure, to take as discordant a position on the EU as Stoiber does. But his sentiments are thought to run in the same direction, though not so far.

Wolfgang Schauble has been widely seen as Kohl's heir apparent; he is majority leader in the Bundestag, a pivotal figure within the CDU, and a very able man who has Kohl's confidence. But the passage of time is narrowing his chances. His physical condition isn't good; he was paralyzed from the waist down after being shot during an assassination attempt in 1990 and is often in considerable pain. Schauble's line on the EU is positive, but he is not thought to equate the national interest with the EU and its progress to anything like the same degree as Kohl. In fact, he is widely judged to take a more "Gaullist" view, that is, a Europe built around a concert of like-minded independent states. He's been quoted as saying, "We gain our identity, not from commitment to an idea, but from belonging to a particular nation, to a Volk."[1]

Probably the most reliably "European" member on the list is Volker Rühe, the minister of defense and one of the few who have held that job in recent years who has not been touched by scandal. He has said flatly that "The nation state is dead."[2] He has fully approved of the deployments of German troops and weapons, notably those in Croatia, that may help to erode his country's cultural passivity and reluctance to be involved in disputes beyond its borders.

Of the four, Rühe's style is best suited to national politics, although his ambition may be overly transparent, and he is a strong and plausible candidate for the succession. However, Kohl dislikes Rühe, and his European bona fides are clouded by his ambivalent view of France, Germany's key partner. In any case, the rivalry between Rühe and Waigel, the two most powerful ministers, has accounted for more than a little of what has gone on in Bonn over the past few years. But neither of them nor anyone else has as yet risked taking a run at the succession, because Kohl, like a monarch of old—"Bismarck in a baggy sweater"—doesn't tolerate any challenge to his authority. He rarely confronts serious opposition from either within or outside. Within, none of the aggressive younger Christian Democrats could be described as a rising star, with the possible exception of Jürgen Ruttgers, the minister for education, research, and technology, who is in his mid-forties and is still something of a new face. Outside, the chief rival party, the SPD, hasn't been a serious threat in years; its internal struggles have battered the party intellectually and ideologically, thereby diminishing its credibility within the country.

Germany may yet steer itself and its partners toward the Kohl vision—a Europeanized Germany within a stronger EU, a few of whose members, starting with France and Germany, might create an inner circle, one capable of making decisions on matters of political importance. Or Germans may allow the larger part of Europe to organize itself, as if by osmosis, around the strongest country, a course that most societies in Germany's position would adopt unhesitatingly; it is the more likely alternative, especially if blended with a variant: a more or less Germanized Europe but one that continues studiously to devolve power onto its states—the *Länder*—at the expense of the federal government. The idea is that a more consciously decentralized Berlin Republic would appear less menacing and hence less likely to foster anti-German coalitions.

Although anti-German sentiments haven't gone away, their relevance matters less and less as Germany's position strengthens. The Dutch, for example, continue to harbor such sentiments, but they also feel culturally closer to the Germans, along with the British, than to other EU members. I asked three senior Dutch diplomats which team they thought an average Dutch family, sitting before the TV, would be cheering on if Germany and France were shown playing soccer. Two of the three answered "Germany," and the third was unsure. The three agreed that British influence, once paramount, was declining. "More and more we are entwined with Germany," one of them noted.

Scandinavians also tend to identify their interests with Germany's. The past notwithstanding, their relations with Germany are rooted in similar ways of thinking. (The Danish-German relationship is somewhat more complicated.) Their schools are in general organized along the lines of schools in northern Germany. Before World War II, most educated Danes and Swedes studied in Germany. Although that has changed, not much else has. "The Portuguese call us English-speaking Germans," observes a Finnish diplomat. Learning English at school is compulsory, but the German language, once the lingua franca, is undergoing a revival throughout Scandinavia.

The hardy perennial and pivotal question for Germany, as well as for France, is what will befall their partnership, the EU's axis. In Germany, the partnership is seen—and has been for nearly four decades—as a war-preventing talisman. And if you are a good German, you carry this talisman around. The other talismans are the D-mark, a stout U.S. military presence through NATO, and, at least until now, the European movement.

Neither side can afford to put the Franco-German partnership at serious risk: France can influence German behavior only through this special link, and Kohl and his entourage have felt that Germany cannot risk the appearance of being left to its own devices in Europe without a strong tie to France. Germany's power, both real and latent, is legitimized by both its membership in the EU and the solid French connection. If the EU continues to decline in importance, as seems likely, Germany's French connection will remain essential, though far more difficult to sustain.

Over time, the tight interaction between the French and German bureaucracies gave the relationship a capillary nature, which is why Chirac's early freewheeling was so disruptive and caused consternation in Bonn. The partnership always started at the top, whether between Konrad Adenauer and General de Gaulle, between Helmut Schmidt and Valéry Giscard d'Estaing, or between Mitterrand and Kohl. The relationships between the foreign ministers and other senior officials in the two cabinets were also central to the relationship, and they continue to be. Mitterrand's foreign minister, Roland Dumas, and Hans-Dietrich Genscher, his German colleague, got on very well and always had tête-à-tête meetings at EU and NATO gatherings; they brought neither note takers nor interpreters, since Dumas spoke good German. Their successors do not possess this kind of rapport.

The Kohl-Chirac relationship settled down after a seriously inauspicious beginning, but it's not likely to develop the trust and intimacy achieved by their predecessors, even though the pair's mandates may well become coterminous. Chirac's mandate runs to the year 2002, and Kohl's fifth term as chancellor, if he has one, will also expire then. They are very different. Chirac is volatile, impulsive, and unreflective—given to taking decisions on the fly. Kohl never takes a decision before he has to—not until he has exhausted his pulse-taking procedure. When he labels some proposal or initiative "irrelevant," it often means he is contemplating a change of his policy in precisely that direction. (In dismissing the idea of postponing monetary union as "irrelevant," for example, he led many Kohl watchers to conclude that postponement lay ahead.)

Of Chirac's numerous mistakes and affronts early on, the most serious was his disregard for the customary practice of consulting Kohl before taking a step that would affect German interests. French nuclear testing was an early and conspicuous example. Bonn had made a major effort throughout the world to enlist support for renewal of the Nuclear Nonproliferation Treaty. Then, in June 1995, just a month after taking office, Chirac announced that France would resume testing nuclear weapons in the Pacific. A wave of anger, along with a sense of betrayal, swept through Germany's political class; Bonn was shocked as well as angered. Ministers wondered aloud how France could expect solidarity if it acted without consulting its partners, Bonn especially. Foreign Minister Klaus Kinkel wrote a piece in a Berlin newspaper criticizing Chirac's decision, but Kohl turned the other cheek and forbade further comment. Still, his entourage pushed him hard to do something, and when the two leaders met in Strasbourg a few days after the announcement on testing, Kohl surprised them by expressing his displeasure to Chirac.

But Bonn felt as if it has more to worry about than Chirac being a loose cannon. It had low regard for most members of his government, aside from the former prime minister, Alain Juppé, who was considered clever and competent. Far more worrisome to Bonn, however, is a growing fear that Germany will be isolated—worry that France and Britain have become status quo players, unwilling to take risks or push the EU's ball very far down the field. Only monetary union has enlisted French support, and it, of course, was originally a French idea and one aimed at keeping Germany's power within reasonable bounds. And if held on schedule, it may create the political equivalent of a train wreck.

If EMU turns sour or ends in tears, the German consensus on Europe will break down quickly. In that case, Germany will probably change course and become yet again a more central European and independent player. Germany will see east-central and eastern Europe becoming a dynamic force in continental affairs. France will have met itself coming back. Briefly, if denied the opportunity to "Europeanize" their country, the Germans are likely to exercise their strength by advancing another agenda, one reflecting a wholly fair but narrower reading of the national interest.

Toward the end of 1995, a member of Kohl's staff offered an aggrieved and gloomy estimate of the state of play. It may have been too gloomy, but not by much and by no means reflecting a temporary set of anxieties. "Germany doesn't want to be isolated," he said. "We need an umbrella. But if that doesn't work, we must act bilaterally in the east. France and Britain are doing nothing there. That is the biggest difference between us and our partners. Europe is stagnating. But change is in the air. It's about the amount of difference in weight we and they [the French] displace. We both will revert to balance-of-power politics. But our dilemma is not wanting to act alone. Russia is sure to come back on the scene. France's problems in the south should not exclude its involvement with the east."[3]

"Our Algeria lies to the east," some Germans say. However, their problem with migratory flow is substantially less acute than France's. In 1992, after a million refugees had descended on Germany, the constitution was amended with language that denied entry to anyone coming from a so-called persecution-free country. The states on Germany's eastern frontier were defined as persecution-free countries, meaning that Germany is now protected from a major refugee influx over its borders with Poland, the Czech Republic, and Austria. These countries share Germany's interest in discouraging the influx. France, of course, has long stretches of vulnerable coastline and no buffers. "If you can solve your problems this way, you don't need integration," says a German newspaper editor, a Euroskeptic.

Not so long ago, Germans felt as if their country and France had no deeper interest than building a European structure to which both societies would bend. No longer. France, they think, regards the EU as a vehicle to be manipulated to its own advantage and especially to constrain Germany. On issues of crucial importance to Bonn—renovating the EU's barely functional machinery—there is little, if any, distance between the French and British positions. And the Germans are still smarting from the shabby treatment accorded them at Maastricht by their major EU partners, France and Britain. Whitehall stands accused in Bonn of having busily fed France's doubts about the EU and indeed of having helped to extinguish the idealism of French conservative political circles with regard to building Europe. Germans are hoping that the Blair government will at some point align EU policy with the prime minister's more comforting rhetoric, but they know that won't happen overnight.

Under Tory leadership, Britain was reluctant to forgive and forget Germany, whereas Germans, by and large, are attracted to British culture and feel as if they have more in common with Britain than with France. "It is unilateral hostility," a senior and distinctly pro-British official in Bonn always said. "The British press, especially the tabloids, sound as they did around 1910—hostile to the nouveau riche Germans. Germans reacted then, but not now." France, he adds, "has created a mythology of French-German reconciliation. The politics of symbolism—German soldiers on the Champs-Élysées on July 14, et cetera. Our political culture owes much to Britain, but there is no British-German mythology."[4]

All countries are capable of pursuing goals that may collide with one another; but the Germans, possibly because of their position in the middle of Europe, do this more unapologetically and with more vigor than others. For example, at one stage in the mid-1990s, they were taking a stronger line on creating a European defense identity than any of their partners, including France, although they have no higher priority than sustaining an American military presence in Europe through a robust NATO; also, Germany has a more passive security policy than its partners and the most passive culture. And only the Germans have tried at the same time both to deepen and to widen the EU. Deepening means trying to maneuver the rest of the egg—integration—into the shell, the Treaty of Rome. As for widening, Germans argue that Poland, the Czech Republic, Hungary, and various other eastern neighbors are fully capable of living within the EU's rules, provided that these countries are granted a transitional arrangement as liberal as that accorded Portugal and Spain when they joined.

Deepening strikes the Germans as unambiguously laudable. Why shouldn't France help? France's leadership kept sounding as if it wanted to fast-forward European unity. But it showed no corresponding sympathy for widening, much preferring the EU as it was, with Germany on the eastern rim and France at the center. But Margaret Thatcher's government seemed to regard enlargement as virtuous, since it would discourage—and perhaps altogether prevent—significant deepening. But after John Major succeeded Thatcher, the British attitude to widening became more ambiguous. And Germans finally discovered that whereas they knew what they wanted to do about strengthening the EU's institutions, the French either couldn't agree on what to do about them or didn't want to do anything anyway.

Early in September 1994, the leadership of the German CDU's parliamentary group published a remarkable paper that met these issues head on. The paper's chief addressee was France. The tone was tough; the paper sounded very like an ultimatum, saying, in effect, either help us build Europe, or accept the consequences. One paragraph deserves to be read in its entirety:

> The only solution which will prevent a return to the unstable pre-war system, with Germany once again caught in the middle between East and West, is to integrate Germany's Central and Eastern European neighbors into the European post-war system and to establish a wide-ranging partnership between this system and Russia. Never again must there be a destabilizing vacuum of power in central Europe. If European integration were not to progress, Germany might be called upon, or tempted by its own

security constraints, to try to effect the stabilization of Eastern Europe on its own and in the traditional way.[5]

The paper recommended that the European Commission "take on the features of a European government." Another controversial proposal called for a "multispeed" approach, one that would create what some Europhiles call a "two-tier" Europe. The first tier, as envisaged by the paper, would be a hard core of states—France, Germany, the Benelux nations—that were prepared to move ahead at all deliberate speed. "Germany and France," the paper said, "form the core of the hard core." But France was described in the paper as opposed to extending German influence by admitting the countries of central and eastern Europe to the EU. The solution, said the paper, lay in "deepening the union prior to enlargement."

Issuing the paper amounted to the most sweeping of Germany's postwar efforts to help create a stable Europe. Authorship was ascribed jointly to Karl Lamers and to Schauble, Kohl's supposed heir apparent. The actual author, however, was Lamers, the CDU's foreign affairs spokesman and a one-man think tank; Schauble was asked to lend his stronger name to the document. In a larger sense, however, it was Kohl's paper; he had seen and approved it at various stages but was an offstage presence and was granted "deniability," as the head man always is, after the paper had appeared. Curiously, he wasn't consulted on the timing of its release and reacted angrily; the paper appeared just after the federal election campaign had begun.

Although the paper had been in the works since the preceding January, at no point was the often ignored and deeply aggrieved Foreign Ministry informed of what was under way. Through Lamers and Schauble, Kohl was telling Germany's partners, "We Germans have options. You others pick one for us. But make sure you pick the right one. We don't want to have to pick the wrong one. We are the EU's giant, with 80 million people and 30 percent of the GDP, but we are prepared to give away pieces of our sovereignty, even to be Gulliverized. But you must meet us halfway."

A major brouhaha followed. A hard core of the few? What is to become of the second tier, the many? A federal Europe run by the Commission? No government, including the intensely Europhile Dutch, seemed willing to go nearly so far or even to say anything nice about the paper; most expressed themselves in terse but negative terms. Many diplomats reckoned that Lamers et al. had done everyone a favor, first by distributing a set of ideas to which most Europhiles could rally, and second by putting governments into the awkward position of having to respond to this high-minded text.

It was especially awkward for the French; in one way or another, they had espoused most of the paper's ideas. "Everyone in the government is embarrassed," said Jean-François Poncet, a highly regarded former foreign minister. He noted that the conservative bloc, of which he is a member, accepted the ideas in the paper.[6]

Not so France's leadership. It didn't have to reply to a nonofficial paper, but the response came nonofficially. While then Prime Minister Robert Balladur was in Bonn meeting with Kohl at the end of November, a long article signed by him appeared in the French daily Le Monde. "An enlarged Europe comprising a greater number of states could not be federal," it said. "That would mean extending . . . the domain of [EU] decisions made by majority voting. Thus, the five big states representing four fifths of the population and wealth could be placed in a minority position. They will not allow that."[7]

In a sampling of reactions that I made, Hungary's foreign minister, László Kovács, said, "My first reaction was negative. I saw this as the kind of language you see from the French, never the Germans. The tone was too emotional. But then I saw that the paper summed up the realities. So on the whole, I think it was OK."[8]

The hard core didn't include Italy, one of the six founding members of the European Community. Giuliano Amato, a former Italian prime minister and one of Europe's wiser and most respected political figures, said, "I see the need of a two-tier Europe. We need a hard core, but Italy will be in the second tier. We Mediterranean powers are lesser lights. Despite the shrill Italian reaction to Lamers-Schauble, it was a statement of Germany's commitment to Europe."[9]

Most officials of most member governments can accept, in principle, the need for a two-tier structure, chiefly because nothing is likely to happen that isn't pushed by a small hard core and sheltered from the weak and the naysayers. Enlargement, too, is fully accepted in principle, but every Europhile knows that an even larger structure would have to be protected from so-called blocking minorities by a hard core—a kind of directorate.

Asked why the paper had gotten such a negative reaction, its author, Karl Lamers, said, "The French saw it as too much German weight in too small a club [the hard core]. The language may have confused them. It looked as if we were excluding others. We were only starting without them."[10]

Amato saw irony in what was happening to the French-German link. "Formerly," he said, "the EU could go forward only because Germany was weak and France ascendant. It's a different game now." He seemed to mean that Germany was calling the shots—to the extent anyone was.

By Christmas, however, the comment about the Lamers-Schauble paper had all but died out. A few months later, Kohl and his CDU colleagues were surfacing another proposal, one that was neither very bold nor very interesting. It drew little, if any, hostile reaction—or much reaction at all—and was quickly forgotten. What was remembered instead is that Europe's strongest and best-intentioned power had for one moment challenged—actually warned—France and others to do something for Europe and had then drawn back at the first show of resistance.

There was a fragment of precedent for Germany's initiative. In April 1991, Genscher had sent eyebrows shooting up by telling fellow EC foreign ministers, during a discussion in Luxembourg of deepening and widening, that Germany was making a "European offer." It was offering, he said, to pool its strength and resources with those of its partners. Do please take up our offer, he warned, while there remains in Bonn a leadership that you can work with. The reaction to his warning wasn't good. "It was a disreputable argument," a senior British diplomat told me shortly afterward. "He was saying, 'Either move at our pace or we become unreliable.' That was arm-twisting."[11]

As it happened, Genscher's warning was empty. So, it appears, was the more carefully thought out and meticulously prepared Lamers-Schauble initiative, which bore Helmut Kohl's imprint. He remains deeply concerned about what his successors may do or not do. The rest of the egg, he feels, must be maneuvered into the shell on his watch. It won't be.

The Economy:
A Productive But Idle Society

Besides having Europe's strongest economy and dominant currency, Germany is the world's second largest exporter and has the most productive labor force. But how to reconcile the stereotypical German worker—an industrious, highly skilled craftsman—with the idler that he or she has also become? "We are the world champs in vacations," says Herbert Henzler, McKinsey and Company's German chairman. "Social costs are paralyzing us. We've become hedonists. Our amenities industry soaks up ten percent of our GNP."[12] Germans have the world's highest labor costs, and they work less—thirty-five hours per week—than workers anywhere else. Germans have forty-two days of paid annual holiday, another first within the industrialized world. Their thirst for holidays strikes disconcerted outsiders as relentless.

It's become a commonplace that Germany has the world's oldest students, youngest pensioners, and most expensive workers. Yes, they are indeed highly productive. The question is how long the so-

ciety can continue to pay these labor costs without slashing the social safety net. Kohl's CDU is itself split on this question. And not
all Germans, least of all the generation of the 1960s, think that
economic growth is necessarily a goal worth pursuing or making
sacrifices for. Others argue more plausibly that it's not the welfare
system that has put the economy under pressure but instead the
$600 billion that has been transferred to eastern Germany.

Shopping hours provide one of the better illustrations of a lan-
guid, self-satisfied society. The unavailing efforts made from time
to time to lengthen them have become an international joke. Previously the law was that shops could not remain open after 6:00 or
6:30 P.M., depending on where they were located. On Saturdays,
they were obliged to close no later than 2:00 P.M. At long last the
law was changed, effective November 1, 1996. Now shops may
stay open until 8:00 P.M. during the week and until 4:00 P.M. on
Saturday. They must still remain closed on Sunday.

Optimists and partisans of the status quo argue along the following lines: The system has served us well, and continues to do
so. Our constitution makes us all responsible for one another. It
opens by declaring that "The Federal Republic is a democratic and
socially responsible federal state." So long as the economy continues to grow, surgery won't be required. The recession of the early
and mid-1990s was a blessing in disguise because it gave business
and government some leverage vis-à-vis the unions and thereby
helped diminish their power. It also made credible industry's threat
to move plants eastward toward lower labor costs. Moreover, our
businesses are already paying the EU's highest corporate taxes
[nearly 65 percent]; any increase would surely be a blow to their
confidence. Give credit to those among our great companies such
as Daimler-Benz and Krupp that have coped effectively with recession by cutting costs and restructuring. Finally, Kohl will want to
be remembered—and should be—as the chancellor of unification,
not as the one who applied a lot of stick and darkened people's
lives and expectations.

The harsher view sounds like this: We urgently need a financial fitness program at all levels—federal, *Länder,* and so on. One party, the CDU, is in control at the federal level, and the SPD is in the majority at the *Land* level. The post–World War II social contract that has been so successful will have to be rewritten and accepted on all sides. Otherwise, we will be watching our deficit soar and our economy sag. We need a 2.6 percent increase in real growth each year to maintain the status quo in the welfare system, and we haven't had that much growth in years. By the end of the century, nearly a fourth of our population will be over 60 years old. Today, each pension is financed by three employees (who contributed 18.7 percent of their gross income to the pension funds in 1990). But by the year 2020 the ratio may be one to one, with employees obliged to contribute 35 percent of their gross income. By the year 2000 the ratio of people older than 75 and those 20 years of age will be one to fourteen, as compared to the end of the nineteenth century when it was one to seventy-nine.[13]

Kohl knows he must do something and has managed to take one slice from the tumescent welfare system. In April 1996, he proposed cuts in the social spending budget totaling about $33 billion. Some cuts were scheduled to take effect in 1997, while others amounted to delaying increases in welfare benefits. Just before the Bundestag's vote in June 1996, a mass demonstration was staged in Bonn by members of the big unions, although not much of a fuss was made because there wasn't much for them to be upset about. The package raised the retirement age, after the turn of the century, from 63 to 65 for men and from 60 to 65 for women; during the first six weeks of sick leave, some workers would get 80 percent of their salaries instead of 100 percent; instead of enjoying government insurance–paid visits to spas of four weeks every three years, workers would have to be content with three weeks of this indulgence every four years.

The cuts in the package finally approved amounted to about $16.5 billion. According to Waigel, the budgetary savings would bring the German deficit down to 2.5 percent of its GNP, below the 3 percent dictated by monetary union. The skeptics demurred, noting that the effort to meet EMU's convergence criteria would drive unemployment up by another 2 or 3 percent, which, if true, would also drive the deficit back up because the welfare costs of unemployment are so high. Germans used to say that 1 million unemployed cannot be tolerated. Now they have 4 million and so far are tolerating it. Some of them are reminding one another that the Spanish and Italians have had 15 to 20 percent unemployed and have endured. We, too, must adapt and learn to tolerate high unemployment, such people are saying.

Germans, by and large, think they are still doing pretty well, mainly because in a sense they are; also because they outperform their European partners and feel as if their standards are higher. But all of Europe is a slow-growth area and lags behind its chief global competitors in innovation, advanced technology, and knowledge-intensive industries. Germany, for example, is being outperformed in East Asia even in products such as autos, where it normally does well, and despite building assembly plants in major overseas markets. At least 30 percent of its cars are being made elsewhere, causing a huge loss of jobs, especially in Baden-Württemberg. But German cars do not stand comparison with those of Toyota, Honda, and Nissan; they continue to be admired for their technology and other attributes, but have become less competitive, partly because of high production costs. "We are falling further behind every day in the race to stay competitive in a global economy," said Hans Olaf Henkel, president of Germany's Federation of Industries.[14]

Investment at home is steadily declining and is expected to continue moving outside the country to lower labor costs. Moreover, unemployment is spreading, partly because small and medium-sized German companies—a traditional source of strength—are creating major subsidiaries in Italy and Turkey. Those left behind are beginning to have trouble competing. Baden-Württemberg, a region of enormous strength, is carpeted with small and medium-sized companies, and Dirk von Häften, director-general of this state's foreign economic office in Stuttgart, estimates that about 98 percent of them have fewer than five hundred employees and an annual combined turnover of no more than 200 million D-marks.

Inevitably, many "Wessis" (former West Germans) see the financial costs of unification as sapping the economy's strength. But that is not the case, according to closely involved people such as Kurt Lauck. "The question, quite bluntly," he says, "is not whether the price of unification is proving to be too high, but whether Germany is aware that many of its economic problems antedated unification, that the first 'early warning signals' were already beginning to be apparent almost a decade ago." [15]

The concern of Germans with their negative distinctions—highest labor costs, youngest pensioners, and so on—is sharpened by the sight of the U.S. economy briskly adapting to change and outperforming those of all the EU members. In late September 1996, a cluster of big German companies, led by Daimler-Benz, decided to do something about lowering their own costs. They startled the unions and the Kohl government by announcing an unprecedented hard line against their workers. Relying on a new law, the companies took aim at various employee benefits, including sick pay; it would be cut 20 percent. (German workers are entitled to full pay for six weeks of sick leave, a benefit exceeded only by their Dutch counterparts.)

It seems that no one, including Kohl's government, had expected the new law to be applied against existing contracts. The unions threatened strikes and a hot autumn. One of them, IG Metall, called a one-day strike that is believed to have cost Daimler-Benz 200 million D-marks, or more than the company expected to save in a year by cutting sick pay. Siemens instantly changed its mind about following Daimler in this dicey move. Other firms announced that they wouldn't be making changes in sick pay either. And Kohl indicated his view that existing labor contracts overrode the law he had struggled to have adopted. Some business and political leaders in other EU member countries were left wondering whether they could do something similar, but more successfully. Kohl may have been left wondering whether the episode would affect the chances for achieving monetary union on schedule.

The German economy's greatest strength was always metal bending—building high-cost, high-quality products such as autos and machine tools, with the entire product line rooted in solid basic science. German brand names were and remain synonymous with quality, a source of national pride. But critics expect to see much of this metal bending capacity headed sooner rather than later to the rust belt. Not to worry, other Germans feel. They can continue to buy the technology they may require, or set up subsidiaries in technology-intensive areas such as Silicon Valley in California—places where they won't be bugged by shrill German environmentalists.

But if Germany is to make its way in the world market, this stubborn aversion to innovation will have to give way. Germany has stood aside from most of the various major advanced technologies that sank commercial roots in the 1980s, including the information industry, new materials, and genetic engineering. Ironically, the first computer, a mechanical device, was invented by a German, Konrad Zuse, in 1936. He started a business producing electronic computers but was obliged to give it up in the 1960s. He died in December 1995. Germans also claim to have invented the compact disc. Kohl himself has cited the example of the fax machine, invented by Siemens AG but exploited with vast success by Japan.[16] Germans are currently in the vanguard of advanced environmental technology but of few other fields.

German chemical companies have invested in biotechnology, but mainly through American companies located in the United States. Ulrich Langer, a chemicals analyst at Commerzbank in Frankfurt, was quoted as saying, "Biotech is almost nonexistent within Germany. Public opinion is still very much against it, so German companies find they have to go abroad, to the U.S. or

Japan."[17] The resistance to biotechnology lies mainly, though by no means exclusively, with the politically powerful Green movement. Green groups around the country have filed lawsuits to stop work in biotechnology, and elected officials are creating barriers to companies trying to do work in this field.[18] Gene manipulation has ugly and troubling overtones for Germans, who cannot forget the genetic experiments carried on by the Third Reich. Still, bankers see it as an industry that may be worth $100 billion in the year 2000. And the net effect, especially as seen from Bonn, of resistance to competing at home in this field and other domains is to export jobs and investment while adding to a brain drain. Sometime in 1995, the chairman of the giant conglomerate Siemens announced that all of its corporate taxes for the previous year had been paid abroad, none in Germany

A deeply conservative society has created an economy that appears to be as risk-averse as it is muscular. Change isn't excluded but comes slowly and belatedly when it does come. The service sector is still too small. The economy remains too guildish—there is too much stress on apprenticeships. And it is injuriously overregulated. Another serious deterrent to innovation, change, and economic vitality is the dominant role of banks in corporate governance. They tend to like things as they are, and compared, say, to the United States, risk capital in Germany is scarce. "A company like Microsoft would never have a chance in Germany," said Joschka Fischer, leader of the Green Party.[19] Because the banks there exercise proxy votes on behalf of some of their customers, they can control firms without holding large stakes of their own.[20]

Briefly, the entire system will have to be loosened up. Polls show that Germans judge the French economy to be stronger than their own. It impresses them as being further along in restructuring (which it isn't) and further along in exploiting advanced technology (which it probably is). The director of the German Patent Office has warned that by the year 2005 the country's formidable economy will have slipped to the world's eighteenth strongest.[21]

Germans and most of Europe were stunned during the spring of 1997 by a blast from an unexpected source—President Roman Herzog. The country's ruling class, he said, was defaulting on its responsibilities to do what had to be done. "The lack of courage is overwhelming," he said. "Crisis scenarios are growing. A feeling of paralysis has settled over the whole society. . . . What is wrong with our country? Put plainly, the loss of economic dynamism, the enfeeblement of society, the unbelievable sense of mental depression. You get the impression that pessimism has become a general state of mind, and that is extremely dangerous."[22]

East and West: Still Divided

Few, if any, governments in the modern era have had to face changes in domestic and foreign policy on the scale that Bonn confronted in 1990. West Germany had been evolving into a kind of post-nation-state—blending itself into a more or less supranational European Community and fully dependent on NATO.

The 16 million new citizens hadn't had the mellowing experience of membership in a community like the EC or of being consenting members of an alliance like NATO. On the contrary, their experience with an alliance—the Warsaw Pact—had been one of being exploited and made subservient. More important, probably, after sixty years of misrule and oppression, first by the Nazis and then by Moscow's puppet regime, eastern Germans weren't shy about asserting themselves. Their expectations ran high, but they also added a distinctly insular, if not xenophobic, flavor to their country's style. They had nothing to apologize for, they felt, since after enduring six decades of darkness they had brought about a miracle—a bloodless revolution.

The idea of unification, however, disconcerted the western Germans. By and large, they hadn't really envisioned or even seemed to want a unified state. They had tended to equate the division of the state with the division of Europe. Reunify Europe, the feeling went, and the two Germanys would be reunified, or at least reconciled while remaining separate political entities. What the Wessis knew for certain was that their country had flourished separately, thanks in great part to the ties it had forged with France and the rest of the European Community. Many of them scoffed at, or in some cases resented, the notion of a secret agenda—of wanting to fuse the divided nation into one authentic heavyweight situated in the middle of Europe. Germany's neighbors to the west and east, not to mention the two superpowers, would oppose any such move. Or so it seemed.

It is tempting but deeply mistaken to think of Germany as being like other places, only better run than most and more prosperous. In fact, this is a society that has spent 600 billion dollars since unification in a massive effort to absorb its eastern portion, while simultaneously investing huge sums in other parts of the former Soviet empire further east. (Compare this performance with the unwillingness of undertaxed Americans to pay a few cents more for their gas.) It's not as if this remarkable transfer of resources to eastern Germans were a sentimental gesture. The two groups still do not like each other. But it doesn't matter. Historically, Germany's various tribes, wherever they were located, never were fraternal; but at least they now know that they make up one nation, even if the sense of nationhood isn't strongly felt. Goethe and Schiller doubted that Germany was a nation or could function as a single state. Bismarck talked of tribes rather than nations. "He had no regard for any traditional state except Prussia— perhaps not even much for her," wrote A. J. P. Taylor.[23] In his memoirs, Bismarck himself said, "It is as a Prussian, a Hanoverian, a Württemberger, a Bavarian or a Hessian, rather than as a German, that he [a German] is disposed to give unequivocal proof of patriotism."[24]

At most times, Germany is an enigma. Some Germans are optimistic; postmodernism for them, they say, is being surrounded for the first time by only friendly faces and lacking only serious problems and disagreeable choices. Yet they impress various German watchers, along with some among themselves, as being despondent and confused, wondering whether their identity lies within the nation, the European edifice, or possibly something larger and more global. Many favor a strong reassertion of German sovereignty.

Monetary union is for some a panacea and more—destiny's instrument for belling the cat—that is, the welfare system—and saving everyone's bacon in the end. Others equate EMU and losing the D-mark with castration or "Versailles without war," as some have called it. Germans of this opinion—and there are many—ask why they should give up the D-mark in order to calm neighbors who worry excessively and unnecessarily about their strength. "Underneath there is the deeper matter of sovereignty," writes Timothy Garton-Ash, one of the most astute Germanologists. "It is one thing to surrender sovereignty in order to regain it," he continues. "But has Germany now regained sovereignty only to surrender it? Even for the world's most dialectical nation, this may be a twist too far."[25] In Bonn, there is a temptation to have a place at the top table—to be a permanent member of the U.N. Security Council. Elsewhere, much—probably most—of the society is indifferent to Germany's seating arrangements.

Unification has imposed some significant changes. The eastern Germans have tilted the religious balance, making the country a good deal more Protestant. They have also upset the geographical balance between north and south, which is more sensitive in Germany than elsewhere in Europe, except Italy. The eastern Germans may help to sustain the national aloofness to defense or retard efforts to turn it aside.

Unification has dictated a preoccupation with domestic affairs. It lends itself to phrasemakers, namely, "a collision under one roof"; "a marriage of inconvenience." "Our Mezzogiorno" is how some western Germans refer to the eastern region. "The exemplary openness and civility of the old Federal Republic have not yet been restored across its larger territory," writes Garton-Ash. "This failure is not simply a case of easterners exhibiting the pathologies of post-communism. It is as much a problem of the condescending and at times frankly neocolonial attitudes of westerners toward eastern-ers. There is more than a grain of bitter truth in the joke that when in 1989 the East Germans started chanting, 'We are one people,' the West Germans replied, 'So are we.'"[26]

From the start, the western Germans have tended to define the problem as one of financial aid, according to easterners, who see it as far more complex. According to Jürgen Kocka, a history profes-sor at Berlin's Free University, the eastern German birth rate fell by 60 percent and the marriage rate by 65 percent between 1989 and 1992. "Declines of this magnitude are extremely rare in history," he writes. "Only the Great wars offer similar examples."[27] It is, com-mented *The Economist,* "as if unification had sent family life into a state of shock for three years."[28] Also, easterners feel as if their in-stant fellow citizens in the west haven't understood that forty-five years of Communist rule shaped their attitudes in ways that can't be changed overnight.

How long it may take for west and east to converge stylistically, economically, and politically is an imponderable. Guesses vary from one group to another and from place to place. Opinion is sub-jective, arbitrary, and highly impressionistic. Kohl spoke at first about "flowering landscapes," but he may have been thinking of Dresden, Leipzig, and Potsdam. Elsewhere, in the five new *Länder,* few landscapes are in immediate danger of flowering.

Some Germans say that unification will have arrived when they no longer have to consult an autobahn map of the eastern *Länder.* Such people like to add, with a bit of hyperbole, that every eastern German has visited western Germany, whereas only 25 percent to 30 percent of western Germans have visited the east, most of them for no more than one day. Whether "real unification," as it's com-monly referred to, is the society's highest goal, as many claim, or a rhetorical goal, is unclear. What is clear is that it is a distant goal.

"The eastern part of the country must play by new rules still not fully understood, let alone mastered," says Anne-Marie Le Gloannec, a distinguished French authority on Germany. Interestingly, she feels that the biggest divide lies not between Ossis (former East Germans) and Wessis but between the Ossis themselves. "It is the east Germans who left for the west who are most quarrelsome," she says. "More of the fights and controversies are between them and the other east Germans [those still there]," she says. "And the mood of the east Germans is volatile. It has swings—from optimistic to gloomy."

Mme. Le Gloannec takes a sanguine view of Germany. "It is a compelling but cumbersome society," she says, "and it works very well. It is the most stable and most democratic society in Europe. That latter quality is what makes it cumbersome but also provides the inner strength." As for increased regionalism, or federalism, she says, it "will have a strengthening effect as it loosens the structure. Germany is like a Russian doll, the various parts neatly fitting together."[29]

Statistics don't shed a lot of light, although they are used by both optimists and pessimists to describe eastern Germany's direction. Economic growth, we hear, is rising steadily—faster, of course, than in western Germany, where the baseline is so much higher. But we also learn that in 1994 the new *Länder* accounted for only 1.8 percent of total German exports.[30]

"I tell them the truth—that it will take us fifteen years to catch up," says Kurt Biedenkopf, Saxony's esteemed leader. "I've always told them the truth, year in and year out," says Biedenkopf, who left the west for the east because he wanted to help heal the country's split.[31] His candor accounts in part for the unchanging popularity of Saxony's "King Kurt," who, with no illusions, talks of gradually restoring its pre–World War I distinction of having Europe's highest GNP and being Germany's industrial powerhouse. Germany's deepest cultural and industrial roots lie in Saxony and Thuringia.

Biedenkopf is an optimist, according to many, who think it will take a minimum of twenty years and probably more for the east to draw more or less even. Yet, several Wessis, watching the huge transfer of resources, anticipate an economic boom in the east. Within five years, according to some forecasts, the east will have become the most productive and modernized part of the country. Envisaged are new autobahns, magnetic rail links, major auto assembly plants. And by the year 2000, a comprehensive fiber-optics network will have given eastern Germany the world's most up-to-date communications. Various thoughtful and experienced Germans feel strongly that in making over eastern Germany, new techniques and various reforms should have been introduced and a model created—one that could also have been applied to western Germany and speeded up its own adaptation.

Traditionally, northern and southern Germany have been more clearly divided than east and west, and in some ways they remain so. And the shift in the German economy's vigor has so far been mainly northward, toward Hamburg. Studies by various European research institutes show northeastern Germany as the only part of the country with a rate of growth that is keeping pace with northern Italy's. Hamburg is providing much of the boost; it is a center of distribution of products from Pacific Rim countries to European markets. Sweden and Finland have joined Denmark as members of the EU, and Hamburg is benefiting from this enlarged Scandinavian presence. But more important, as well as more interesting, is the opening of markets to the east and the return to Hamburg of its hinterland. This hinterland stretches to Dresden and beyond to Prague, all of it international waterway. A strong interaction between Hamburg and Dresden has developed, and Hamburg has again become the Czech Republic's port city.

According to Biedenkopf, Saxony also has more interaction with Bavaria than with other eastern *Länder,* partly, he says, because of the CDU's dominance in Saxony. All but one of the other eastern *Länder,* he says, are governed either by the SPD or by coalitions. Still, while Saxony may be the brightest light among the eastern

Länder, it remains as much a product of the past sixty years as they do. Like the others, it lost markets in the east after unification and struggled to find new ones. And it found itself not just toeing a line handed down overnight by a brand-new center of authority in Bonn but having to bend to a novel and even more distant authority in Brussels.

"Saxons do not know much about the EU," says one of Biedenkopf's senior civil servants. "When they first heard about these rules and regulations coming out of Brussels, they were incredulous." Saxony, he feels, is far from ready to adopt a European identity if that means also adopting the EU.[32]

Although the latent tension in relations between the eastern *Länder* and Brussels rarely comes to the surface, it did so in the form of a nasty, three-party dustup during the summer of 1996. Biedenkopf was tempting Volkswagen to make a new car in Saxony, where unemployment is a massive problem, by offering subsidies worth about $61 million. The European Commission protested, arguing that the subsidies were a breach of rules governing competition. In Bonn, Kohl exploded when Biedenkopf announced that he was taking the Commission to court. In the end, Saxony lost the argument; the subsidies were blocked. Still, it may not be the end altogether. Opinion polls ran heavily in Biedenkopf's favor, and baronial Euroskeptics such as Edmund Stoiber have entered the fray, noting that Germany is much the largest financial contributor to the EU but has far too little to say about how the money is spent and about what goes on in Brussels.[33]

The decision to move the capital from Bonn to Berlin was controversial. One looks west, the other east. One is understated and memorable only as Beethoven's birthplace. But as the federal capital in the postwar/Cold War era, Bonn was a great success. Returning Berlin to its former status of capital is judged unnecessary by many Germans. Also, numerous Wessis will see themselves as losers in the move as the Ossis begin to find their voice. The move will help with that but may add to the tension between the two groups.

At least as many other Germans see the move as a very good one, and for a variety of reasons. One is that it will, in theory, give the Ossis a surer sense of belonging to the nation. Another is that Bonn as capital city has the defect of its virtues; that is, the main currents of German society do not flow freely through this small city on the Rhine.

At a different level, the signs of weariness or impatience with Germany's restricted role in Europe will become stronger as the political center moves to Berlin. We can expect to see more clearly the consensus on the EU changing; more stresses and strains on relations with France; and pressure for Germany, a sovereign entity, to push its national interests independently.

More strikingly, the move will show the country and its capital for what they were and, to a considerable degree, still are—two very dissimilar societies sharing a capital city that is actually two very different cities. The people of West and East Berlin have starkly different attitudes and styles; they think differently, dress differently, behave differently.

Berlin was always an exciting, high-energy city, and it still is. It resembles New York in the kind of people it attracts. With the Wall a relic of the past and the nation unified, expectations for Berlin run high. Besides becoming Europe's political capital, it would, as in the days of Weimar, become yet again the cultural center and mainspring of the artistic avant-garde. Or so it has seemed. But the Weimar analogy is deceptive, as Paul Goldberger, the chief cultural correspondent for *The New York Times*, has convincingly pointed out:

> Weimar Berlin was a true burst of culture, a staggering moment of dancing on the edge that could not have lasted. Its beginnings were made possible by the sudden openness of what, until the Weimar Republic was declared in 1918, had been a closed and oppressive society. There was a sense not only that the world could be made anew but that it had to be—that Ger-

many, having lost the war, was given a blank slate on which to write its future.

Of course, the new Berlin has also been defined by a sense of release at the outset. But after the initial euphoria came a marked decrease of artistic energy. There was a profound urgency to life in Berlin before 1989, as East Berliners and West Berliners faced one another across a wall that was brutal in its silence and as looming in their consciousness as a mountain. . . . Now, Berlin copes more with the pains and pleasures of adjustment to bourgeois, democratic life. It is an adjustment that is full of complexities, though not necessarily the sort out of which great art is made. . . . In a new Berlin, what could be as compelling as the wall? No architect in the world could make a new symbol to equal it . . . it insinuated itself into every citizen's life, every moment of every day . . . [even] after unification, the city still feels the vastness of its void."[34]

Drifting

Germany is in aimless transition. Its political parties are steadily losing strength. So are the unions, which once produced political leaders but do so no longer. Church membership is in a steep decline. The rest of Europe is also in transition and has most of the same problems. But Germans, who are more prone than most to see a half-full glass as half empty, do not, by and large, recognize that they are better positioned than most to do something about their problems. Germany today, as Anne-Marie Le Gloannec points out, is Europe's most stable and among the most thoroughly democratic countries. One wonders how large a part of the society grasps what it has achieved. Or whether, and if so when, the society will acquire a sense of purpose and direction that accords with an unfamiliar preeminence in Europe's affairs.

For the first time, Germany is a united, prosperous society with fixed, undisputed borders. Among the effects of this, some Germanologists feel, are increased self-absorption and introspection. What is Germany all about? What should we be doing? These are questions that come easily to Germans. Already some of them are asking, What will Germany look like in fifty years?

Like people elsewhere, Germans are looking for solutions to their problems, but they are probably more resistant to innovation—to new ideas—than others, even though just adjusting to unification gives them more to think about than is true of most of their EU partners. *"Keine Experimente"* (No Experiments) was a campaign slogan used successfully by the Christian Democrats in the early 1960s and comes close to capturing a diffidence that is not just western German but national. Michael Mertes, a senior adviser to Kohl in the Bundeskanzleramt (Chancellery) and one of the most acute observers of his nation, characterizes what Germans want as "change through stability." He and others wonder whether a consensus on basic national values can be achieved in the current environment. "Are there," he asks, "articles of faith that might constitute an 'all-German' political credo, different from the mere exorcisms inspired by *Angst,* or the simple worship of the deutsche mark? The answer depends on whether the Germans will be able to develop a calm patriotism based not only on their indivisible history (not excluding its darkest chapters), their common cultural traditions, but also, and most importantly, on shared democratic values, civic responsibility . . . an active sense of solidarity and togetherness.

"This is the true challenge of normality," a condition neither Germany nor Europe has known for the greater part of the twentieth century.

" 'Patriotism,' " continues Mertes, "is a word greeted with enormous reservation by post-national-minded Germans. In fact, reunited Germany's real, though unacknowledged, problem may be the weakness of its republican consciousness, for which an enlightened patriotism might be a remedy." Having been fully sovereign only since 1990, Mertes observes, Germany "is not yet endowed with what might be called mental sovereignty." He cites a "culture of reticence." In defining national interests, he says, Germans must start to "exclude defensiveness as well as assertiveness, cheap moralizing no less than cynical *Realpolitik*."

The term "power politics" (*Machtpolitik*), Mertes suggests, is out, and "moral politics" (*Verantwortungspolitik*) is in. "When the German Government, supported by an all-party consensus in the Bundestag, successfully promoted the international recognition of Slovenia and Croatia at the end of 1991 . . . Germany was exerting power, clearly by diplomatic means. In Germany, this was not considered an act of power. For Germans, only their intentions counted, and these were good, meaning moral. The idea that Germany was taking advantage of her strengthened position as a reunited country was felt to be a hurtful accusation." But Germany's allies in Europe and America regarded the step—Germany's biggest and most consequential postwar initiative—as wrongheaded and deeply troublesome.

" 'No experiments,' " Mertes says, "turned out to be a recipe for a thoroughgoing and dramatic modernization experiment. Since reunification, this no longer applies: remaining wedded to the West German status quo will not do with regard to the greatest experiment that the country has faced in its postwar history. This is a message that mainly the West Germans must understand; for their Eastern compatriots, momentous change has become an everyday experience."[35]

It's hard to quarrel with any parts of Mertes's analysis. But the likely consequences of what he prescribes have to be recognized: the process by which Germany moves away from what he calls a "culture of reticence" and regains its "mental sovereignty" is likely to disappoint Europhiles (of whom he is one) and bear out the Euroskeptics.

German politics offers few, if any, clues about the country's future direction. Politics at the national level is a muddle. Kohl's Christian Democrats, a lesser force than in earlier days, seem to have become dependent on the aging of the population; one third of its supporters are over sixty. In the last federal elections, the

Christian Democrats did best with women over fifty-three. Those who vote for the other parties are younger, but the German society is, of course, aging.

In Germany, the parties perform a more established, or institutionalized, role than they do in most other countries. They run foundations, for example, and these, along with their other activities, are financed in large part by the state. Each party receives a government subsidy based on the number of votes it receives in elections to the Bundestag, *Länder* Parliaments, and the European Parliament. Industry, too, helps to broaden the financial base, Today, however, every German party, except the Greens, is losing membership. And leaving aside Kohl, the one-man band, only the Greens have a leader, Joschka Fischer, who manages to act like a leader, even though his party is often racked by internal disputes and may not have much more room for growth. As for the Social Democrats, they have lost the last three federal elections with three different leaders. Their senior figures tend to attack one another as vigorously as they attack the opposition.

Just what is weakening the parties isn't clear and may not be for some time. The European issue is probably not a factor. The ripple effect of unification probably is. None of the established parties, for example, has known how to deal with a new arrival on the scene—the Socialist Unity Party (PDS), the successor party to the Socialist Unity Party of the former German Democratic Republic. By 1994, eastern Germany had become the battleground. A great many eastern Germans felt that the PDS, unlike the established parties, was an expression of themselves. The Greens were better organized in the east than the others, but they did far less well than the PDS. And the problem posed by the PDS was and is especially hard on Social Democrats, first because it caused a reemergence of an old fault line, with some of the party faithful wanting to cooperate with the left, and others, as in the past, favoring the center and a mainstream approach to issues.

The Social Democrats also suffered because, compared to the

hard-charging new party, they impressed the electorate as being just what they are—exhausted and out of ideas. The strong showing of the PDS in the east left some Christian Democrat notables worried, too. They saw the Social Democrats, in some places, as being sandwiched between themselves and the PDS. And some CDU people actually discussed—though very privately—how they might help the Social Democrats, their traditional rivals, cope with this troublesome legacy of unification. One of them put it this way: "They [the Social Democrats] had a hard time with their left wing in the old days. But they were able to open to the center and break out of the thirtieth percentile. There was no danger of trouble from their left wing. But now those people [eastern Germans mostly] who voted for the PDS are saying, 'There was nothing wrong with socialism except for the people in charge of it.' The Social Democrats just do not know how to deal with this problem. They have forgotten."

The PDS provided its enemies in both major parties with some good talking points. In the 1994 elections, Kohl borrowed a phrase that Kurt Schumacher, a great SPD figure of the 1950s, had used to good effect against his hard left, by calling the PDS "red-lacquered fascists." And Kohl charged that his SPD opponents, instead of continuing to me-too him, would cooperate with this crowd of unreconstructed, hard-line socialists. The Kohl strategy worked pretty well: the Christian Democrats actually did better in eastern Germany than did the SPD, which, of course, was competing with the Greens and the PDS for the entire left of center.

The clearly good political news lies in the sharp decline and virtual free fall of the far-right parties. They have become bitterly divided within and among themselves. People who might have drifted in their direction were retrieved by Kohl's adroit management of various hot-button issues, including immigration. The danger posed by the extreme right is far less in Germany than in Austria, France, Belgium, and Italy.

What is of slowly rising importance are the political attitudes and preferences within the eastern *Länder;* these are sure to bear on German domestic policy, European policy, and perhaps foreign policy, too. The parties, as they strive to regroup and get healthy, are trying to figure out just how much weight to give these attitudes and preferences. Geography may help to moderate immoderate tendencies, or it may awaken anxieties about the new Germany drifting into what Timothy Garton-Ash describes as the "old *Mittelage* of the Bismarckian second Reich. . . . This Germany lies more to the west than did the Bismarckian Reich," he writes." A glance at the historical atlas shows Germany sprawling across East-Central Europe, with Prussia stretching into what is now Lithuania and the Russian territory of Kaliningrad (formerly Königsberg). Today's political map shows a compact territory west of the Oder and Neisse rivers and the diamond wedge of Bohemia. Germany still faces sensitive eastern issues, but the country's center lies westward."[36]

Still, some of these sensitive issues directly involve eastern Germans, and among the uncertainties is how they will manage their porous border with their neighbors and former allies farther east. Through this border come an array of problems, from most of which Germans were once shielded by the Iron Curtain. "The new threat from the east must be recognized," says Biedenkopf, who as Saxony's leader must concern himself with the longest section of the border. "It is disorder, creeping disorder," which, he says, began with the breakdown of the Soviet Union. He cites an "influx of criminal energy." Germany, he says, "is wide open to this but doesn't understand its vulnerability. It assumes a cultural environment that stretches west to east. That is an illusion."[37]

Germany watchers are in most cases agreed that the 12 million or so expellees and refugees who entered the country shortly after World War II have on the whole been a constructive influence. "Their integration," Mertes says, "drastically diminished the tribal and confessional homogeneity of the regions that took them in."[38]

"Germany is not an immigrants' country," Kohl has declared.

However, it is one of Europe's most ethnically diverse, and will become more so, partly because the law will enable numerous ethnic Germans to enter, partly because Germany will have to import workers as it exports jobs to reduce labor costs; also, Germany has the world's second lowest birth rate.

Foreigners now make up close to 9 percent of the population, compared with less than 3 percent elsewhere in western Europe. Between the end of the war in 1945 and unification, close to 15 million people emigrated to West Germany. And while four in ten of these foreigners have now resided in Germany for at least fifteen years, most live on the outer fringes of society because the requirements for citizenship keep them there. A new edict, adopted early in 1997, requires German-born children of foreign parents to acquire a residence permit. A great many foreigners, as required by law, live in group housing so that authorities can keep track of them.[39]

The tougher immigration laws are now keeping down the number of refugees and asylum seekers. What will become of those who already are there is still another uncertainty. The same can be said of how much and what kind of influence they will exercise when and if their status improves.

A separate and very different problem involves integrating the Ossis, who, as Klaus Bade puts it, "were confronted [by unification] with the alternative of unconditional adjustment or progressive estrangement."[40] As always, geography, history, and latent power are presenting Germany with some far-from-easy choices. But until Wessis and Ossis can recover their common past and reach agreement on a national identity and purpose, the choices either will not be made or will largely be made by events. The process of full convergence may be the work of a generation.

Briefly, Germany needs time, a little luck, and, above all, understanding. Its agenda of domestic and European concerns is overloaded. In one of the clearest looks at Germany by an outsider, Martin Walker of *The Guardian* noted that "the era of German complaisance is ending, not through a return to self-interest, but through systemic exhaustion. The expectations of the United States, of the European Union, and of the old Warsaw Pact cannot all be met by a population that is aging so fast, and reproducing so little, that, within 25 years, half of its citizens will be over the age of 60. . . . The new Germany now faces so many competing demands . . . that through sheer overstretch Germany is about to become the problem."[41]

For most of its half century of history, the Federal Republic has been led by strong, commanding figures. But post–Kohl Germany will be leaderless for the first time in decades. The adjustment will create additional stress and uncertainty. Kohl has provided clear, sensible direction. Beneath the surface, however, some new tendency, or direction, is slowly being formed. A compassionate, benign, still-passive, still-divided nation may be on the verge of arousing itself.

Germany is the only country in Europe that hasn't reached the limit of its reach or isn't depleted. It is lagging in some important ways, but at some point it will strive mightily to close the gap with the world's pace setters and may very well succeed. Meanwhile, the country is adrift. And thus, the larger part of Europe is also adrift.

CHAPTER V

FRANCE AND BRITAIN: L'ENTENTE AMBIGUE

Shortly before closing out a long and brilliant run as Britain's foreign secretary in June 1995, Douglas Hurd said, "In our interests, in our assets, in our view of Europe, in our hopes and fears for the outside world, there are not two substantial countries as similar as France and Britain."[1] What Mr. Hurd didn't say was that Britain and France are the only two members of the EU with serious traditions of nation-statehood to protect. Most of the others find in the EU a makeweight for their own deficiencies as free-standing entities. Germany's long shadow and a shared interest in heading off serious reform of EU institutions have pushed London and Paris closer together for the time being. But it's not likely that concerns such as these will align them more securely or comfortably.

The tie between France and Germany has for years been perhaps the closest and most important relationship between major countries anywhere. It was solemnized in a kind of European High Mass as General de Gaulle and Konrad Adenauer formally interred the turbulent past in a bilateral treaty concluded in 1963. France, they tacitly agreed, would be the leader of a renewed Western Europe built upon the French-German reconciliation.

Until 1990, nearly thirty years later, this arrangement endured and prospered. In France, however, the post–Cold War era, along with a new decade, began badly. German unification was a shock. Not since the struggle for Algeria in the 1950s and early 1960s had official Paris seemed as confused and depressed. The year 1990 should have belonged to the memory of de Gaulle, who was born one hundred years earlier and is one of his country's sacred handful of epic figures. De Gaulle became France's *rassembleur* during World War II and again when the Algerian crisis drove the country to the brink of civil war. However, his centenary was darkened, partly by a Socialist president, François Mitterrand, who was talking like a European federalist and at times even acting like one. Of the blows that Gaullism has suffered, the spectacle of France seemingly at the forefront of a drive to subject Europe's nation-states to the discipline of the communal institutions in Brussels that de Gaulle despised was for a time among the hardest. Harder still was the prospect of France and Germany gradually exchanging the role of *primus inter pares* within the European Community.

To be more or less obsessive about German power was normal for a French nationalist of de Gaulle's vintage and formation. De Gaulle could recall that three times in the space of a lifetime Germany had invaded France. American power might threaten to dim France's light throughout the world, but America was not a primordial threat to France or her real rival for the leadership of Western Europe. Germany was, or could be. America would one day go back to being a Western Hemisphere and Pacific power, leaving Europe to the Europeans. Then as before, Germany might again be the most powerful state in Western and central Europe. As the

Cold War ended, France's force of nuclear weapons no longer provided a political edge, if it ever really had. An unusable military instrument could hardly offset the expansive power of the D-mark.

During the early 1990s, the French professed to want a federal Europe, seeing it as a potential match for the United States and any Japan-led Asian bloc that might eventually emerge. They continued overreacting to German unification. It seemed not to matter that inflation in France was edging just below the German level—for the first time in nearly two decades—or that France was recording an unprecedented trade surplus with Germany. What did was the deep anxiety that Germany would supersede America—sooner rather than later—as Europe's dominant influence. Never mind that this heavy American influence and presence, which had been essential during the Cold War, impressed Paris as having become anachronistic as well as undesirable; the Americans would soon reach the same judgment, the French reasoned—wrongly; they would return their military forces to the United States and in effect jettison their commitment to Europe's security.

As before, defense was the source of much of the tension among NATO's Big Four—Paris, Bonn, Washington, and London. The French had been trying to create what they and others call a European "defense identity," largely at the expense of NATO, and hence of American influence. "Defense identity" is an odd term, one that Washington has derided, since it is vague and hardly robust-sounding, as, say, "defense capacity" would be. But France has pushed the notion in one form or another since the 1990–91 period. Then as later, Washington resisted, and German leadership was put into the middle. The latter was always reluctant—understandably so—to choose between America, Europe's chief source of security, and France, Germany's partner in building Europe. Bonn has sometimes dealt with this recurring dilemma by telling Washington and Paris what each wanted to hear, even when the messages were contradictory.

The defense debate grew heated in the summer of 1991, with

various European members of NATO, led by France, saying that since the Soviet threat was fading away, America's mission was over. Washington was criticized for being unwilling to accept the consequences of the ending of the Cold War. NATO was compared to the March of Dimes, an institution in need of a cause. "NATO now ressembles the Church in the era of Galileo" was a comment that caught on in some capitals. A few members of Congress complicated matters by suggesting that American forces should remain in Europe because it was a good place to park them, as the war against Iraq in the Persian Gulf had shown.

The row over defense split the alliance. The British, Dutch, Danes, and Portuguese favored little more than token alteration of the status quo in NATO, whereas Italy, Spain, Belgium, and Greece came down on France's side in the argument. And so, finally, did the Germans, who, it seemed, had decided that Washington wouldn't rock their boat on this issue. They were right, although Washington was as annoyed with them as with the French. After all, the United States, unlike the others, hadn't questioned unification and had shown no nervousness about it, whereas Germany's neighbors, whatever they said, had been and remained nervous; this was especially true of France. Kohl had not forewarned Washington, Paris, or London of his historic purpose, but when he signaled it to the Bundestag on November 28, 1990, only the Americans, who by then judged unification to be in the cards, had come to his support. Actually, it was more than support. President George Bush and his advisers were instrumental not just in interceding with Soviet President Mikhail Gorbachev on behalf of unification but also in maneuvering his acceptance of an enlarged Germany as part of NATO. Moreover, the Bush people did what they did without asking for, let alone getting, anything from Kohl in return; this impressed diplomats as odd.

Bonn drew comfort from Washington's increasingly obvious calculation: Germany was already the most important of America's partners; a unified Germany would be a source of stability during a period of change, provided that the enlarged nation continued to be a member of NATO. Briefly, in the summer of 1991 Bonn was taking Washington for granted and electing to give priority attention to its European partners, starting with France. In this new era, France was the vital partner; first, in burying once and for all the fear of a united Germany, and second, in anchoring their joint prosperity as Germany began looking east—investing heavily in the equally compelling cause of stabilizing eastern Europe.

In Paris, this calculation was given a different spin: unification and the abrupt collapse of the old order were seen as perversely offering Germans an alternate focus—central and eastern Europe—for their foreign policy. Also, the sheer weight of this Germany had almost overnight become a dynamic that was shifting the tectonic plates of French policy, even if much of the comment in Paris tended for a time to belie the reality. Once again, the Germans were being described there as unpredictable, potentially unstable, and lacking the political culture that might enable them to do what ought to be done in the new era.

Setting policy had been so much easier during the Cold War. Germany had been confined to a small field of maneuver by the two superpowers, one of them providing the threat, the other the security. France had been free to shelter within the penumbra of the NATO security system and occasionally put pressure on her German partner by taking some modest initiative vis-à-vis Moscow. France was a member of the two best clubs, one of which—the European Community—it dominated. The other one—NATO—was dominated by the Americans. Now the dominant member of the all-European club is Germany, not France, although Germany takes care not to make a point of its growing strength.

Briefly, the end of the Cold War narrowed Paris's field of maneuver. In principle, France must accommodate Kohl so as to embed Germany in a European system in which France still has influence. There may not be a lot of time for this. The younger post-Kohl leadership may be less disposed to confine Germany within the EU, and it is expected by many Germans to take a more independent line. The pivotal question was and is whether France will bend far enough toward Kohl to allow the EU to acquire political scope at the expense of member sovereignty.

General de Gaulle's faithful need not have worried so much about the federalist sounds made by Mitterrand or the steps he took in that direction, most of them in the 1980s, a time when France was still the EC's top dog and could call itself the "motor of Europe." But trying to play that role after German unification was more demanding; it seemed to mean having to build up the institutions in Brussels at the expense of Paris. Thus, in the 1990s, French leaders, first Mitterrand and then Chirac, have tried to maintain France's freedom of maneuver and preserve the illusion of her power. Or, as Dominique Moisi has written, "France wants a strong Europe, but with weak institutions that will not undermine its claim to continue to act as a *Grande Nation*."[2]

Mitterrand was a narcissistic, endlessly complex, deeply paradoxical figure whose motives were often obscure. He sprang from the traditional clerical right of French political life, and as he moved across the spectrum—absorbing as much punishment as gain—an aura of mystery formed around him. Stanley Hoffmann noted "his deliberately cultivated resemblance to many ambitious and complex provincial characters in French novels, from Balzac to Mauriac, and including Barres and Montherlant." Like de Gaulle, Mitterrand fostered his own mystique, along with a tendency, less pronounced, to equate his destiny with the nation's. But since 1944, as Hoffmann has also written, "he was . . . driven by a hostility to General de Gaulle so deep and so constant that he could not even bring himself to mention de Gaulle's name when he celebrated the fiftieth anniversary of the end of World War II in Berlin." But Hoffmann gives Mitterrand credit for breaking with the "Gaullist heritage" in the 1980s, in part by helping "to remove many of the obstacles to the single market."[3]

At no point in the new era was Mitterrand willing to match his

Europhile rhetoric, or the lofty goal of tying down France's potent neighbor, with deeds of consequence. French sovereignty would not be compromised. Monetary union, which means giving up the French franc and an independent central bank, might seem to have been an exception but wasn't. France's elite has pushed for monetary union, as noted in Chapter 3, in order to regain a measure of sovereignty that had been lost to the Bundesbank and the D-mark. Also, the French public has liked the idea of being at the table with the Bundesbank and others, just as it liked the idea of a French general being in Bosnia. When asked, the French have made clear their aversion to one country's currency being allowed to dominate the currencies of its neighbors. (Polls taken in 1996 suggest that as much as three fourths of the population favors monetary union.)

Other signs, however, were interpreted by Germans as evidence of a diminishing French commitment to Europe. The referendum in France on approving the Maastricht Accord, which after all had been Mitterrand's idea, was very nearly defeated. With the startling, though quickly forgotten, Lamers-Schauble initiative, Kohl's people sent what a prominent Parisian and former official called "a piece of registered mail to France which had to be answered." And everyone in Paris, he said, "put a negative spin on the paper even though stripped of the rhetoric and tone it was what we said we wanted."[4] The paper was designed as a historic gesture—as proposing a last clear chance to build what, in effect, would be a Europeanized Germany. It warned that unless the addressee—the Élysée Palace—accepted its thrust, France and Germany could "drift apart."[5] In Paris and other EU capitals, Kohl seemed to be saying, "Take Germany while it is there to be taken. Go ahead and tether us now. Don't wait. My job is to fufill the legacy of Adenauer, and, like him, I look first to France."

France's reaction was more clearly and harshly negative than expected, least of all by the Germans. The Germans had run up their true colors, according to France's right-wing fringe, by pushing for a federal Europe, with the European Commission becoming an embryo government. The Gaullists of the center right also reacted harshly. They saw the *"noyau dur"* (hard core) of key countries that the Germans were pushing for as being really nothing more than a D-mark zone by another name. It didn't seem to matter to the Gaullists that by then the French-German partnership was being held together mainly by the prospect of monetary union, an enterprise that Germany was certain to dominate. The Lamers-Schauble paper, said one highly experienced Paris-based ambassador, "is the end of idealism about Europe on the French right."[6]

Dejected French Europhiles, while fully agreeing with the German paper, reproached its authors for their take-it-or-leave-it tone and for being too explicitly clear, that is, proposing in so many words that the European Commission take on the aspect of a European government. That seemed to be inviting trouble. So did naming the members of the hard core (France, Germany, and the Benelux countries), thereby also identifying countries such as Italy that were being excluded. Far more important, however, was the concern among Europhiles that the rest of their country's political class had lost sight of reality. The only way for France to exercise major influence in Europe, they feel, is by strentghening the European structure. The first victim of a weakened structure, they say, would be France. Germany, they point out, will insist on enlarging the EU. But unless its institutions are adapted and strengthened, Europhiles argue, a larger club will be dysfunctional.

Nearly four months after the German paper surfaced, French Europhiles called on their government for an official reply. The call came in the form of an article written by Dominique Bocquet, secretary-general of the French section of the Mouvement Européen, an influential EU advocacy group. "If the two partners in the Franco-German couple were to drift apart," the article warned, "Paris would see its hand in international affairs greatly weakened . . . it is surprising that the recent proposals by . . . Helmut Kohl's party have not been welcome . . . as good news . . . all kinds of language subterfuge have been used to postpone the time when we, the French, will give an answer to this document. Does this mean that the pressure from some fanatical anti-European quarters is such that France needs to preserve the image of an uncertain Germany as an alibi to hide its own European ambiguities?"[7]

Britain actively fed French doubts, especially those of the Gaullists, about the German initiative. Actually, it was at this moment, with the Mitterrand era drawing to an end, that the British and French began developing what Germans saw as a sinister dalliance. Britain had assumed that with Germany unified, France would feel the need for improved links with London (and Washington, too). Neither side was deceiving itself—creating fanciful goals such as reviving the entente cordiale. But since anxiety comes easily to Bonn, the Paris-London flirtation was seen there to threaten the French-German tie. It doesn't, or shouldn't, even if various deluded Tory MPs have chosen to see all this as actually foreshadowing another entente cordiale. Whitehall knows better, and the French won't overplay the British card. Still, German Europhiles, from Kohl on down, worry with reason about what amounts to an Anglo-French veto on their efforts to give the EU some semblance of a political vocation. A meeting between Chirac and Major in October 1995 aroused more comment in the German press than in either the British or French press.

France, like Britain, was becoming a status quo player. Conservatives in Paris and London were seeing eye to eye on such questions as whether to strengthen the Brussels institutions. Their answer to more power for the Commission or the Parliament was no, but yes to more power for the Council of Ministers, who, of course, represent the member governments. "On political questions, it will be be France and the U.K. against Germany," a senior British diplomat commented in late 1994."[8] He wasn't exaggerating. Also, the French could not have been unaware of the monologues to which Kohl subjected visitors, especially Americans, about how Germany was obliged to walk lower so as to make France seem to be walking taller—to feel itself more of an equal.

In London, French thinking seemed obvious: France was not about to walk back its special relationship with Germany. But France wanted to keep it in balance, which meant casting about for new friends. The only new friends that mattered enough to advance this purpose were Britain and the United States—those meddlesome Anglo-Saxons whose relations with their French ally were often edgy, rarely close, and just occasionally productive. But France had few other options. A French-led coalition of Mediterranean states was an option, one that might be developed. But its political weight would hardly balance a bloc of northern and central European countries of which Germany would be the dominant influence.

A Tie That Binds?

All sides depended on the special French-German link. None of the parties, including Britain, wanted to see the two countries going their separate ways as in the past. But by building up its relations with France, Whitehall could see Britain becoming more important to both Paris and Bonn. In some ways, Britain had more in common with both of them than either did with the other. In a strategic sense, Britain and France, unlike Germany, still play something of a political role in the world and deploy military forces of the kind that give the role credibility.

Over the years, numerous officials in both London and Paris, noting shared Anglo-French attitudes on various strategic issues, tried in vain to narrow the gulf between them. Until then, Britain had stood accused in Paris of competing with the Germans for being *les meilleurs élèves transatlantiques* (the best transatlantic pupils—of the Americans, of course). In late 1994, the climate began to improve, chiefly, though not exclusively, in the area of defense. The process began formally in a summit meeting in November 1994 between Prime Minister John Major and Mitterrand at

Chartres. There they agreed to form an Anglo-French air group—a unit that would be kept combat-ready, hold joint training exercises, operate from alternating headquarters, and maintain a planning staff of five on each side. The group was designed to deploy forces that could react quickly. The change in France's course was being closely watched by those most interested and affected, not just Germany but also Russia. When Mitterrand and Major met, Andrei Kozyrev, who was then Russia's foreign minister, also paid an official visit to France, an unusually long one; he was in Paris for a week. Kozyrev's main message was roughly the following: There are two ways of organizing Europe: the American way, with Germany at the center; or with a structure built around France, Russia, and Britain. The message was interesting, but it didn't resonate. The European states, France included, had outgrown shifting alliances and other games of the past.

Further progress in Anglo-French relations was recorded eleven months later, when Major held weekend talks with Jacques Chirac, Mitterrand's successor. Chirac announced afterward that the Franco-German link was a "necessary but not sufficient" condition for building Europe, which, he added, "we will not build . . . without Britain." Major characterized the meeting as "a breath of fresh air."[9]

In subsequent meetings, Chirac and Major announced arrangements for the Royal Navy and the French Navy to exercise and train together. "Britain," said Major, "has a wider range of joint projects with France than with any other country."[10]

France had just begun to see Britain as beginning (1) to accept that it is a European and middle-size power (even though it lacked a coherent European policy) and (2) to see the special relationship with the United States not as London would like it to be but as it is—less special than before.

Britain, according to one of its closely involved diplomats, "sees a triangle with two long sides and one short side," which, he said, "is the Franco-German relationship. The long sides connect us with the other two. Lately, the side betweem Britain and France has gotten somewhat shorter, the one between Britain and Germany less so."[11]

Defense is and may remain the tie that binds. "We cannot deal with European defense without Britain," says a Paris-based French general. "The Germans emphasize institutions, the British emphasize capacity. We are closer to the British approach."[12]

By then the French also felt that some American presence would be needed in Europe—that it was a matter of rearranging the defense burden. But how? Playing the British card was one thing. Playing the highest card—the American—was quite another; would France—could France—do it? Doing so would mean, minimally, returning to NATO's military structure, not necessarily in a single bound but step by step. That would be hard. The institutions of Paris, starting with the "Quai" (Quai d'Orsay), as the Foreign Ministry is generally known, were all but genetically programmed against having an *intime* relationship with America. Drawing closer to Washington would mean playing junior partner to America's senior partner, as Britain had elected to do during and after World War II. France had always declined any such unequal arrangement, judging it to have cost Britain influence as well as free hands. Far better, as de Gaulle insisted, to touch glasses all around but drink from one's own. His legacy included the perception of an imperial design in American purposes; Britain was judged a stalking horse for Washington and was to be denied a serious continental role until it gave up any rival claims or pretensions to power that might jeopardize French primacy in Europe. De Gaulle insisted on an *"Angleterre* [England] *toute nue"* (stark naked) before he would admit her into Europe.[13]

That thinking gave way in the mid-1990s to some practical considerations. Early in December 1995, President Jacques Chirac took France partway back to NATO's military fold, a move that was wholly consistent with a variety of national interests. The bureaucrats of most member countries were not surprised; the French had been edging toward the move for some time. Its political logic reflected a hardheaded calculation that had begun with German unification. Defense is an area in which France can stay well ahead of Germany. Also, after the Persian Gulf War pointed up numerous deficiencies in France's military structure, an embarrassed general staff began to press for reestablishing ties to the NATO system. Then Bosnia put French forces into the awkward position of being under NATO's operational control without being part of the command structure.

A budgetary motive also lay behind Chirac's initiative. The pressure on defense spending in France was and remains very serious. In the first five years or so after the Cold War ended, France maintained its defense spending at ludicrously high levels. The new regime then began making up for lost time by cutting heavily—too heavily, according to various political figures, who worry that deep cuts will create upheavals in some places where large numbers of workers are being laid off and, in general, increase the threat to social peace.

The step toward NATO could probably not have been taken except by someone like Chirac, who has latitude that his predecessors lacked; it derives solely from his being a ranking member of the Gaullist family and securely anchored to its tradition. Mitterrand was depicted by the cognoscenti, with conscious irony, as the last Gaullist in the Élysée Palace. However, whereas de Gaulle sought to use the European movement as a device for imposing French leadership, especially over Germany, Mitterrand tried to use the EU itself as an instrument for tethering Germany.

De Gaulle and his legions were able to distance themselves from transatlantic orthodoxy at no risk to the security of France or of Europe itself. The Gaullists could take for granted America's commitment while expelling NATO from France, withdrawing from its military structure, and adopting an abrasive style that held appeal for the French people. But French chauvinism is a diminished chord. And with the Cold War a receding memory and the

American commitment judged less certain, the French leadership has had that much more incentive to adopt a more sensible, less standoffish approach to NATO.

Still, about a year after signaling France's partial return to the NATO structure, Chirac reversed the decision. The dispute he contrived to justify his turnabout is described in the following chapter. Quite clearly, however, he felt that France's grave economic and social ills had put him and his government under pressure so extreme as to call for a diversionary move, and with it a scapegoat. Germany would hardly do as the scapegoat, and for different reasons, neither would Britain. For a Gaullist, it could only be America and its "velvet hegemony." NATO, America's club, would have to wait a little longer (maybe forever) for the return of its most stalwart European member.

Chirac is an original—a Gaullist to his shoe tips who likes America and its works. He is wholly comfortable and at ease with his various American contacts, a characteristic that should not be allowed to obscure his purpose. Like de Gaulle, he'll try to maintain France as a player in the center stage of world affairs. Like de Gaulle, Chirac reckons that keeping France in an active, high-profile world role means presuming to speak for Europe as well as France when he thinks he can. Also like de Gaulle, Chirac sees the great purpose as requiring gestures taken unilaterally and without consultation, along with a willingness to clash from time to time with the world's only remaining superpower. Early in World War II, when he was leading the Free French in London, de Gaulle would observe that the Anglo-Saxons can only lean on something that offers resistance. It remains a natural Gaullist tendency but provided better theater in de Gaulle's day, a time when the French were less absorbed with internal difficulties or worried that a new president was making them worse.

A Fragile Society

Those first six months—May to October 1995—were very bad for Chirac and for France. A tough decision had lain in wait for him, but that was hardly a secret, and he had had plenty of time to think about it. Either he could invest more money in the economy and thereby create jobs; or he could impose financial austerity, in which case he would give French people the impression of being led. Chirac chose option one. "We will ultimately be judged by our capacity to produce a deep and lasting movement of job creation," said Alain Juppé, Chirac's prime minister, a few weeks after they took office.[14] By deferring the inevitable—tough decisions on the economy—Chirac was perceived as weak and unwilling to shake up a country that badly needed shaking up. He squandered about forty points of goodwill and made an uphill task that much more arduous.

Seen from within, France's woes were worsening. Unemployment was hovering around 12 percent and rising higher than in the large industrialized countries except Italy. Taxes in France were the highest in the nation's history and, again, the highest of the major industrialized states. By October, Chirac was facing a threat to public order. Serious people, starting with Prime Minister Juppé and Robert Balladur, who had preceded him and then run unsuccessfully for president against Chirac, were saying privately that France was at the edge of a May 1968–style upheaval. All sides wondered what Chirac would do. This time he surprised most people, including Paris's watchful diplomatic community. They had expected to hear again that "people are more important than statistics." But instead of trying to relieve the pressure by spending more money, Chirac declared for austerity. His top priority, he said, was paring France's budget deficit to 3 percent of GDP.

By then, it had been borne in on him that more than the French economy required a dose of austerity. The survival of the special

Franco-German relationship was being equated, however unwisely, with achievement of monetary union. By his unguarded and volatile behavior, Chirac had done harm to the special link. Not only had he failed to establish rapport with Kohl, but it appeared that he had gone out of his way to give offense, chiefly through failure to consult. Moreover, contact between Paris and Bonn at all levels of government had been drastically curtailed. All that had to change. France's commitment to EMU would have to be made credible. An exigency could be met only by putting about and heading the economy toward the Maastricht criteria.

It hardly mattered that Chirac was not an admirer of monetary union or even the EU. Then as now, he was between the upper and nether millstones, having laid down mutually exclusive commitments: producing growth and jobs had been campaign promises; meeting the EMU criteria would cancel chances for better times but was now a solemn commitment to Kohl; with the economy continuing to weaken, France would need Germany's support. Only 25,000 new jobs were created in France in the second half of 1995, compared to five times that number in the preceding six months.[15] However, maintaining a low public sector deficit is much harder for France than for Germany. For twelve years, France had struggled to sustain the *franc fort,* a pun on Frankfurt, home of the Bundesbank. Having a strong franc meant yoking French economic policy to the Bundesbank and its interest rate policy, which was set high so as to prevent the heavy costs of unification from producing inflation.

Europhiles in France and throughout the EU had hoped that Jacques Delors would occupy the Élysée Palace. Delors had resigned as president of the European Commission, where he had served for ten years and with greater distinction than any predecessor; he became France's foremost and most effective voice for European unity. Delors was universally admired; although nominally a Socialist, his presumed candidacy appeared to have the support of a sizable segment of France's center right. He was ahead in the polls when, on December 12, 1994, he surprised and disappointed his following by announcing he wouldn't run.

Since Delors offered no reason, an awed and strikingly respectful press tried explaining his decision. "He has never been a power seeker," offered *Le Figaro*. "He has too high an esteem for politics." And *Libération* said, "Delors's noncandidacy is like a bucket of icy water on the heads of a band of agitated people. It gives dignity to politics." *France Inter* was even more aglow: "Here comes a major European politician, well known all over the world, who declares that not one ounce of the power of the presidency is worth a single lie to the voters. One's first reaction might be annoyance, but in truth, it also makes one dream, and it is always through dreams that politics improve."[16]

None of the candidates who ran took a strong or even a straightforward position on whither Europe, except for the racist xenophobe and leader of the National Front, Jean-Marie Le Pen. The major political camps were divided. "We no longer know where we are going," one senior figure was quoted as saying. "But, wherever it is, we are convinced that we are all going there together."[17]

The lasting impression of the presidential election was not Chirac's victory in the second round; he was expected to win. It was Le Pen's strong showing in the first round; he got 15 percent of the vote; he ran abreast of the mainstream party candidates in some areas and won outright in Alsace. Le Pen's score was an unpleasant surprise. Why, it was asked, had he done so well in Alsace, a region where, presumably, the protest vote should not have been a dominant factor, as Alsace has lower unemployment and higher consumption than most of the rest of France? Alsatian villages that have yet to experience immigration voted for Le Pen.

The far right is not likely to lose ground, and some signs point to it gaining more at the expense of the mainstream parties. Their vulnerability was pointed up in a closely watched by-election held in October 1996 in Gardanne, a normally Socialist stronghold outside Marseilles. The seat had been held by Bernard Tapie, a high-stakes wheeler-dealer and former government minister who had resigned after being convicted on bribery and tax evasion. In his place, the Socialists were running Bernard Kouchner, another former minister and a national figure who was expected to do well but didn't; with just 13 percent of the vote, Kouchner was the heavy loser in the first round, although the center-right candidate, with 16 percent, did scarcely better. The voters left themselves a choice of extremes—the Communist candidate or the National Front's. Kouchner urged his supporters to vote for the Communist, who was the local mayor and also had the backing of the Greens, dissident Socialists, Trotskyites, and other left-wingers. He beat the National Front candidate in the runoff.[18]

Even if strictly local matters worked against the mainstream parties, their combined vote of 29 percent was a shock. The impact of the Front on the 1997 legislative elections was a still greater shock. The Front emerged from these as a force with about as much popular support as either of the two mainstream conservative parties and an expanding influence on the outcome of national elections. The Front had arrived. What the two extremes—left and right—have in common was outright opposition to the Maastricht Accord and a single European currency. An alliance between Le Pen's National Front and other, less thuggish right-wing political elements, could spell further trouble. And if—still a very big if—such an amalgam managed to join forces with, say, Charles Pasqua, a prominent right-wing Gaullist, its reach might extend to more than 30 percent of the electorate and even create the possibility of forming a government. Pasqua is a political force and serious Euroskeptic who acquired a high approval rating by becoming the scourge of immigration when he was employment and interior minister in the last government. The theory is that an alliance between Le Pen and others of the far right could obtain 25 percent of the vote. Right-wing Gaullists, starting with Pasqua, could supply the rest.

Although the far right cannot come to power on its own—not

unless France descends into a Weimaresque mess—the political class has no answers to Le Pen and his allies. The major parties are muddled and directionless. Their credibility is in a steep decline. As an article about Le Pen observed, "The traditional parties of both the left and the right spend a great deal of their energy—simultaneously denouncing Le Pen as an antidemocratic philistine and pandering to his voters by seeking to co-opt his issues."[19]

For some time, France has shown signs of being the most fragile of Europe's major societies. It has been undergoing a serious identity crisis, asking what it means to be French; whether the nation is truly independent; what should be done about the flow of refugees; how to deal with non-French people who declare themselves French. The society is losing confidence in itself and in the EU as well. France's position in much of Francophone Africa is declining, a victim of special-interest groups and the flawed but unbending views of the French military. *"La morosité"* is the term used on all sides in France to describe the mood. The fear of what a rapidly changing world holds in store for France and its people is widely described as *"la crise."*

No one problem, event, or series of events has produced this national depression. Immigration is only one difficuty, but a critical one. A society that tends to be chauvinistic and sees its country as the most complete nation-state is less well equipped than most to deal with mass immigration of people as different from them as most North Africans are. In February 1997, former Prime Minister Alain Juppé called publicly on the French left to help him stave off the National Front's campaign to end all immigration—legal and illegal. Intellectual and cultural elites were already in full cry against a provision of the Juppé government's immigration bill, which would have required people hosting foreigners from outside the European Union to report their guests' departure to the local police. "We still have not exorcised the shame (of Vichy)," conceded Juppé, a reference to ordinances aimed at searching out Jews in World War II. The controversial provision was amended in a form acceptable to those who had opposed it. According to newspaper reports, however, public opinion supported the provision in its original and disquieting form.

"If we want to send the Arabs and Africans and Asians back to where they came from, it is not because we hate them; it is because they pollute our national identity and take our jobs," said Bruno Megret, the deputy leader of the National Front, around this time.[20]

Many, perhaps half, of the Muslims residing in France are French citizens. Most have integrated, or tried to integrate, into French culture and French life in its most obvious aspects, including language, dress, and so on. In April 1995, France's National Institute of Demographic Studies published the results of a two-year study on the assimilation into French society of foreigners and citizens of foreign descent. Both immigrants and naturalized citizens were reported to have made a genuine effort to immerse themselves in French culture. For example, nine out of ten youths of Algerian origin consider French to be their native tongue. Even if they can more or less understand Arabic, one out of three cannot speak it. Sons and daughters of working-class families do better than their parents. Marriages between cousins are now extremely rare, and families intervene less directly in the choice of a spouse for their child. Mixed French-Algerian marriages are on the rise.

The study's research was described as dispelling "the myth of Muslim homogeneity in France. Almost half of the Algerian immigrants questioned declared that they either had no religious affiliation or did not practice their avowed faith. The finding corresponds to the behavior of French youth in general."[21]

Major newspapers applauded the study. "Sweeps away clichés about immigration," said *Libération*. *Le Monde* hoped it would "lead those in the public eye to abandon their provocative and politically expedient rhetoric in favor of statements about immigration based on fact."[22]

Five months earlier, *Le Monde* had published an authoritative poll on Muslim attitudes toward French society. Ninety-five percent of the respondents felt it was possible to be fully integrated into French society and still practice Islam in private. Sixty-six percent disagreed with the proposition that the more integrated into French society one is, the less Muslim he is. Seventy-eight percent disagreed with the idea that Muslims should benefit from a special status for marriage and divorce. Seventy-two percent agreed that French secularism allows any faith to be expressed.[23]

The reality, according to one experienced French journalist I spoke with, is that "although most Muslims are integrating, or trying to integrate, into French ways and culture, with language and dress, the perceptions of French people are very different." The latter, he said, "cannot reconcile their perceptions with the reality. It's dangerous. The false perceptions breed reactions and incidents."

France's deeper problem, many argue, is an invincibly hierarchical system that over the years has created a sense of alienation that is steadily widening. Ordinary folk feel themselves manipulated by a state apparatus controlled by *hauts fonctionnaires* (high officials), who are products of an insular, archaic, and elitist system. "It is a small, incestuous, and monopolistic world," writes Stanley Hoffmann.[24] Among the by-products is a social malaise that breeds skepticism about the democratic process and stifles hope for a better future. It is believed to account in part for the stronger support of extremist groups in France than is found in countries such as Germany and Britain. It probably lay behind the upheaval that took France to the abyss in May 1968, events for which there was no obvious cause or explanation; the country was peaceful and prosperous. The spring weather was balmy. But what began as student demonstrations in Paris erupted into generalized chaos that swept the country. Established authority, both public and private, was routed. De Gaulle's regime was on the edge of collapse, and for a time it appeared that any moderately well organized opposition could have taken power without firing a shot. But there was no cohesive or sensible opposition, only a contagion of shrill protests and speeches that sounded mindless even at the time.

Adding to the current sense of disillusion is corruption, both public and private, on a disconcertingly broad scale. "In which country have the heads of the biggest construction company, the biggest investment bank and a big car firm all been charged with various illegal practices in just a fortnight?" asked *The Economist* early in 1996. After naming the guilty parties, the article observed that "over the past year, five former ministers, two former party leaders, the heads of France's biggest water utility, second-largest retailing group and third most important industrial firm have been charged or sentenced in connection with scandals."[25]

Like other hard-pressed welfare states, France is trying to adapt to a new era and altered circumstances without overwhelming the tolerance of society and risking social peace. It's harder and more confusing in France, though, because the role of the state there is more important than anywhere else; cutting back the state means cutting back the 5 million people employed by the public sector and the taxes abosrbed by the welfare administration at all levels of government; it all amounts to nearly half of the country's national output. France is schizophrenic; people resent the control exercised over their lives by their extended core of elitist officials while feeling secure and protected by the state's oversized role.

"The figures are terrifying," Juppé also said in February 1997. This time he was talking not about immigration but about public pensions and the ratio of active workers to retirees. Transport workers in several big towns had been staging strikes aimed at cutting the work week from thirty-nine hours to thirty-five without loss of pay, and retirement on a full pension at age fifty-five. By and large, French people are not intimidated by the prospect of retirement and having to fill the gap it leaves. Nearly two thirds of the French (and eight in ten public workers) support lowering the retirement age from sixty, the state's pension-qualifying age to fifty-five. The government had already caved in to truckers who demanded retirement at fifty-five after an injurious twelve-day strike in November 1996.[26]

The French will resist efforts to trim their *acquis*—the benevolent welfare system. The society "increasingly seems to equate its welfare state with its very identity," wrote Roger Cohen of *The New York Times* in a revealing piece on the source of France's depression.[27] Sooner or later it will have to shrink. What will replace it?, the French wonder. They are beset by fear—the fear of being directionless, of having lost their compass. The press reflects the pervading anxiety. One sees cover stories in the major news magazines, with headlines such as "Where Are We Going?" "Is France Disappearing?" "Will China Devour Us?"

This bit of theater is playing out while France, unlike other, less fragile states, must painfully reconcile itself to cutting a lesser figure in Europe's political affairs as German influence grows. The French dilemma has a perverse quality. France doesn't need monetary union but does need an infusion of economic growth. Preparing for the first probably means blocking progress toward the second. Polls illustrate the conflict; most people, it seems, do not want to give up the *franc fort,* the gauge of French parity—or illusion of parity—with Germany. But most people also expect things to get worse, and two thirds of those polled have expressed themselves as "dissatisfied with the way the country is being governed." Eight out of ten were recorded in September 1996 as wanting economic policy to change.[28]

That same month, Pasqua and other Gaullist notables said the same thing, although they disagreed sharply over just how to change the policy. Pasqua, who has a voice that carries, wanted to pump demand into a flat economy by means of a huge government loan. People had just returned from their summer vacation to hear that a heralded economic rebound hadn't materialized. Official forecasts of growth for the year had been scaled back from 2.8 percent to 1.3 percent. And the latter figure in fact seemed to be a whistle in the dark; the 1.3 percent forecast, said the budget minister guardedly, was "not yet impossible."[29]

An increasingly unpopular leadership was, of course, preoccupied with EMU—more exactly, with bringing the public sector

deficit down to 3 percent in 1997. For a start, the budget for government spending in 1997 would be frozen at the level for 1996,
which in real terms would work out to a cut of about 1.5 percent.
Such a cut, if achieved, would be the first since the start of the
Fifth Republic in 1958.[30] David Buchan, the Paris correspondent
of the *Financial Times,* wrote, "The 1997 budget is arguably the
most important fiscal plan a French Prime Minister has ever
drafted, because it is the basis on which France will be judged fit—
or unfit—to join EMU." This budget, Buchan added, was rather
less austere than it seemed, because it would contain some tax
cuts. The government, Buchan said, "wants to use the bait of lower
taxes to try to persuade its electorate to accept a slimmed down
state.

In late April, Chirac surprised all sides by calling legislative
elections; these had been expected a year later—in the spring of
1998. Although the government held eighty percent of the seats
(464 of 577), Chirac was sailing close to the wind; the unemployment numbers were doleful; the opinion polls shed little light on
what was likely to happen but were not encouraging; every percentage point drop translated into thirty to forty seats lost. The
Juppé's government was defending a dismal record of mistakes and
nonachievement. Indeed, the government's only asset, apart from
its large majority, lay in the feebleness and disunity of the Socialist
opposition. It was hard to see the Socialists, whether alone or allied
with the Communists, as an alternative to any sitting government,
no matter how unpopular. They produced a surge during the campaign, identifying with Tony Blair, or trying to, drawing energy from
his big win a month earlier and trimming their commitment to
EMU.

The press asked why Chirac had dared the country to reject his
program and his government. He wanted, he said, a new *élan*—to
bring France "farther along the road of change."[31] This was a
doughy way of saying he wanted a political cushion for the tight-
budget policies dictated by EMU. The voters, of course, rejected

Chirac's new road, even though, ironically, he had made very little effort to nudge the country in that direction.

The French state is counter-cultural, resisting innovation and protecting state-owned companies from market forces. In the private sector, business failures, like unemployment, are rising. Capitalism, as practiced in France, simply isn't working. The overall tax burden won't decline appreciably below the 1996 level of 45.6 percent, higher than what other similar societies must endure. Most economists don't expect unemployment to begin to fall before mid-1998 at the earliest.

Still, if the preparation for monetary union has gone forward within an aura of unreality, French commitment to the goal was always genuine. A society more prone than most to flirting with revolution—one that was feeling a lot more pain than it was accustomed to—was to be subjected to more pain. How, then, to deal with an increasingly irresistible force, EMU, and an immovable object, the French system? Chirac's strategy was and is German-based. Kohl was expected to do his considerable best to generate some growth in the German economy, and France's economy would be lifted by a rising German tide. The growth would allow both countries to take the steps required to meet the EMU criteria. And suppose France managed to whittle its public debt down almost but not quite to the magic number, 3 percent of GDP? Suppose the actual French figure was, say, 3.5 percent? The treaty says that a candidate for EMU must demonstrate substantial movement toward the required figure. Would 3.5 percent be judged close enough? What about 3.8 percent? In short, how much indulgence could the chancellor afford to show France in 1998, a year of federal elections? Some economists and others in the gallery were guessing that Kohl would have to be flexible, if only because Germany, too, might not make it all the way down to 3 percent, meaning that he might have to show some indulgence at home, too.

At a deeper level, France's leader assumes that Kohl will be indulgent because he has a need to carry on serious business with Chirac. Assuming Kohl's candidacy and reelection in the fall of 1998, he and Chirac, it bears repeating, will be in tandem until the year 2002. And Paris expects Kohl, the apostle of a Europeanized Germany, expected to try, with Chirac, to take the European Union beyond a point of no return during their coterminous tenure.

Those may be the right assumptions, but they ignore an intriguing question: If in 1997, the testing period, France succeeds in meeting the 3 percent criterion with a socialist government, or is judged close enough, what will happen afterward? It's one thing to do something difficult and out of character for a period of months, quite another to sustain the experiment. France might, on December 31, 1997, have met the fitness club's compliance rules. But what about afterward? Could France's socialist government, or any other, stay the course? Probably not, many would argue. It might also prove to be the wrong course, or at a minimum, the wrong time to take it.

No End of a Muddle

Not long before Prime Minister Anthony Eden and his coconspirators in Paris set into motion their misbegotten Suez campaign in 1956, he dispatched an observer to Messina, where the Continental Six were laying the foundations for the Treaty of Rome. Eden took a jaundiced view of what seemed to be going on there. And so apparently did his observer, who famously commented, "I leave Messina happy because even if you continue meeting you will not agree; even if you agree, nothing will result; and even if something results, it will be a disaster."[32]

The ignorance and hubris gathered in that reflection all but defy comprehension. Eden's observer was reflecting what was then a typically derisive British view of whatever the continentals might be up to. Eden himself was soon to be driven from power by the

Suez folly, which had a sweeping effect. For a start, it did more harm to relations between France and the Anglo-Saxons, especially the Americans, who caused it to be aborted, than any other episode in the postwar period. France's latent mistrust of both Washington and London came to the surface. Washington was seen to have betrayed its chief allies. Britain had lived up to the French pejorative *perfide Albion* by abandoning France and Israel at the first sign of disapproval in Washington.

Suez, as Hugh Thomas wrote, destroyed the entente cordiale, "which thus died, as it was born, over Egypt."[33] Among the lessons drawn by the Conservative Party's mainstream was that never again could Britain permit herself the luxury of a major row with the United States. Paris drew a different lesson: France—make that Europe—must develop the means to run its affairs without interference from Washington. America was Europe's ally, not its sovereign. Briefly, the heavy deposit of frustration left by the Suez affair produced much of the energy that led to the creation of the European Common Market, forerunner of the EU.

Part of Britain's Conservative Party, while fully committed to the so-called special relationship with America, felt about as strongly that Britain should take part in the joint effort by France, Germany, Italy, and the Benelux countries to overcome centuries of strife and disunity, not to mention two civil wars in this century, by huddling within a common structure. The sentiment grew and created an issue. The issue split the country and both its main political parties, the Tories most conspicuously because they have held office over a far longer stretch than the Labour Party has. For thirty or so years now, their party has been blown this way and that by a kind of prolonged identity crisis. Is Britain part of western Europe, an appendage of the United States, or a larger, more insular Sweden? Joining the European Community in 1973 didn't answer the question, since Britain has always kept one foot outside the structure.

From the other side of the English Channel, it appears that forty years or so after Suez put the handwriting on the wall, the

British people, by and large, still do not feel that they are part of a European community. In 1962, Dean Acheson, perhaps tactlessly, read the handwriting aloud: "Great Britain has lost an empire and not yet found a role." Across the British spectrum the reaction was splenetic. Prime Minister Harold Macmillan linked Acheson with Napoleon and Hitler as one of those who had guessed wrong on Britain.

The six original members of the EU have been especially resentful of Britain's unwillingness to break with the past and its old tendency to involve itself with Europe only when it feels a need to restore a comfortable balance of power. What the continentals haven't fully understood, or accepted, is that experience has made the British wary of Europe. After being made for a time to feel a supplicant, especially by de Gaulle, Britain was rejected by and then excluded from the EC for many years. This feeling of denial extended even into the Foreign Office.

In the 1990s, French and German leaders have in one way or another been absorbed by the adjustment to a new era. But Britain's Tory party, whose leadership has been in charge during this period, has ripped itself apart on the issue of just how European the country can or should be. "Europe has replaced Socialism as the enemy from which the Conservative Party now derives its identity," wrote Professor John Gray of Oxford in *The Guardian*.[34]

One may wonder at the unreal nature of the quarrel. An island people, perhaps overburdened by a proud history of standing alone and surviving, might at this stage prefer to be moored off Long Island but knows that it is part of western Europe and has no place else to go. The problem lies in demonstrating one's Europeanness; that comes hard, as a piece in the *Financial Times* made clear: "British politicians, business people and bureaucrats have long tended to regard the EU as a tiresome consequence of a Common Market, to be suffered but not celebrated."[35] Early in 1995, Lord Howe, a pillar of the Conservative Party's inner circle and a former foreign secretary, described John Major as a hostage of the Euroskeptics. The party's division, he said, was dragging British foreign policy "into a ghetto of sentimentality and self-delusion." For Britain to be excluded from the heart of Europe's decision making, he said, would be a "national tragedy of huge proportions."[36] In the end, Howe put this concern ahead of his loyalty to Margaret Thatcher; for years, he had served first as her chancellor of the Exchequer and then as foreign secretary. If she had a right hand during her tenure, it was Howe. But he resigned and then attacked her European policy in a speech to the House of Commons, an act that led to her eventual downfall.

Before Mrs. Thatcher arrived at Number 10 Downing Street, the debate over Britain's role in Europe was no more unmannerly than most others. She sharpened the tone, and there was a lot of handbag waving at the Brussels edifice during the early and middle years of the decade during which she bestrode Britain. But her government was not then obstructionist and was actually taking steps to make the EC a more sensible and workable organization. In an interview with me in the fall of 1985, Mrs. Thatcher's jumbled feelings about Europe were expressed: "Yes, there are times when you can see the French-German axis at work," she said. She was referring to a recent meeting of EC leaders in Milan at which a sensible British proposal had been rejected. "The whole thing was small-minded," she said. "I wonder if it is surprising—because we were never beaten, we were never occupied, and they [the French and Germans] were either not victors or occupied. . . . We must just forget about it and go on. And so what can I say. . . . We do go to endless trouble to be constructive. Europe will mature."[37]

It wasn't until the latter stages of her tenure that Mrs. Thatcher began to fully indulge her latent hostility to the EC and, according to many, to the other Europeans themselves. The chief targets for her displeasure were Germany and early steps toward monetary union. By 1990, the year of her abrupt decline and fall, Britain had drifted out of Europe's political mainstream and was being marginalized even further. From London, it looked as if George Bush had decided that America and Germany should be "partners in leadership," a phrase that Bush had actually used in Bonn in June 1989, four months *before* the Berlin Wall fell and eighteen months before unification. Bush's words reverberated in every European capital and sent a frisson of concern, if not alarm, through London and Paris.

By then, Mrs. Thatcher had apparently concluded that only a rigorously independent policy could prevent Britain from becoming a bit player in a German-dominated Europe. And a more integrated Community, she felt, would just tie Europe that much more closely to Germany. In mid-July 1990, Nicholas Ridley, her trade and industry secretary, delivered an astonishing anti-German diatribe in *The Spectator*. Although Mrs. Thatcher was believed to have been unaware of Ridley's ill-advised initiative, his feelings clearly matched her own. The ensuing flap cost Ridley his job and Mrs. Thatcher an ideological soul mate whose departure was widely seen as among the most serious political reversals she had experienced as prime minister. But even worse jolts, largely of her own making, lay just ahead. There remained to be seen only how fast and how ingloriously the Thatcher era wound down. Barely four months after the Ridley affair, she was pushed out of Number 10.

Thatcher's Shadow

Not long ago, the Conservative Party was centered on broad acres and old institutions—schools, the army, and the Church of England. It was run by the gentry—aka knights of the shires—who were by and large decent chaps who belonged to good regiments, where they learned to look after the men before they looked after themselves. Lesser orders and society in general were treated with a paternalism that contained some genuine compassion and was devoid of ideology.

Like Mrs. Thatcher, John Major was a product of the lesser orders and always despised the traditional Tory paternalism. He wasn't just her successor after she was shoved aside by her peers in November 1990; he was her invention. He had impressed her as being dry as dust but rigorous and reliable on issues that mattered to her. That he was a man of ordinary gifts with no apparent leadership qualities didn't seem to matter. Mrs. Thatcher assumed, wrongly and for no particular reason, that Major was "one of us"— the code she used to distinguish herself and "fellow revolutionaries" (also her term) from mainstream members of the Tory party.

Major was a victim of circumstances. His front-bench experience was negligible. He not only wasn't ready for the highest office when he acquired it; his mighty patron was shocked and devastated at having to give it up. Thus, Major inherited not just a share in the worst of Europe's postwar recessions but also the intrusive and unforgiving presence of his predecessor, who was now known as "Lady Thatcher." She still commanded the loyalty of a cluster of Tory back-benchers in the House of Commons. For them, she remained an iconic figure, cut down by a stab in the back—a deed for which this crowd still holds many of her former ministers accountable and which some of them continue to see as a crime against the state.

Mrs. Thatcher exuded strength, partly because she had a clear vision, even if many of her fellow Conservatives were never comfortable with it. The problem for any successor was that no one could become as dominant as she had, because no one could see the way forward with the kind of clarity to which she had laid claim, often thunderously. "We've got socialism by the throat!" she would say. "We will destroy socialism here and in the world!" She left no dragons for Major to slay. She had neutered the trade unions, privatized the inefficient companies that Labour had nationalized, and put paid to Labour's notions about income redistribution.

The party still lies within her shadow. She and her claque of Europhobes (a better term than "Euroskeptics") have split Conservatives more deeply perhaps than at any time since the 1840s, when Disraeli and Peel divided them over the issue of the Corn Laws. They were—are—largely self-made businesspeople, many of them from the suburbs, who cut their political teeth in the Thatcher years. They see the EU as the next dragon to be disposed of, and never mind that instead of uniting the party, as the other dragons did, the issue of Europe still divides Conservatives.

Ironically, the most conspicuous Europhobes are those traditional bastions of support for the Conservative cause: *The Times, The Sunday Times,* and the *Sunday Telegraph.* An Australian, Rupert Murdoch, owns the first two, along with *The Star,* the biggest and among the shrillest of the tabloids. A Canadian, Conrad Black, is owner of both the *Sunday Telegraph* and the somewhat less tendentious *Daily Telegraph.* Major can claim to have been treated shabbily, or worse, by them all. Alas, from the start, he read and remembered and brooded upon all the negatives in all the stories about him. His ministers and advisers urged him to read the press less and more selectively. They felt he could have done worse than emulate Mrs. Thatcher, who claimed to read the press very little and to rely chiefly on a prepared digest.

Before Tony Blair took over the helm of the Labour Party, Labour was judged so weak that some of the press took over the role of opposing the government. I remember in the pre-Blair era asking the editor of a major newspaper that normally supported Tories if that was true.

"That's how it's worked out," he replied. "Labour can't do anything."[38]

Another of the ironies is that *The Guardian,* which normally supports Labour, rarely the Conservatives, was admirably objective in its coverage of Major, taking a more measured view of him than the nominally Tory press. The *Financial Times* and *The Independent* were similarly detached and measured. But the Tory press had to decide which wing of the Party to support, and that also meant taking a position on the Maastricht Accord. Murdoch's papers sided with the Thatcherites, and most of the Tory press has to one degree or another opposed Maastricht.

Major's circle of irony was completed in July 1993, during what seemed to be a debate over whether to ratify the Maastricht Accord. The real stakes, however, were the control and direction of the Conservative Party. An astonishing coalition lined up against Major on an amendment to the accord that would have forced Britain to accept the so-called social chapter—a provision that imposes EU-wide standards on workers' rights and wages. At Maastricht, Major had deftly arranged for Britain to be excluded from the social chapter, which, he'd said, would have saddled Britain with the heavy social costs and higher wage structures of the continentals. "Socialism through the back door" was how Tory Europhobes had characterized the provision. Major could never have imposed it on them, even if he had wanted to. But that summer, these same people joined Labour and the Liberal Democrats, a small, centrist, and strongly pro-EU party, in support of the amendment. Even by normal parliamentary standards, it was a rich brew of hypocrisy and cynicism.

Nobody won the vote on the amendment. The speaker broke what had been a tie by casting her vote with the government. Major had held just enough of the Tory renegades to avoid defeat. It was a brief respite, however. Just a few minutes later, another vote was taken, this one a motion to ratify the accord, and this time the government lost.

The press cited the government's defeat as the Labour Party's greatest triumph after fourteen years in opposition and four successive election defeats. But Major had one more card to play—what his people called the "nuclear option"—and he played it that afternoon. He linked a revised motion to ratify the accord with a threat to resign as prime minister, dissolve Parliament, and call a general election. It was enough to bring the Tory rebels back into line. With the tide running heavily against their party, few Tory MPs wanted to confront their electors. "Turkeys never vote for

Christmas" was the comment one heard and read repeatedly that evening and over the weekend.

Major became the leader partly because he was the choice of the Thatcherites, but also in part because the majority had wanted an emollient figure, someone who could both heal the divisions and provide leadership. But except for brief moments, he wasn't able to do much healing or leading. He was often and aptly described as "punching above his weight." The Tory party was all but out of control when Major was anointed. His often pathetic and usually unavailing efforts to find and then steer a course between its Europhobes and Europhiles tended to dramatize the polarity rather than bridge the differences.

The greatest of Major's several mistakes lay in refusing to fire ministers who flaunted their disloyalty by openly opposing his European policy, such as it was. Major saw the choice before him as uncomplicated but brutal: he could have taken on the Europhobes and run the risk—though it was not great—of having them rebel and formally split the party. But in not taking them on, Major watched his party plunge itself into a turmoil worse than any it had experienced since the days of Stanley Baldwin, in the mid-1930s.

Symptomatic of the craziness and paranoia of the Tory party was the "mad cow" episode, which played out over the spring and summer of 1996. Tories, not all of them Europhobes, reacted to the affair as if yet another continental cohort was assaulting not just Britain's sovereignty but an enduring staple of its way of life—roast beef. Another Finest Hour had come round. "Major Goes to War at Last," proclaimed the *Daily Express*. "A showdown rarely seen since the Battle of Britain," said the febrile *Sun*.[39]

The issue turned on whether Creutzfeldt-Jakob disease, aka mad cow disease, had been transmitted to people through tainted animal feed given to British cattle as protein enrichment. John Major's government was unwilling to do the drastic culling judged necessary by other EU members, which felt that Britain was doing the bare minimum. More suspect cattle—British imports—were slaughtered in the Netherlands than in Britain. Aggrieved EU members imposed a ban on British beef products that would last until London could show that it had the problem in hand. That would mean slaughtering enough cattle to remove the problem from the bovine food chain.

For whatever reason, Major's government did not consult with Brussels when the link between mad cow disease and humans began to draw attention. Other EU members saw Britain's apparent indifference as symptomatic of its attitude toward the EU and, indeed, Europe itself. Britain's partners were not just enraged but baffled by what seemed Britain's inability to understand the damage being done to them; meat consumption fell off dramatically in EU member states; German meat sales were down by one half for a time. But the British government showed itself equally aggrieved, either believing or choosing to believe that its partners were acting out of malice. Playing to hysterical Europhobes, Major retaliated by announcing a policy of noncooperation with all EU decisions. Britain, in effect, was boycotting the institution, vetoing every EU initiative that required its concurrence. British diplomats in EU capitals were embarrassed, not for the first time but rarely so completely. "We used to watch [Britain] with amusement, then with bewilderment and now with silent despair," said a member of Helmut Kohl's entourage.[40]

"How," asked *The Economist,* "can a country that puts vaccinated family pets from abroad into quarantine for fear of rabies object when its partners ban British beef for fear of a mad-cow disease that has been and still is disproportionately present in British herds? . . . How . . . [can] Britain cooperate with NATO and the Commonwealth, despite bans on British beef imposed long ago by America, Australia, Canada, and New Zealand?"[41]

The EU offered to pay 70 percent of the costs of slaughter and disposal, with Britain to pay the balance. Britain eventually accepted the offer and lifted its boycott. But the EU's ban on British beef products remained, and the threat to humans from mad cow disease became clearer. The episode has reinforced pressure in some EU capitals, including Bonn and Paris, for a more flexible EU structure, one that would allow a hard core of member states to proceed with further integration and leave behind fence-sitters such as Britain.[42] Germany has a powerful interest in reshaping the EU along such lines, as reflected in the Lamers-Schauble paper. Briefly, the ripple effect of the Tories' antics during this wacky episode may be far-reaching and inimical to Britain's interests, depending on how these are defined in Whitehall and Number 10.

Conservatives of moderate hue tend by and large to support a strong EU and a strong British presence inside it. But, like Major, most of them sat back and did nothing to restrain their xenophobic, little-Englander colleagues. On the front bench, not even Douglas Hurd rose to the occasion before retiring, as he easily could have done. This puerile performance by sober and moderate Tories recalled the better example set by Roy Jenkins, who, in 1972, resigned as Labour's deputy leader so as to oppose the anti-European bias of other members of the shadow cabinet. Lord Jenkins and sixty-eight other Labour MPs backed Tory leader Edward Heath on joining the European Community. This gesture is believed to have cost Jenkins his chances to become Labour's leader later on.

In 1993 or 1994, Major would have gratified many colleagues on both sides of the European issue by quitting. Numerous mainstream Tories reckoned that after fourteen years in power, they were burnt out, and the polls seemed to show a public thirsting for a change in leadership. Had Major actually stepped aside at that time, his successor, quite possibly, would have been Kenneth Clarke, chancellor of the Exchequer and the Tory front bench's most conspicuous Europhile, as well as its brightest light. He is the best performer in Parliament, according to a poll of MPs on both sides of the House. Clarke was—is—as unlike Major as Major was unlike Thatcher. Actually, Clarke is unlike most politicians anywhere, first of all because he usually says exactly what he thinks, a tendency that has often caused him trouble—trouble that has, however, invariably left him unworried and unharmed. "It wouldn't be the end of the world if Tony Blair became prime minister," he said during the period when the gap between Labour and and the Tories was steadily widening. When Clarke is asked if he would like to be prime minister, he usually says, "Of course; so would all six hundred and fifty members of the House."

Clarke is a lawyer from the West Midlands; he was born in 1950 and is one of a number of gifted, upwardly mobile Tories from lower-middle-class origins. Like some of them, he is a former president of the Cambridge Union. Clarke is relaxed and amusing, wears down-market clothes, and can be politically incorrect as well as indiscreet. Although prone to earthy and picturesque language, he also uses very good, precise language. And behind the matey exterior lurks as tough a political operator as the Tories have deployed in recent years; Clarke is a natural brawler, who in his several ministerial jobs speared various sacred cows, including teachers, policemen, and nurses. He is singularly uncompromising. "My views," he says, "are as constant as the northern star."

Most of the comments one hears about Clarke from politicians, civil servants, and reporters who know him are positive and rather alike. "A big beast of the jungle" is a comment often made, usually as a way of contrasting Clarke to Major and other unremarkable but equally ambitious figures. The net impression is of a high-quality character who, although aggressively irreverent, is at least as gifted and at least as bold as any of the leading figures in British, or indeed European, politics.

The line on Clarke contains just one "but" clause: "But would Thatcherites accept him?" In the 1993–1994 period, some of them would have accepted Clarke; they knew him to be strong, competent, and good at bashing Labour. They also knew that Clarke had the confidence of the City, which has shared his pro-EU position and respected his strength. As chancellor, Clarke was beginning to steer Britain through what has become an extended period of non-inflationary economic growth. Opinion divides on whether Clarke could have functioned as leader of a united Tory party. My own feeling is that he could have. Among those who disagreed was the writer of a column in *The Economist* called Bagehot. "The question," he wrote in December 1994, "is not whether Mr. Clarke is up to leading the Tories. He is. The question is whether the Tories are up to being led by Mr. Clarke. They aren't."[43]

The question—or one of them, anyway—was whether Britain's economic recovery would balance the strong anti-Tory tide, much of whose force was drawn from the degrading spectacle the party had made of itself. By 1995–1996, the infection within the party had spread to the point that there was probably no alternative to Major, certainly no one to his left on the European issue and probably no mainstream Tory. Aspirant successors to his right—Michael Howard and John Redwood—did not command respect and had never impressed the gallery as particularly competent. The other and more credible right-wing contender for the leadership was Michael Portillo, who is considered competent but lost his seat in the Labour rout.

By election time 1997, handicappers were betting on Malcolm Rifkind, who had replaced Hurd as foreign secretary, to be the next leader. Rifkind, a mainstream figure of known competence who once upon a time was aligned with the party's pro-Europe faction, began hedging once he smelled the leadership. And then he, too, lost his seat.

In the long run-up to the 1997 election, mainstream Tories took the measure of Tony Blair. They judged him competent and unlikely to make mistakes of the sort that would help them. They also saw that Blair, though shrewdly noncommital on the single currency, was unambiguously pro-EU and keenly alert to the danger of allowing Britain to repeat its routine follies of talking down to European partners and affecting indifference to the European cause. As a practical political matter, Blair was indistinguishable from most mainstream Tories on the European issue and on some others. Among the dangers, as Tories of all stripes recognized, was that

Blair, if elected, would drive the younger, suburban members of their party—the Thatcher intake—to put more blue water between them and Labour by moving further to the right and to even more extreme positions on Europe. That activity, in turn, could split the Conservative Party in the formal sense and prolong its stay in the wilderness. Many Tories had been reckoning that a Labour government, or a coalition of Labour and Liberal Democrats (Lib-Lab), wouldn't last long—that the electorate would quickly tire of the new crowd and come back to the familar fold. But that calculation was certain to fall apart if the Europhobes succeeded in splitting their party.

What befalls the diminished Tory party in the years ahead will depend on who prevails, the shires or the suburbs. Shire people are centrist—Tories of a familiar breed, accustomed to governing and going with the flow. They have never been ideologues. In the Thatcher era, the products of these different cultures were called "Wets" and "Drys." The typical Wet (a derisive public school term that Mrs. T. adopted) favored cautious, moderate policies and opposed major cuts in public spending and other drastic remedies demanded by the Drys; anyone who could be judged "one of us" was ipso facto a Dry.

Which side does prevail won't be clear for some time. The question of Europe and Britain's place in it has generally held center stage since the de Gaulle–Macmillan era. It won't be settled overnight.

Turning the Page

Monetary union will agitate Tories and Labour alike if Germany and France keep the project on course or limit the duration of any postponement. But the Tories' agitation will exceed Labour's. Blair has tamed a once unmanageable, self-destructive party. Its huge majority in the House of Commons frees his hands—up to a point;

the party whips have an easier time enforcing discipline when so many of their back-benchers are thirsting for a limited number of preferments. However, it won't take long for the Blair era to acquire some of the trappings of normalcy. The government will make mistakes. No one of its members, including Blair, has had one day of prior government experience. Also, Blair's top tier isn't conspicuous for breadth of talent; the second tier is judged better, but the people there will have to wait their turn. So Blair can be expected to spend a fair amount of time putting out fires, at least in the early stages of his tenure.

The contrast with the Tories is interesting. Five members of Major's government, including Clarke and Rifkind, are out of office for the first time in eighteen years—a modern record. (Lloyd George held office continuously for seventeen years.)

Well before Blair's election, his advisers on Europe were focused on an EU summit, which took place in Amsterdam a month or so later. Britain's partners had already concluded that Blair probably wouldn't take Britain into EMU on the first wave but might do so on the second. (Treat Britain as a "Pre-In," some of the Blair people were saying.)

Blair couldn't bring much to Amsterdam beyond attitude. He wanted to show that his government, unlike Major's, was committed to the EU and most of its works. He advocates enlarging the club. And he favors more majority voting but not, it seems, on the hot-button issues—immigration, justice, defense, and foreign policy. The other EU members hope that Blair's congenial attitude will gradually make Britain a better "European"; but they know that the British people are, on balance, Euroskeptic and, thanks mainly to Tory Europhobes, confused about European issues.

As for the Tories, if the burden of membership in an apathetic, all but immobile EU can tear them apart, how will they cope with a proposal to replace the pound with the euro and allow the Bank of England to become a mere branch bank in a European central banking system? The British people voted in the last election, without knowing what either party actually thought about the dominant issue, monetary union. Tony Blair had distanced himself from it during the campaign. The two key figures in his shadow cabinet, Gordon Brown and Robin Cook, were to be on different sides of the issue. But party leaders on both sides have known that staying out of EMU could handicap Britain. Foreign investors, especially Americans and Japanese, might begin to equate Britain with the less disciplined crowd making up the EU's second tier—the countries that couldn't qualify for EMU. American investments in Britain are larger than in all of Asia and three times those in France or Germany. About 40 percent of Japanese investment in Europe has been directed to Britain.

In the runup to the election, Blair devoted considerable time and energy to showing British business leaders that he could be trusted on EU matters. But he couldn't enlighten them on what he would do about EMU or how far he might eventually go in supporting reform of the EU institutions. He himself probably won't know until he has had some experience in leading the country and some success in dealing with other, less treacherous issues.

One such issue involved the Bank of England, which, unlike America's Federal Reserve and the German Bundesbank, has never been able to set interest rates; British governments always reserved that power for themselves. But remaining aloof from EMU would add to existing pressure to liberate the Bank of England, a move that has been judged long overdue by most central bankers in other countries. And with the other key European countries on the verge of being tucked up in a tightly controlled Euro-Fed, a detached Britain would be hard pressed to protect its anti-inflationary credentials if the government could still manipulate interest rates for political ends, as John Major did in the run-up to the 1992 election. But just five days after arriving in office, Blair both surprised and delighted the business community and his fellow European leaders by yielding virtually all the power to set interest rates to the Bank of England. It was a shrewd move; Blair was pledging himself to anti-inflationary, free-market policies by taking a step that not even Conservative governments had been willing to take.

As for EMU, leaders of both parties were on notice that the City was getting ready for it; specifically, British bankers would be preparing for the retail use of euros. Quite clearly, a situation in which the financial community was moving in one direction, while the country itself remained either on the fence or resolutely outside Europe's mainstream, would be awkward, to put it mildly.

Assuming monetary union goes forward more or less on schedule, the City would like to be in on the ground floor; the alternative, say worried Europhiles, would be watching the Bundesbank organize an institution that Britain would probably be joining at some stage anyway but would be unable to influence. Let's not worry about this now, argue the Europhobes. EMU won't fly, they say, if only because the bar was clearly set too high for too many. We've won the argument, they add. The EU is not extending its reach and should give up trying.

The Europhiles feel that Britain, as one of the three main EU members, should be where the action is, not in spite of the risks but because of the need to control them. Indeed, if EMU is a flawed project, it may not be reparable without Britain's involvement. And if it can't be repaired, the EU itself may spin into irreversible decline. It needs workable institutions, to which a European central bank would have to be somehow accountable. To expect their arrival anytime soon requires a leap of faith. Nothing of the sort is likely to happen unless (1) Britain lifts its veto on political steps forward by the EU and (2) the other members proceed on a separate track without Britain, in which case all sides, including Britain, would be the poorer. That probably won't happen anyway, since France's reluctance to confer power on EU institutions comes close to matching Britain's.

Britain's stunted role in EU affairs does injury to all of Europe. When not being difficult, Britain is often the organization's most sensible and moderating influence, pragmatic when it should be, creative when imagination and innovation are needed. The people

Britain sends to Brussels are among the EU's most resourceful and productive, despite the obstacles to their work that are thrown up in London. Some EU members, including Germany, feel closer to the British outlook and style than to the French.

Briefly, Britain has steadfastly denied itself and Europe much or most of the benefit of its EU membership during the larger part of the Tory dominion. "Everyone knows the British can't make good cars," some Germans like to say. (Those with long memories may substitute "tanks" for "cars.") "But diplomacy is what they were supposed to be good at it. They are making a mess of it." The meaning is clear: if Britain is worried about German power, it should not weaken but rather strengthen the EU and use it to keep Germany's clout within acceptable bounds.

Doing both argues for a strong and unprecedented effort by Blair to put Britain's relations with Germany on the strongest possible footing. With the EU stalled, France in a bad way, and Germany groping, Blair should exercise some leadership by pushing to extend the EU eastward, and doing so, if possible, with the most interested of his partners, Germany. In a Mori opinion poll taken in May 1994, British voters selected Germany as the most reliable member of the EU bloc, an outlook that must have troubled the Tory party's German bashers.[44]

It's been quite a while since British diplomacy accomplished anything notable or memorable. A clever Whitehall would have used 1995–1996 as a time in which to begin hedging against the prospect of serious political trouble in Europe. Specifically, Britain's diplomacy should have equipped itself with a plan to protect France, Germany, the EU, and, yes, Britain, too, not to mention their all-important special link and the EU itself, from the possibility that monetary union does not go forward; or that it goes forward and founders; or that it breaks too much crockery as it goes forward.

"One of the great fallacies of postwar British diplomacy has been the supposed need for Britain to 'choose' between Europe and the United States," wrote Sir Robin Renwick, whose reflections should be heard. Renwick was a highly regarded British diplomat who retired as ambassador to Washington in 1995 after having also served as head of the Foreign Office's European Department. Unlike some colleagues, Renwick never prophesized, let alone advocated, a federation of European states. But Britain's decision to keep its distance from the EU, he says, "was a far more fatal error than Suez. It enabled the European Community to develop as a continental system, with France dominating its institutions. . . . Britain has influence on American policy to the extent that it still has some power and influence itself in various parts of the world."[45] Senior officials of successive U.S. administrations have put it more bluntly: Britain's influence in Washington will be no greater than its influence in Europe.

CHAPTER VI

UNTHREATENED YET
INSECURE

A s they ponder security, governments are having to accept that the certainties of the Cold War era were an anomaly— that the more turbulent, less predictable world of today is both normal and one with which nobody currently holding power or office has had prior experience. And with no explicit threat confronting them, the NATO governments are beset by a variety of problems, both current and latent. Some of them have roots in bygone days; some are novel. How to think about such problems, how to deal with them? Also, policy makers must grapple with competing priorities on a scale far exceeding any agenda that confronted leaders at any time during the Cold War. Most western governments appear to agree, for example, that Russia—the sick giant—should take on a role that accords with its potential reach and impact on European and world affairs; the capitals that are likely to influence the deeply interactive affairs of North America and Eurasia most strongly in the years ahead are Washington, Bonn-Berlin, and Moscow (after an extended and possibly chaotic recovery in Russia).

However, most members of NATO have either endorsed, acquiesced in, or won't oppose expanding the alliance to include at least some countries of central and conceivably eastern Europe. And there has developed serious, if predictable, tension between accommodating Moscow's resistance to the idea and extending the western security system uncomfortably close to Russia's frontiers. But Russia doesn't object to the EU expanding eastward, a step that EU members say they favor and are committed to, although they are in no hurry to take it.

With the end of the Cold War, it was inevitable that the major tasks confronting the western system of joint institutions would be generated by societies lying to the east of Germany. Some of them, starting with Poland, the Czech Republic, and Hungary, equate membership in the key western institutions with being able to sustain themselves as parliamentary democracies. Stated briefly, the countries of central and eastern Europe, including Russia, are forcing the West to redefine itself. They worry seriously that what becomes of them will be decided over their heads, as in the past, by the strongest, most determined powers. They fear the unknown, which, they think, will involve domination by some condminium, probably Russo-German or—though less likely—Russo-American. Throughout the Cold War, Polish leaders struggled to convince Moscow that they were being more hostile to West Germany than were any of their neighbors, including Walter Ulbricht's German Democratic Republic (GDR). Poland and its neighbors to the south will do whatever they can to discourage another Rapallo, although Munich and Yalta seem to be equally worrisome metaphors.

Nationalism is now and will continue to be a problem in parts of Europe. In repealing a half century of experience, Mikhail Gorbachev did more than release an empire and fling Europe and the world into a new era. He reawakened ethnic and nationality groups, including many in his own country, which in the past had often fought one another. The borders in most of Europe, especially in central and eastern Europe, are recent and arbitrary.

Like Germany, Russia sees itself as menaced by the past—its own and, in a sense, Germany's; many Russians, as well as non-Russians, see Weimar Germany as the right metaphor for a military colossus that was swept into a state of turbulence and insecurity by a tide that caused it to abandon the Cold War and break apart. The difference, as Christoph Bertram, foreign editor of *Die Zeit*, has noted, is that the Germany of the 1920s, although demoralized by defeat and depression, was already a modern industrialized state in possession of institutions that Hitler was able to exploit.[1]

Russia watchers are split between those who counsel patience and those who see only trouble on the horizon. For a thousand years, Russia was ruled by men not by laws, we are reminded by the advocates of patience. Between the end of tsarist rule and the end of the Soviet system, there was no period of enlightenment. And, of course, the argument continues, Russians have no experience with due process. Yet in the brief time since the Soviet Union self-destructed, the Russians haven't done badly. They have a constitution. Their leaders have called nine elections, which may not have been above reproach but were nonetheless held on schedule, the results not seriously challenged. Voter participation in the elections is increasing—up to 60 to 70 percent in the past two elections.

Also, Russia is in the first stage of capitalism. It could be called the feral stage, with robber barons everywhere and wholesale privatization of institutions, including the army. Nonetheless, we do see a market economy emerging—raw, flawed, strongly flavored by gangsterism, but, according to some big players on the investment scene, the world's most exciting new market. The Russian stock market outperformed all other "emerging markets" last year—

surging 156 percent in dollar terms. "Russia is in the process of becoming one of the great markets and economies in the world," said David Mulford, chairman of Credit Suisse First Boston Europe. "Established institutions can't afford to be away."[2]

According to some worldly Russians, Russia is a surreal country where the highly improbable becomes real. Moreover, for a time we heard dire forecasts of upheaval, revolution, and restoration of strongman rule, not to mention a military takeover of Ukraine. None of these fearsome expectations has been borne out.

At least not yet, reply the pessimists and worst-case thinkers, a large group. A big part of the overall problem, they say, is that there is no *there* there—no voice or institution that can speak for Russias and deliver. We confront instead, they say, a chaotic society lacking centralized direction and dominated by a medley of competing elites and clans, each with its own corrupting agenda. A criminalized state is emerging. The breakdown and collapse of the Soviet system created a disorder that is spreading.

The trouble with this line, according to those who reject it as simplistic and exaggerated, is that it reflects only the thinking of the Moscow intelligentsia, a group of people who are reacting to what they see around them, not to what is happening beyond the city limits. What they don't see, some Russians and non-Russians observe, is a pronounced shift in the society's focus away from Moscow to the provinces and provincial ways. What they may also fail to see, or register, is a rising middle class in Moscow itself, along with the spread of prospering small businesses there that sustains it.

"Many of Russia's twenty-one republics and forty-nine *oblasts* are doing far better today than under Communist rule," writes Frederick Starr, a notable as well as knowledgeable moderate on Russia. "The government's financial infrastructure may be crumbling," he adds, "but scores of private banks are thriving. Thousands of senior administrators who kept Soviet-era trains running on time, both literally and figuratively, now work in private firms that are turning handsome profits and are able to lobby effectively in Moscow for policies favorable to their needs." Starr, too, counsels patience, observing that "for the last six years Russia has been in the midst of a revolution far more massive, all-embracing, and swift than nearly all the other great revolutions of the modern era. Among those aspects of Russian life undergoing a transforming upheaval have been the national borders, form of government, structures of society, economic institutions, the political system, and values, both public and private. These changes are occurring not seriatim but all at once. Is it any wonder that the country appears to be on the brink of chaos?"[3]

With so much change occurring at so dizzying a pace, it's hard to see whether the net effect at any given moment may be plus or minus. The mixed picture shows people in their mid-thirties in Moscow and St. Petersburg taking to capitalism like ducks to water; it also shows Russian army officers selling weapons under their command in order to feed their families and their troops. In March 1997, President Boris Yeltsin turned over authority for reform to a new team composed of two young men whom he appointed first deputy prime ministers. One of them, Anatoly Chubais, was forty-two and a known quantity—the toughest and most resourceful member of the Yeltsin entourage. The other, Boris Nemtsov, has been widely seen as a prodigy. Only thirty-seven when appointed by Yeltsin, he had been a highly successful provincial governor. Four years earlier, Yeltsin is supposed to have pronounced Nemtsov a future president of Russia.

Nemtsov has said that he would go back to Nizhniy-Novgorod after two years if the situation hadn't clearly changed for the better and a coherent governing authority hadn't been established. He and Chubais may not have that much time. The fragmentation of authority within Moscow is cited by some Russianologists as reminiscent of the latter stage of the reign of Nicholas II, the last tsar. "My government is responsible for nothing," says one prominent and well-connected Muscovite when asked what the leadership may do about this or that problem. He was referring to national security policy, of which there is little, or none, except for what may be in Yeltsin's head at any given moment when he is in Moscow and in control. A lot of different notions and projects are pushed in the name of national security by various interest groups.

Seventy years of Soviet misrule left a blasted, morally bankrupt society, say those who hold the darker view. Russia is now, they say, in the middle of an identity crisis, wondering if it can again become a great power, or whether it is a European power, or a Eurasian power. And what are, or should be, Russia's borders? What are the external threats to national security?

Actually, there are none; Russians are living within a more benign environment than any they have previously known. Just solve our problems, they tell their leadership. Still, old habits die hard, say Russia's skeptical critics. "Better the French as enemies than the Russians as friends" became a fashionable view in the early days of the Congress of Vienna in the early nineteenth century. The other, more widely held view is that for the first time in four centuries Russia has no designs on central Europe. The Russian government is trying to preserve its current military establishment with a third or less of the resources it might need. Russia today is a threat mainly to itself, certainly not to societies in central and eastern Europe that were victimized in the past. The danger from Russia lies not in irredentist goals but in its instability and volatility, much of which is traceable to humiliation and frustration.

Russians may feel a need to regain their identity as a great power, but after centuries of imperialism, they have probably lost their imperial thirst. At this time Russia is not capable of launching a military campaign outside its borders. The campaign in Chechnya, in which more Russians than Chechans were killed, silenced anyone who might have wanted to divert attention from domestic woes with foreign adventures.

If western capitals elect to see Russia as the now or future problem, Russia may become the problem. For the time being, Russia is necessarily self-absorbed; it sees internal disintegration as the serious threat. Russia's frontiers have shifted north and east since the collapse of the Soviet Union. Disputes between the regions may sharpen, and additional conflicts are expected to arise from competition for energy and water or over cultural and religious divisions, which, of course, tend to inflame fundamentalist forces. "If you want to help us, help Russia," Václav Havel used to tell visitors. "The nearest Russian troops are nearly a thousand miles away."

The chief external goals of the centrist and liberal political establishment in Russia are predictable and hardly objectionable; they amount to a craving for the status of a great power, which translates as a place for Russia at the center of arrangements for European security; a role in world affairs over and above Russia's participation in the U.N. Security Council and partial involvement with the feeble G7 (the club in which the main industrialized nations try to sort out their common problems); a sturdy and productive bilateral relationship with the United States. Russia may lack most of the attributes of a great power, but it cannot help still thinking of itself as one and, indeed, as a partner of the West. It is hard for Moscow to equate its problems with some former republic with those it may have with Japan or India or, above all, with the United States.

Russia is not a world power. It is a potentially great power that is currently "power lite" and engaged in a long strategic retreat. Russia sees itself as the only country with vital interests in both Europe and Asia, but it feels isolated from both. Gorbachev often spoke of a "common European home" and at least once of a "common Asian home." The cost of losing the Cold War was high, and it is Russia, not the Soviet Union, that is paying it. China, meanwhile, is emerging as a major power and a long-term threat to Russia. Cultural Islam is having a revival. NATO intends to occupy space that Russians are accustomed to influencing, if not controlling.

In lieu of a steady policy, Russia is setting up scapegoats to blame for its domestic chaos. Other countries and institutions, including even the International Monetary Fund (IMF), are accused of trying to undermine Russia's position, make off with the Russian patrimony, and seize control of the economy. Nonsense of this kind complicates efforts by other governments to develop coherent policies toward Russia.

It's hard enough as it is, trying to help Russia help itself and watching its leadership all but losing control of problems that concern everyone. First and perhaps foremost of these is the calamitous state of Russia's military establishment. As the Cold War ended, forty divisions of Soviet soldiers withdrew from Germany, eastern Europe, and the Baltic states. A large part of Russia's military budget was earmarked for construction needed to house and sustain the returning troops. But the program is running out of money and energy.

It will fail, according to Sergey Rogov, director of the Institute for USA and Canada Studies in Moscow. "It's impossible," he says,

> . . . even if you mobilize the entire Russian economy, to do the job in such a short time. . . . You have to add on top of this . . . the lack of housing for 200,000 officers. . . . Lack of training for the officers who had to retire as a result of reductions. Lack of training for civilian jobs and lack of housing for them. Malnutrition for the draftees and abuse of draftees by elder soldiers, which is still widespread. This has led to a situation where the military forces, instead of being one of the elements in the system of protection of national security interests, become to some extent a threat to Russian national security. . . .
>
> "The Russian military is divided and fragmented like the population in general. . . . In Chechnya, the army crossed the Rubicon. It didn't want to do it. It was pushed. Thus, the army was engaged in a very dirty and bloody war which in fact was a civil war. Fighting against their own fellow citizens. . . . The fighters on the Chechen side were mostly former Soviet soldiers and officers with whom the Russian military were together just a few years ago. I think this made a tremendous psychological

impact on the Russian military. Thus, if next time the politicians will ask the military to intervene, I am afraid that the military will intervene, but it's not clear at all on whose side.

However, Rogov also expressed doubt that the "Russian military want to act as an independent political force and want to take power in their hands. I don't think that there's a real threat of a military coup d'état in Russia."[4]

None of the Russia watchers disputes the gravity of the military's plight. The government hasn't the funds to pay, or even feed or clothe, many units. Nor can it demobilize them because there isn't enough money for housing and transitional arrangements, for example, job training. Just turning troops and their officers into the streets is out of the question. The army is running out of conscripts, but moving to a professional army is not an option either because the government couldn't pay the recruits—not enough, anyway—or provide incentives in the form of education and training. In the scramble to feed themselves and their families, officers take second jobs; they tend to go off to their other job immediately after roll call. Some have turned to crime: selling weapons; using military trucks and even airplanes to transport drugs.

In mid-February 1997, Russia's then defense minister, Igor N. Rodionov, appealed for more money to support the armed forces. He described the state of the armed forces as "horrifying." "If things go on like this for another two years," Yuri Baturing, secretary of the president's advisory defense council, had said a few days earlier, "we may have a navy without ships, an air force without planes and a military industry incapable of producing modern weapons." At this same moment, a defense and policy institute that draws together business leaders, members of Parliament, and journalists proclaimed "the present state of the Russian army . . . as a catastrophe."[5]

Moscow's dilemma is multiple. Sustaining the army would bankrupt the economy. Not sustaining it could lead to the army's disintegration, with many units signing on with regional warlords. Factionalism is already rampant. Apart from the regular forces, there are at least twenty-two military groups serving under commanders who are in some cases serving themselves and who in the main are considered unresponsive to centralized control. Some of the irregulars belong to paramilitary groups, others to official organizations such as the Ministry of Internal Affairs (successor to the KGB), whose militia has grown from about 45,000 to an estimated 260,000. Banks and other financial groups maintain armed security forces, as does Gazprom, the oil and gas behemoth, which has not only a private militia but armored vehicles. No one, including the government, seems to know how many men there are under arms, including those who belong to the Russian armed forces. Again, comparison is drawn to the last tsarist regime: a sick leader, a vague national security policy, and an army that is being fragmented and to some degree privatized. But the tsar's problem was, of course, even more serious: he was also fighting a war.

Only by turning the economy around can the military problem be solved. But it isn't happening. Huge sums of money are sloshing around the economy, but the money isn't being turned to productive use and creating economic growth. Only by printing more can the government pay its unpaid troops. Doing so, however, would create unacceptable inflation and further problems with the IMF, which in the fall of 1996 suspended payment of a $10 billion loan, mainly because the government can't collect its taxes. Tax revenues for the first nine months of 1996 amounted to 65 percent of the sum budgeted. A third of the Russian economy is off the books, and as Clifford Gaddy, a research associate at the Brookings Institution, has written, "the tax system is a mess. New taxes are introduced and others abolished, rates are raised or lowered, exemptions are granted and withdrawn at a dizzying pace. This unpredictability has been detrimental to economic development and business creation." When the government cracks down on delinquents, Gaddy adds, the first targets are "little guys—the small businesses" and next the "relatively honest taxpayers who already pay some, though not all, of their taxes."[6] Russia has no more urgent need than a coherent and workable tax code.

Russia's economy is further burdened by the continued presence of Soviet-era companies—socialist dinosaurs—which have staying power in a troubled nation whose quality of life is declining. The dinosaur provides essentially free housing and a cradle-to-grave kind of security of which wages amount to just 30 to 40 percent of the package.

Some of Russia's military commands, notably the Strategic Rocket Forces, are being paid, although often quite belatedly. The same may be said of the forces deployed around Moscow and capable of getting themselves there in a hurry. The risks arising from the decline of Russia's armed forces can't be measured. The Soviet leadership always worried actively about "Bonapartism," and seventy years of strong civilian control of the army may have institutionalized the practice. Professional Russia watchers don't exclude a coup but do not expect to see one, partly because they can't see where it might originate. A revolution cannot be made without a revolutionary party.

Aleksandr Lebed once had a plan for raising a "Russian Legion" from within the armed forces, and he warned that the miserably treated soldiers might stage a "mutiny."[7] Lebed has been widely seen as a figure of authority and a potential kingpin. But his star has faded, according to some. He wagered everything on Yeltsin's departure from the scene, and that didn't happen. Lebed, it is believed, won't become a serious political figure again unless Yeltsin does leave the scene a lot sooner than expected—that is, well before his mandate expires. Meanwhile, they add, Lebed has no party to lead, no funds to organize one, and no obvious ways with which to maintain a high profile.

Other Russia watchers take a different view; they see Lebed as a work in progress, a man endowed with an aura of leadership and a wholly natural can-do style that separates him from his equally ambitious and determined rivals. When Yeltsin is resting and not on the scene, Russians sense a leadership vacuum, and they are right. Yeltsin rules by limiting the fields of maneuver and power of those around him. Thus, the argument goes, Russians want some durable character to take charge and crack the whip. If Yeltsin falters, whether politically or physically, only Lebed may be able to take the helm, unless an even more convincing whipcracker comes along.

The Gravest Threat of All

To say, as I did a few pages back, that Russia is a threat mainly to itself is wrong in one crucial aspect: Russian nuclear weapons and weapons-grade nuclear material are a vastly greater threat today than they were during the Cold War. Some veterans of the Cold War, not all of them occupational "cold warriors," may disagree. But it was never likely then that either superpower would make a calculated nuclear strike against the other. Then as now, the chief threats were two: first, that some new entrant into the nuclear club might use one and, second, that a misreading by either superpower of the other's actions could provoke a missile launch. In short, there are two ominous variables. One is the spread of nuclear weapons and material, especially to some terrorist group; the other is the vulnerability of Russia's command and control structure.

The danger of weapons-grade nuclear material seeping out of Russia is expanding rapidly. It has already happened on a few known occasions—known only because the prospective sales were thwarted. For all one knows, other attempts may have succeeded. What's clear is that in a society whose scientists, technicians, and military officers are badly paid and, in many cases, badly off, the temptation to flog nuclear material is at least as great as the undoubted rewards for success. We know that the Soviet Union never inventoried its weapons-grade material (Russia is estimated to have about 1,200 tons of highly enriched uranium and 150 tons of plutonium. Producing a nuclear weapon used to require 30 pounds of weapons-grade uranium or 10 pounds of plutonium; now it takes less.)

We've discovered that security in some Russian nuclear installations exists barely, if at all. And we must suspect that in today's *sauve qui peut* Russian environment the line between selling non-nuclear weapons and selling nuclear material is one that many people would cross. There are endless examples of people who are well placed to do the wrong thing and do it. To cite just one, the commander of a paramilitary group sold rocket engines to China without notifying the only company that possessed the authority to make the sale.

So far, the western governments haven't treated this threat that confronts them all with the priority it cries for. In Washington, efforts by the executive branch and Congress have been too little and too slow in developing. A task force concerned with the subject reported late in 1996 that "current American policy, substantially constrained by Congress, has clearly been inadequate in encouraging the necessary Russian assistance that would make possible rapid progress in implementing anti-leakage measures. . . . U.S. programs have been set up in a way that precludes swift action and provides little Russian incentive to be forthcoming."[8]

Less obvious and less discussed than the "loose nukes" problem but nearly as serious is the danger of nuclear weapons used by accident or inadvertence. That, too, is a graver problem now than it was during the Cold War, and it was serious enough then. "Never before have so many nuclear weapons coexisted with such unstable conditions," noted the task force report cited above.[9] The reference was to Russian weapons, but it is American weapons and the American command and control system against which the Russian force is targeted.

On the day Rodionov was calling the state of the armed forces "horrifying," he also warned that Russia's nuclear forces could become "uncontrollable."[10] The risk of nuclear weapons being taken over and misused was always seen by experts as distinctly theoretical, not a cause for serious concern. What did worry and still worries closely informed people is the hair-trigger nature of the command system, which has never been widely understood, even in Washington and even inside the government. During the Cold War, each of the superpowers was determined not to absorb a first strike from the other if it could be prevented. However, a crisis would have generated huge and confusing flows of information. The effect would have been chaos. Either side could have been misled by radar blips and/or intelligence intercepts, or even reports from moles within the other's apparatus. False alarms couldn't be excluded, if only because there were some which, had they occurred during a crisis or moment of high tension, could have made matters much worse.

While much of the Russian press was dismissing Rodionov's warning as "hysterical," a colonel named Robert Bykov joined the debate. Bykov had served in the Soviet strategic rocket forces since 1959; for ten years he had supervised his country's military satellite program; from 1976 until 1992, he had served on the general staff, on the defense minister's staff, and then on Russia's chief defense committee. "My extensive experience," he wrote, "allows me to state in all certainty that Rodionov is right. . . . The designers of this system are long retired or worse, but the system remains the principal element of control over the strategic missile forces." Bykov then quoted Rodionov as having said, correctly, "The psychological fatigue of the officers of the strategic missile forces is building up." And, Bykov adds, "Few people have paid attention to these words by the minister for the simple reason that very few realize the danger of the unstable psychological state of the officers on routine duty at strategic nuclear control stations. . . . Let me assure you that all the statements by members of the general staff about the impossibility of converting the control system from the routine to full-alert or combat mode without the verification . . . of attack on Russia are sheer bluff."[11]

The concern, briefly, is the state of readiness of the missile forces. It is too high. The danger was never cold-blooded preemption but rather one side becoming fearful that the other side was launching, or about to launch, its weapons and therefore electing to empty its own silos.

A preeminent authority on command and control procedures in the United States is Bruce Blair, a senior fellow at the Brookings Institution. Blair is also very familiar with Russia's system. Among his concerns is an agency, called Impuls, which designs and manages Russia's command and control network and is located in St. Petersburg. Impuls, Blair says, has its share of the problems afflicting most other Russian agencies; its people are not being paid and the best of them are moving on.[12] Since the breakup of the Soviet Union, Blair writes, "the risk of a breakdown in the control of [Russian] nuclear weapons has grown." Blair has a long list of reasons for his grim assessment, including these:

- [A]s the cohesion of the Russian military weakens, the danger of unauthorized actions by weapons commanders and custodians grows.
- Convulsions at the top of the nuclear chain of command in Moscow could occur, given an unstable political system that still lacks effective institutional checks and balances. This weakness may be compounded by the general staff's possession of the codes that enable senior officers to initiate a missile attack independent of political authorities.
- Russia's nuclear strategy . . . still rests on a philosophy of "launch on warning"—that is, launching Russian missiles *before* incoming enemy missiles arrive . . . the inherent danger of this quick-draw posture is compounded by the deterioration of Russia's early warning network, which is falling on hard times like the rest of its military infrastructure.
- Russian military planners are looking at a steep decline in the combat readiness of Russia's least vulnerable forces—submarines at sea and mobile land missiles in the field. . . . If Rus-

sia faced a foreign missile attack and if their current strategic forces were not launched promptly on warning, then only a very small fraction of their arsenal—and possibly none—would be able to retaliate after absorbing the attack. Compounding Russia's problem are the new D-5 missiles on U.S. Trident submarines, whose accuracy and short flight times reinforce Russian reliance on quick launch.[13]

Curiously, nuclear weapons have never been exposed to the same degree of scrutiny by American public opinion as other issues. If they had been, topics such as protracted nuclear war or limited nuclear war, which once preoccupied America's nuclear priesthood, would have been lost in ridicule.[14] We used to think, reasonably enough, that a more benign environment would remove, or at least narrow, the risk of a nuclear weapon or weapons being used. The irony is that the risk has become considerably larger.

Europe's Keeper

A reliably good relationship with Washington is what all European governments—major and minor, France included—are seeking to maintain or develop. Among the perverse effects of the Bosnian affair, however, is the extent to which it has persuaded Americans that Europeans could and should have bestirred themselves to settle it. Europeans, conversely, had all but determined that they could no longer rely on America because two administrations had seemed to be dodging serious involvement with the conflict in the Balkans, breeding ground of Europe's wars. Anyone who reviewed the behavior of American and European leaders in the early days of the fighting could be excused for judging it irrational or worse. At first, all of them saw it as a problem for Europeans to deal with. Geography argued for that, and so did history. European powers may have failed in the past to cope with turmoil in Yugoslavia, but that was before France, Britain, Italy, and, above all, Germany were cemented together in a single community. Moeover, since the larger part of Yugoslavia's trade was with the EC countries, it seemed as if they had leverage. Desert Storm had been mainly an American show. Yugoslavia would become a test for a community that was segueing into a common foreign policy, or trying to.

There was no argument from Washington, where involvement in Balkan troubles was judged to carry huge risks and little chance for political gain. There developed a strong preference not just for letting the Europeans manage Yugoslavia but for pushing them to do so. Various senior officials argued that Europeans would fail the test and would thereby be reminded of their continuing need for a strong American presence. That, of course, is what happened, to the ultimate cost of all parties.

Perhaps unavoidably, America continues to rank high on Europe's list of anxieties. A sizable segment of American opinion, some of it centered in Washington, has wanted to reap a peace dividend, in part by spending a lot less for European security and, in the bargain, writing off NATO as a relic of the Cold War. Europeans can only hope for the best, aware that the larger part of the U.S. foreign policy community feels as they do about the importance of the American presence, not to mention NATO as the essential vehicle for this presence. Briefly, it isn't a potential threat from Russia or anywhere else that most worries European governments but rather the prospect of America reducing its role in their affairs.

A debate on NATO—its purposes and role—may at some point be required. The argument for sustaining the United States' commitment to European security, along with NATO itself, is straightforward, if less self-evident, than during the Cold War. There remains a military purpose in that the alliance is judged a deterrent to and protection against any aggressive tendencies that could threaten member countries. Also, for now and the foreseeable future, any European-based coalition that is engaged in more plausible contingencies such as peacemaking or peacekeeping ventures outside the NATO area will require, at a minimum, the intelligence and logistical support that America provides.

American forces deployed in Europe cost about $2 billion more than if they were deployed in the United States. This investment may be considered among the best returns on the defense dollar since, as before, it allows America to defend some vital interests on other than American soil. Without NATO, America would barely have been able to wage the Gulf War.

At a more political level, NATO and the American role are seen as discouraging any tendencies toward renationalization of defense within the alliance that might arise from hard times and a breakdown of institutions. The temptation to renationalize is not and isn't likely to become a problem, but European societies cannot avoid thinking about the so-called forces of history. Without an American presence, Germany's neighbors would worry about being dominated. France, in particular, needs to feel comfortable about its partnership with the Bonn-Berlin Republic. As for Germany itself, without a credible American involvement, it would surely concern itself with a potentially renewed threat from Russia and the lurking instabilities in east-central Europe. With Germany then beginning to provide for its own security, Russia, whatever its difficulties, would respond in kind. Briefly, nationalism could be revived in western Europe, revanchism in Russia. We could begin to see the reappearance of competing coalitions of the kind that did so much damage in the past and that the multinational structure was designed to discourage.

America is a European power, as two world wars and now Bosnia have demonstrated. The departure of the explicit threat they shared hasn't lessened the stake of either Europe or America in their relationship. The United States' interest currently lies in trying—helping—to contain and limit the uncertainties that run across all of Europe now. If Europe's moorings weakened again,

Washington could become dangerously muddled. As in the 1930s, the temptation for America to draw in on itself would be strong.

Inevitably, the habit of close consultation between Washington and its chief allies has shown signs of serious wear; it has at times broken down, notably over Bosnia. And the inability or unwillingness of European states to manage this and other woes has created a deepening melancholy. Briefly, Europeans are wondering whether their problems may not be too much for them.

Passive Germans

Perhaps inevitably, much of what Europeans once took for granted is under heavy pressure. We see a decline of confidence in those icons of the post–World War II order, the European Union and the ultramunificent welfare state. Whether the fortunes of the European movement have crested, at least for the time being, is a debatable proposition. If they have—if the European Union is unable to develop more cohesion—there will be increased pressure on the Franco-German relationship. Pressure on the welfare state is adding to the difficulties of both countries. Both must also confront the uncertain prospects for a quieter time in the Balkans.

Germany and France, however, remain the societies that matter most. One is the strongest by any measure except military power, although it does have one of Europe's two largest armies. The other has the most disposable military power and the most reliable inclination to use it in defense of its interests. Arguably, American interests, along with all Europe's, would suffer if either France or Germany elected to go its own way or was isolated from the other.

With a bit of luck—that is, absent some seriously destabilizing development—the special Franco-German link should survive the current difficulties, even though others, probably more serious, lie ahead. (It recalls, some say, Woody Allen's comparison of a relationship with a shark's need to keep moving forward.) And given the habit of routine consultation at the leadership level, the arrival of President Jacques Chirac in the Élysée Palace put the collaborative habit under serious strain. For the first several months of his presidency, France seemed free-floating, with no one at home in Paris for Germans to talk with. It was a shock. The situation has greatly improved, but whether Chirac develops the collegiality with Chancellor Kohl that has characterized the relations of virtually every German chancellor since Konrad Adenauer with his French interlocutor will depend on whether they continue to regard their interests as being alike.

Like its neighbors to the east, not to mention Russia, Germany has veered into an intensely transitional phase. Prior to unification, it reaped the benefits of passivity. As a divided frontline state with a past to overcome, its economic policy could serve as its foreign policy. The role of benign and deferential welfare state came easily, and Germans drew a high measure of comfort and security from their membership in the West's two best clubs: NATO and the EU. Unification changed all that. Overnight, Europe's center of political gravity shifted from Paris to Bonn, and Germany was once again positioned to play a dominant role.

European security will, of course, be strongly influenced by how Germany exercises its influence. The mist that obscures the question—a more Europeanized Germany, a more Germanized Europe?—blurs the prevailing German attitude toward security. The attitude thus far reflects a studied disinterest in security problems that is only natural in a society bent on absorbing the lessons of history. Unification is said to have sharpened the attitude; the 16 million–strong new citizenry appears to be not just passive but moralistic and insular. Germany is not unaccustomed to being the strongest regional power, but never in the past, as noted, has it been able to look around and see no hostile neighbor. Russia has withdrawn a half-million troops from central Europe and is in the novel position of not threatening any of its neighbors. Still, some part of the German political class—though probably not a large one—feels as if the country, although unified, remains a frontline state, exposed to latent instabilities farther east and the possibility of a neoimperialist impulse taking hold one day in Russia.

The refusal by Germans to be drawn into disputes and crises elsewhere at times conveys a whiff of self-righteousness that has provoked some allied capitals, notably Washington. Paris doesn't mind, since the Germans' passivity plays to France's claim to have a world role—as being willing and able, unlike Germany, to project some power. "We have no understanding of power," says one senior German official who is close to Kohl. "It is seen here as a negative."

Outsiders have commented on what strikes them as a lack of respect by today's Germans for institutions, starting with the armed forces, the police, and other organizations, including large companies, that possess an aura of authority. Germany's experience with its most notorious institutions—the Stasi, the Gestapo, the Wehrmacht—is supposed to explain this disdainful attitude.

As recently as two years ago, German officials who deplore the passive culture and feel that the Bundeswehr should be helping other allied armies control chaos were deeply pessimistic; they felt it would take at least a generation to overcome the society's reluctance to send troops on missions outside the country. Some members of the fellowship of Germany watchers who are themselves German still feel this way. Others sense a marked shift toward a more orthodox view of security. They point to a ruling by the Constitutional Court in 1994 that, in effect, allows the government to send troops to participate in peacekeeping missions authorized by the United Nations and NATO; any such deployment requires parliamentary approval.

In June 1995, the Bundestag did approve Kohl's decision to send eight advanced German combat aircraft—Tornados—to do electronic jamming in Bosnia. The debate was serious and free of polemics; the leadership of the major opposition parties, including the Greens, supported Kohl. Most of the editorial comment was favorable. The outcome of the debate provoked no exuberance on the winning side but rather a sense within the chamber that a precedent had been set. A bit later, the government was able to commit forces to help with implementing NATO's peacekeeping arrangements in the former Yugoslavia; about 4,500 German troops were sent to Croatia to clear mines, repair bridges, and help with logistics; another unit was assigned to the international staff in Bosnia.

What might be called the last hurdle was cleared just days before Christmas 1996, when the Bundestag approved plans to deploy up to 3,000 combat troops in Bosnia; these units—infantry and armored reconnaissance forces—became the first German combat troops sent abroad since World War II. They were the fourth largest contingent among 31,000 soldiers drawn from more than two dozen countries to join the international peacekeeping force there. The Social Democrats and Greens, the main opposition parties, voted with the government to approve the mission.[15] Volker Rühe had already tested the public reaction to the other moves noted above and discovered little opposition to them. Karsten Voigt, the Social Democrats' chief spokesman on defense matters, said, "There is no longer any reason why German troops should not have the same rights and duties as any others."[16]

Skeptics play down the high court's decision and these subsequent initiatives, arguing that whoever is chancellor will decide to take some adventurous step not because he or she has the authority to take it but because the step makes sense and/or the politics don't argue against it. But the skeptics say that Germany doesn't have the forces for anything like a full-blooded role and isn't developing them. To the contrary: Germany's defense spending isn't just low but continues to be much lower than France's or Britain's. In 1995, German defense spending as a percentage of national output was 1.7 percent; both France and Britain spent 3.1 percent. (The U.S. number is 4.0 percent.)[17]

The number of draftees coming into the Bundeswehr is smaller than the number of eligible people who, by claiming to be conscientous objectors, can obtain deferments by signing on for terms of public service. (For now, the army is roughly half professional, half conscript.) Moreover, the length of service for draftees, who can go home on weekends or even live at home, has been reduced from twelve to eleven months; that isn't enough, according to military people, who say it doesn't prepare people to be combat-ready.

When the Bundeswehr was created in 1955, conscription was seen as the army's link to the society; no one wanted to see another professional army. Military training was based on the principle of *innere Führung* (inner leadership). Forty-one years later, in February 1996, France's Chirac startled Germans by announcing that his government would phase out conscription and create a fully professional armed force. Germany, Kohl said at once, would not follow suit; it would maintain conscription and the principle of the soldier as "citizen in uniform," but he expressed the hope that France would keep a "substantial presence" of French troops in Germany.[18]

Germans are upset and defensive about the French move, about which they weren't consulted and which they see as signaling a conscious decision to move away from territorial defense—the German posture—to so-called global force projection. All this confronts Bonn with hard questions about how to size and structure the Bundeswehr. Bonn must also worry about the Franco-German Eurocorps, since France may insist on earmarking it for credible contingencies, for example, missions outside the NATO area.

At present, the Bundeswehr is an army designed to defend German interests on German territory, and it depends on the United States for logistical support. Left to itself, the Bundeswehr probably couldn't support a force of more than 10,000 if deployed outside Germany.

A German-Dutch corps was created in the summer of 1995. During the run-up to joint operations, Dutch Army units, which are fully computerized, were surprised to find their German counterparts still relying on paper and pencil; the Dutch concluded that for the Germans, security held an even lower priority than it did for them.

As seen from Bonn, the threats to Germany are a potential security vacuum in east-central Europe and the possibility of anti-German coalitions being formed. "If America withdrew its forces, we would instantly encounter a constellation of anti-German forces around us," says an experienced member of Kohl's entourage. "Germans are taking America's commitment to Europe for granted," he adds. "As ties within the EU become more important, the relationship with the U.S. becomes weaker. But Americans are either here because they belong here or as guests. They are not guests. America is a European power. The issue is whether we can maintain a conscript army. It is as if the threats have all gone away. They haven't. We are very vulnerable."

Germany's tie to America is obviously less burdened by the past than its relations with neighboring societies are. And as noted, the American role is a source of comfort for Germany's neighbors. But with the certitudes of the Cold War barely remembered, Germany cannot afford to take American public opinion, let alone Congress, for granted. More and more, Europe's strongest power will be seen as having the least willingness to match its economic reach and prosperity with measures to enhance stability in unstable areas. Congress is likely to serve notice on America's allies, starting perhaps with Germany, that America, too, feels overstretched and is confronting pressure to redistribute resources earmarked for defense, not least for defense in Europe.

Coalitions of the Willing

Bonn is probably exaggerating the danger of the prospect of anti-German coalitions developing. Whenever in the distant or recent past Europe's power balance was tilted toward one power, as it is now tilting toward Germany, other states would form coalitions to preserve, or try to preserve, an equilibrium. This pattern isn't likely to develop again, if only because the EU represents and symbolizes the refusal by members, including the strongest of them, to replay deadly balance of power games. Moreover, America is no longer a watchful observer of Europe's balance of power but rather, as a self-declared European power, part of it.

Within the EU, coalitions of another kind will and should develop; "coalition of the willing" is the fashionable term for an inner tier of member countries, whether of NATO or the EU, that elects to perform tasks that other members couldn't or wouldn't take on. Germany's willingness—at least at the official level—to give up the deutschemark—reflects a deep reluctance to exercise dominance. On security matters, least of all, will Germany lead or act alone, certainly not as long as the United States continues to play its current role. The question is whether a better division of labor between the United States and Europe could be achieved—whether Europeans can find a way to assume a larger part of the responsibility for their own security.

Various experienced and committed Europeans have felt over the years that the EU's big three—Germany, France, and Britain—acting jointly and pooling much or most of their defense capacity, should develop a tridirectorate for security. Any such instrument could be closely linked to NATO but available for use in contingencies that did not engage vital American interests.

A second and better-known approach would amount to movement, at least partway, toward a favorite goal of a large part of Europe's foreign policy establishment: a bilateral military alliance between the United States and the EU. Europe's "pillar" would be the Western European Union (WEU), an organization created early in the Cold War years by France and Britain and committed to helping with coordination on security matters. Germany joined a few years later, and there are now ten members. Lacking military assets, this paper organization has drawn much derisive comment, for example, "a cluster of filing cabinets staring at one another." For a time, the WEU headquarters were in London, where it reminded one continental diplomat "of a seedy old hotel in Bournemouth run by the daughter of the deceased owner."

The trilateral approach has the merit of logic but is unlikely to yield results—at least in any formal sense—in the years directly ahead. The key variable, as before, will be America's role—Washington's willingness to stay on course. Given a continued U.S. presence, Britain will feel little need to create a European defense capability that amounts to much or that would carry the risk of suggesting to Americans that Europeans were preparing to take charge of their security. To a lesser but still considerable extent, Germany and France would be reluctant, or at least find it difficult, to move toward a defense directorate. With European budgets continually being squeezed, governments in Bonn, Paris, and London will be hard pressed to maintain something approaching their current defense forces, much less invest in the kinds of airlift and intelligence assets that a more or less freestanding European pillar would require and that the U.S. supplies through NATO. Moreover, not until the three capitals acquire the habit of thinking in common on political issues are they likely to move very far toward joint defense forces, still less toward prompt decision making on the use of such forces.

German integrationists from Kohl on down worry with reason about what amounts to an Anglo-French veto on their efforts to enhance the power of the European Parliament and Commission. In short, Britain, along with France, Germany's supposed confederate, is rejecting what Kohl sees as his vocation—to build a politically cohesive Europe linked to NATO.

Yet the Germans are neither predictable nor consistent. All sides expected them to applaud France's partial (and, it appears, temporary) return to NATO or any other step that had the effect of improving relations between Paris and Washington, their political anchors. Also, Germans are acutely aware that NATO works well when these two agree. Yet the Germans, instead of applauding, at first expressed some skepticism, hinting that the French move could be disingenuous. One wondered: Was Bonn worried that France might be building up its American connection at the expense of the special Franco-German link? Or was it worry that Washington might decide that with France moving back toward NATO, America could lighten its involvement in Europe's security?

Among the hardy continuities that are skewing Europe's approach to defense matters is the absence of communication between NATO and the EU; these are two organizations that were set up for the same purpose—to provide security and stability. Their headquarters are located in the same city, Brussels. The key European countries belong to both organizations. Both are confronting similar challenges in a very different era. And their need for each other should be obvious: a fragmented Europe, as distinct from a community of states, would be less able to sustain NATO as a politically effective instrument. But instead of creating productive links, the two institutions shun each other.

Habits developed during the Cold War die hard. At Maastricht in 1991, the EU laid down a so-called Common Foreign and Security Policy (CFSP). But the institutions were not empowered to do more than member states allowed them to do, thus ensuring an awkward, unworkable system; for relevance, it has been compared to the judicial code of the Carolingian empire. Any member can veto consideration of an issue. Once an item does reach the agenda, all parties must agree on allowing a vote, the outcome of which also requires unanimity. Predictably, the system generates a good deal of busywork; there are thirty or so working groups, which in a year may generate ten thousand cables and hold two hundred or more meetings. On the rare occasion when an initiative is actually agreed on and taken, it may die with the biannual change of presidencies. "Foreign policy is the great failure of the EU," says Giuliano Amato, whom some regard as Italy's shrewdest and most distinguished political figure.

The idea of making Europe less dependent on America is deeply rooted. Over the years, various U.S. leaders have told European colleagues that if they wanted to develop a bilateral alliance with America, it wouldn't be a veto from Washington that would stand in the way. Europeans professed to see a veto, however, and they weren't wholly wrong. They were never in a position to rebalance the alliance significantly; perhaps more important, any ambiguity or perceived weakening of the American military presence and commitment would have carried a risk of being misunderstood by the adversary.

Some rebalancing should now be feasible; the administration of President Bill Clinton has signaled its willingness to support whatever division of labor European members could devise and sustain, provided there would be no cost to security. Clinton said as much at a NATO summit meeting in January 1994, and Europeans regarded the offer as serious. And if, as they believed, the United States was preparing to shed some of its obligations, Europe would have to pick up the slack.

At Maastricht, EU members wrote some treaty language that seemed to give them a defense component in the form of the WEU; the two institutions were being tied together, or so it seemed, but actually nothing much happened. France and Germany pushed for the merger, but the British, Dutch, and Italians resisted; they wanted the WEU linked instead to NATO, where Europeans could draw on American assets and thereby avoid having to spend money they didn't have on developing similar assets. The WEU, which is now based in Brussels, still doesn't have an integrated military command structure or much in the way of airlift for moving troops quickly to troubled areas. Nor can it begin to match the kind of advanced intelligence assets that the United States makes available in NATO; it has a staff of only one hundred at its Brussels headquarters.

Curiously, only Germany was for a time pushing to make the WEU the so-called defense arm of the EU. Britain would have none of that, and the idea no longer seemed to hold much appeal for France. But early in 1997, France abruptly joined Germany in proposing that EU members absorb both the WEU and its commitment to mutual defense. It was hardly a serious proposition: The EU's four neutral countries—Ireland, Sweden, Finland, and Austria—were clearly unwilling to take part in a military tieup, and Britain would surely veto the idea. Bonn's position seemed to reflect still another effort to keep the EU flame alive.

In the end, NATO may become responsible for large problems, including potential crises, with the WEU being authorized to take a modest role in peacekeeping operations and humanitarian ventures. And it may fall to the WEU to nominate the deputy supreme allied commander, Europe (SACEUR) who would command the European element within NATO. However, the WEU link that matters will be with NATO, almost certainly not with the EU. As for Europe's common foreign and defense policy, it's unlikely that members will manage to give it any more credibility in the years ahead than they did at Maastricht. Decisions will continue to be taken by consensus rather than majority vote.

A sense of impending crisis was evident in Chirac's decision to move toward NATO late in 1995. France had never excluded the possibility of returning to the alliance's command structure, noting only that it couldn't rejoin it as constituted. Bosnia taught not just the French but also the Americans a lot they hadn't known about the structure and process of decision making. The U.S. military grew to accept the need for renovation, not because of pressure from France but because it needed to be done. With the superpower threat gone, pressure developed to have fewer elements— fewer shoulders bearing stars. NATO's effort to halt the conflict in Bosnia and then to stabilize an inherently unstable situation pointed up the need for a leaner, meaner organization.

Agreement that less is more is progress. Agreement on the design of a lighter, more flexible command structure is more of a reach and will take some time. What France appeared to want was a distinctly European command within NATO, one that would deal with contingencies that didn't engage American interests. By mid-1996, Washington's ponderous bureaucracy was ready to meet the French about halfway. In June, NATO foreign ministers met in Berlin to begin renovating the command structure. Some "Europeanizing" in the form of combined joint task forces was agreed on. The idea was that NATO units composed of able and willing Europeans and placed under WEU command would handle various military contingencies that didn't engage American interests or require direct American involvement.

France seemed satisfied: "For the first time in alliance history, Europe will be able to express its personality," said Hervé de Charette, France's foreign minister. "For the first time we have gone from words to deeds."[19] De Charette's German colleague, Klaus Kinkel, echoed him, saying, "it is neither in the American nor the European interest that we have to call our American friends each time something flares up somewhere." This move, he added, will make the alliance more a "partnership of equals."[20]

Cosmetically, the step taken in Berlin did create an aura of a separate European defense identity, but actually nothing much had changed. Although France had obtained a fig leaf for its long step back to NATO, no one imagined that any coalition of the willing would want to be separated from NATO's senior command structure, if only because American involvement in any nontrivial operation would almost certainly be essential.

That appeared to be among the lessons of Bosnia. Indeed, as Philip Gordon, an authority on security matters, observed, "a classic and sensible example of an American supported but European manned mission would be a force to replace the NATO troops in Bosnia when the Americans leave. Inauspiciously, Europeans reject this categorically as too difficult without the United States."[21] Yet the debate on the "architecture" of European security seemed oddly detached from the drama in Bosnia.

Much remained unclear after the Berlin meeting. Europe had acquired an outlet for its "personality"—Chirac's term—but what sort of outlet? Would the new units be commanded by a European general appointed by the WEU? Or would NATO pick an officer to manage any strictly European operations? In either case, other questions arose: Did Europe need a four-star general running, say, a rescue operation in the Adriatic? Would he be just sitting around awaiting a chance to leap at such an operation? And who would be in charge of planning for these lesser contingencies? Someone closely linked to SACEUR? Or someone whose NATO responsibilities were vaguely defined? In the Pentagon and elsewhere, it was argued that the alliance shouldn't substitute uncertainty, or ambiguity, for certainties that had stood the test of time and periodic duress.

Within three months of the Berlin meeting, France began pressing to settle the issue prior to the next ministerial meeting: in mid-December. Chirac offered a deal in a letter to Clinton. France would return to NATO's command structure, provided Europe's share of the leadership was broadened. Specifically, Chirac wanted to see a European placed in charge of the allied forces in southern Europe, one of three regional commands. It is located in Naples and commanded by an American. The U.S. Sixth Fleet provides most of the command's air and naval muscle. There isn't a lot else, and, given the scale of America's responsibilities in the Mediterranean and Middle East, Washington would not—could not—yield control of the southern forces.

An exchange of letters between the two presidents settled nothing and left an attentive gallery wondering why Chirac had chosen to make the issue a visible test of strength between him and Clinton; giving ground at that level is very hard politically. The answer probably lay in the contesting priorities that underlie French policy. It was hardheaded realism that pushed Chirac toward NATO in late 1995. It was the ethos of France's role in Europe and the world—his Gaullist legacy, some would say—that provoked Chirac's episodic campaign to raise France's profile in the Mediterranean basin—a French lake, as it has always been seen by many in Paris.

Chirac has two sides. He is, first, an old-fashioned French radi-

cal (that is, a political centrist and economic liberal) and, second, a
Gaullist, perhaps even the keeper of the flame. From side one, he
draws a mystical attachment to France's yeomanry. From side two
comes his predilection for operating on a broad canvas. With the
ploy aimed at the southern command, Chirac was rejecting the
idea of a unipolar world, just as de Gaulle had rejected a bipolar
one. He was also indulging a third, impulsive side—his pronounced tendency to act before he thinks.

Concentrating on the Mediterranean must have struck Chirac
as being useful. The Germans weren't there. To the extent that
France could keep its EU partners focused on the Mediterranean,
they would focus less on the more German-oriented part of Europe. And Chirac doubtless felt he had a pretty good case; that
France's profile should be a lot higher in the Middle East and Persian Gulf.

Chirac must also have reckoned that going to the mat with
Washington on this kind of issue might provide a political bounce
at home. France was mired in serious difficulties, and polls showed
Chirac's acceptance level as having fallen to a historic low for
French presidents. In the run-up to the legislative elections he
would have to dig deep for political gain. It was not likely, though,
that the quarrel over the southern command would have helped
Chirac much domestically. The French people already saw their
country as being back in NATO. France, they thought, had already
worked out a better political balance within the alliance. Whether
the balance was what it should be was an issue for specialists, not
voters.

Chirac's maneuvering over the Mediterranean did work to his
advantage in various European capitals, but just briefly. The Germans, starting with Kohl, always want France to feel good about itself and the amount of water it displaces. And most of France's
partners agree that Europe should have a larger role and more influence in the Middle East. Why not, they felt, let France do the
running? These countries have wanted France to be reintegrated

into NATO, and they assumed it would be, however the dispute between Chirac and Clinton played out. But as the months wore on, it showed no sign of playing out; Chirac was unwilling to settle for less than he had called for. His Gaullist side may have ruled out a deal on other than French terms.

Chirac may not at first have grasped the implications of walking back his decision on rejoining NATO. Or he may have merely ignored them. In any case, outside NATO French leadership may feel as if it has greater scope for independent maneuver. But it also has less influence. French leadership felt betrayed by both Italy and Germany, and Germany's ritual support of its special partner was withdrawn, once Bonn saw that Chirac was making a zero sum game of a silly proposition. The hard reality is that by playing at *cavalier seul,* France is simply pointing up Germany's greater strength and influence. Also, Chirac has known for some time that he must restructure and cut back France's defense industry, end conscription, and otherwise save money. Going back on his NATO decision was sure to add to his long list of problems. Still, that is what Chirac seems to have done. From within and without, he has heard strong arguments to retrace the step toward NATO, but he's not likely to do so any time soon, and the socialist government would probably oppose him if he tried.

After decades of talking back and forth about creating "a separate defense identity," this talk between European capitals is still mostly just talk. Europeans express declining confidence in America's commitment, yet seem no more capable than they ever were of developing some cohesion at the decision-making level. Their dilemma is part of and contributes to the larger problem—a mix of confusion, despondency, and self-doubt that for now and the foreseeable future would appear to be Europe's lot.

Bosnia, of course, added to the self-doubt. Europeans seemed unable to affect the course of events or contribute much to the agreement that produced the uneasy peace. Still, Bosnia was a learning experience. The efforts to calm the situation there began

to succeed when a handful of NATO governments showed firm-
ness and addressed the source of the problems more directly.
Bosnia may have signaled the need for a more consciously pragmatic foreign policy, one that doesn't automatically respond to a
new situation by assigning some multinational institution the task
of dealing with it. The United States and its allies will continue to
rely heavily on institutions, particularly NATO, while recognizing
that new fault lines and a diet of fresh crises and uncertainties may
dictate novel forms of diplomacy. Stated differently, coping with
unfamiliar problems will require regular infusions of political will,
as Bosnia has shown; an episodic need for coalitions of the willing
will reestablish this old reality.

Expanding the Clubs

Finland, Sweden, and Austria have recently joined the EU, and the
enlargement process might continue—more sluggishly, though,
than it should. But the east-central European states that appear to
stand at the head of the line for membership, notably the Czech
Republic and Poland, are actually keener to join NATO than the
EU. Applying to NATO impresses them as a more direct and reliable path into the West's institutional structure. These countries
don't expect the EU to become an instrument capable of providing
security; like other Europeans, they look to NATO and the American presence for that. If becoming part of the EU is seen as seriously important, membership in NATO is judged essential. NATO
is an American-led club, with English as the first language; the EU
will be a German-led club. "It would be good to start [this experi-
ence] speaking English," says an influential Czech official. "We
need to eliminate traditional psychological problems [with Ger-
many]. The Dutch and the Danes have had forty years of alliance
experience to get over their problems."

Most such officials feel that moving NATO in their direction
would have the advantage of further committing America to Eu-

rope's security. "Joining NATO is our basic foreign policy," says a Polish ambassador, adding that Poles "see Germany as well entrenched in western institutions. So long as we see that," he says, "we can accept some German leadership. But America's role is the most important thing for us."

The Poles no longer worry about being threatened militarily by Russia. They do worry about becoming yet again part of a security vacuum in which big powers such as Russia and Germany could exercise influence in different ways. Poles want to avoid replaying the past, in which they were bit players in either condominial arrangements or strategic maneuvering they could not affect. As the Poles well remember, in situations of that kind, the small players competed against one another. Enlarging NATO would put an end to all that, they believe.

Václav Havel considers NATO enlargement as even more important than expanding the EU. He warns that if the West doesn't move "quickly to build a new European order and a new world order, others will take the initiative—and then we would all stand astounded." The spirit of Munich is back, Havel thinks. "I do not have in mind some concrete political act," he says. "Rather, I refer to a mentality marked by caution, hesitation, delayed decision-making and a tendency to look for the most convenient solutions."[22]

However, the importance to his and neighboring societies of becoming part of the EU mustn't be minimized. Most of them are making a fairly smooth transition from the cheerless past to parliamentary democracy and the market-driven economy. But it is still a time of transition. This cluster of countries must continue to develop confidence that they can raise their living standards and sustain them. They must acquire unrestricted access to the markets of western Europe, meaning not just a formal removal of tariff barriers there but also the dissolution of hidden barriers and other contrivances. Enlarging the EU will extend their hope and confidence. Not enlarging it could push some of these societies to regain their pride by rekindling nationalism.

Both enlargement processes are laden with difficulties. Most European members of NATO are neither drawn to the idea of enlarging the alliance nor openly opposed to it; the prevailing sentiment is one of acquiescence. France was probably the least supportive of the scheme, and Germany the most conflicted and worried by it. Most European members may favor NATO enlargement for just the wrong reason: It will provide cover for their laggard progress toward enlarging the EU.

The issue has split the American foreign policy community as few others have in recent years. And the split is not generational; retired diplomats and military figures going at least as far back as the Eisenhower administration may be found on either side of the issue, which for a time divided agencies of government and offices within agencies.

The issue has divided senior members of the same party; NATO expansion was described by President Clinton in July 1994 as being "no longer a question of whether, but when and how. And that expansion will not depend on the appearance of a new threat in Europe. It will be an instrument to advance security and stability for the entire region."[23]

A year later, Senator Sam Nunn, who was then his party's preeminent spokesman on defense matters, asked, "Are we really going to be able to convince the East Europeans that we are protecting them from their historical threats, while we convince the Russians that NATO's enlargement has nothing to do with Russia as a potential military threat?"[24]

Enlarging the EU is a less divisive but more complicated issue. It has had rhetorical support in most EU capitals, but in none of them except Bonn is there any appetite for the enterprise. Indeed, nothing is being discussed with any sense of urgency other than EMU, and that is carrying far too much political baggage. If EMU founders, Germany may feel the need for another European project and push for enlarging the EU. But so far, German advocacy is largely hortatory and aimed at bringing EU members, starting with France, into line on this issue.

Of course, Germans do not want to be the EU's, or NATO's, border country; as members of these institutions, the central European states, especially Poland and the Czech Republic, would provide a useful buffer zone and fix Germany in the middle of Europe. But for Kohl, the political downside is serious. The number of German farmers may be dwindling, but at 3 to 5 percent of the population they could, it is argued, make the difference between winning and losing an election. Kohl favors amending the CAP, but gradually—over a period of eight to ten years. And he is loath to commit regional aid funds to candidate members of the EU, given his voters' unhappiness with the costs of both unification and the EU budget.

For Germany to remain the eastern frontier of the EU/NATO structure would suit France very well. As recently as early 1996, however, Bonn and Paris did agree on one point: the processes of enlarging both clubs should be linked. Russia, they argued correctly, has consistently disavowed any objection to EU enlargement. The case for linkage, as put forward by various European leaders, however, would have sounded more convincing if they had done something concrete about EU enlargement. Paris and Bonn have responded on occasion by suggesting that NATO enlargement could also take a lot longer than Washington has envisaged. And it may. Also, Kohl has had mixed feelings about it. He, too, wants to ensure the security of societies inhabiting the historically troubled plain that separates Germany from Russia. But he has worried that the process of ratifying enlargement in the U.S. Senate could provoke a full-blown debate in Washington over NATO itself.

The idea of edging NATO eastward developed in the days that followed German unification, a time when the restless energy of states was released and much of the talk was about devising a new European security architecture. For a brief time, it looked as if NATO would leave center stage and be replaced there by the EC, as the EU was called before Maastricht, and the thirty-five-member Conference on Security and Cooperation in Europe (CSCE). Washington, it appeared, would have to exercise its influence bilaterally and through institutions such as the EC (of which America wasn't a member) and larger groups such as the CSCE (in which America's vote had no special weight). In some European capitals, the question of NATO's mission became pointed; the threat had gone, and the EC's stock was rising. Washington reckoned that NATO could be the instrument for handling regional issues, but Europeans would not then agree to using the alliance as the place to discuss what are called "out-of-area" issues. EC members worked out a tough response to Saddam Hussein's aggression in Kuwait among themselves, not in the NATO Council.

That all began to change as events—the Gulf War, the Maastricht affair, the dismemberment of and conflict in the former Yugoslavia—shifted Europe's focus yet again. Questions arose over the nature of European security. NATO was judged the centerpiece of any sort of architecture, old or new. But questions arose: Would Russia be part of it? Outside it? Alongside it? And what to do about the east-central Europeans and that troubled plain? No one, including the Poles, was worrying about Russia as a military threat; for the first time in three hundred years, Poland was detached from a Russian sphere of influence. But the Poles had already begun to worry about the appearance of new nationalistic forces within the region. And the possibility of some danger from Russia lying ahead—even if well ahead—wasn't being ignored altogether.

As the Poles, the Czechs, and some of their neighbors began to lobby for NATO enlargement, powerful arguments for and against the proposition began to form; in 1994, with the Clinton administration by then committed to enlargement, a fierce debate within and beyond the government got under way. The case for enlargement has centered on the need to develop and maintain stability in east-central Europe; if this region is left unprotected, the argument ran, Germany will set about ensuring its security by national means; Russia will react similarly; and a set of historic instabilities will reappear.

Membership in NATO, advocates argue, would attract broad support in east-central Europe and help political forces there that were committed to parliamentary democracy. Conversely, to deny NATO membership to freely elected governments could imperil further movement in the right direction and help foment protofascist political behavior reminiscent of the 1930s.

Proponents of what is called "neocontainment"—the hard-nosed position—argued for carrying off the enlargement process while Russia was still governed by moderates and in any case too weak to do more than protest. In Washington and a few other NATO capitals, there are elements, both political and bureaucratic, that have an unacknowledged, perhaps largely unconscious, nostalgia for the Cold War. The presence of a geographically defined and familiar adversary—Russia or, conceivably, China, if not both—would clear the air; it would reduce the influence of other political and bureaucratic elements—those that emphasize arms control and conflict prevention; those that see preventive diplomacy and the United Nations as major stabilizers in world affairs. Reinventing an adversary would simplify the task of justifying defense spending on a scale that reaches the comfort level of various parties within the Washington Beltway and their counterparts in Europe.

Underlying the broader, more moderate advocacy case was a sense that enlargement was essential to NATO's purpose and credibility. It would recommit the United States to Europe's security. The reminder from Bosnia that the Balkans constitute an enduring source of conflict was sobering; ethnic tension, whether violent or nonviolent, threatens European security as nothing else does or probably can. Unless societies in central and eastern Europe can become part of a broad security system, they could become weak and unstable, tempted as in the past to make separate arrangements with one of Europe's major players, notably Germany or France. Any such pattern would seriously weaken NATO and diminish Europe's chances of being able to head off crises and small wars.

The case against enlargement has centered largely on Russia's reaction. What, opponents ask, is the threat that enlargement is supposed to counter? A threat from Russia, they argue, won't materialize unless Russia feels threatened itself, and pushing NATO to Poland's border with Ukraine would be perceived in Moscow as threatening. Apropos, isn't there the danger, opponents ask, that expanding NATO to fill a putative security vacuum in this region would strengthen Russian nationalists and weaken reform-directed moderates? The hard-nosed school, its opponents say, should remember the Treaty of Versailles and its effect on German behavior.

Exactly what lines are to be drawn in eastern Europe? ask the skeptics. Where would NATO's eastern border lie? Would Romania and Bulgaria be inside or outside? The Baltic states? And what is be done about Ukraine's security if three bordering states—Poland, Hungary, and Slovakia—all became members of NATO? For Russian leaders, the Ukraine is a red line.

Ukrainians are said to have mixed feelings about having NATO on their border; the prospect scares many of them, causes others to aspire to membership for their country, causes still others to feel that whatever they themselves decide, Moscow should not be allowed to affect the decision. Ukraine, according to some of its neighbors, has understood for some time that NATO enlargement is unavoidable and that Poland would be the first, or among the first, new members.

In June 1995, the Russian Foreign Ministry leaked a planning document prepared by a group of outside scholars—moderates—who have advised the ministry. The document gave nine reasons for Moscow to oppose NATO expansion, among them the prospect of its leading to the isolation and "Weimarization" of Russia. The document went on to state that expansion would "stiffen military thinking in both East and West, and Russia will lose its major benefit from the end of the Cold War: a defacto neutral buffer zone on [its] Western border."

The sense of creeping "Weimarization" had been communicated

a year earlier by Sergei Karagonov, one of the planning document's authors:

> Russia already has many elements of the Weimar situation—a feeling of national humiliation due to the dissolution of the Soviet Union, high inflation, growing unemployment, and the low and falling living standards of large groups of the population. The only factor missing is the feeling of being unfairly treated by other countries. No one could question the right of NATO to widen its membership or of East Central European nations to apply for NATO membership. But the price could be the creation of a fully fledged Weimar syndrome in Russia.[25]

On either side of the Atlantic, some of those party to the debate argued that NATO enlargement should proceed but at a pace that did not interfere with or upstage a related activity called "Partnership for Peace." PFP, as it's known, was launched early in 1994 and designed to promote military cooperation, especially for peacekeeping operations, between NATO and the countries of central and eastern Europe, most of which wanted to join NATO. Its goal, as Catherine Kelleher, a former senior fellow at Brookings who became a ranking Pentagon official, has written, "was to buy time and stability, particularly against a premature offer of membership in NATO. . . . Moreover, it was a visible, positive channel through which to engage the 'willing,' those states that by their behavior would approach NATO standards and express similar values."[26]

By the end of 1994, twenty-three countries, including Russia and Ukraine, had joined PFP, and it was becoming controversial—criticized both because it denied immediate membership in NATO to various aspirant countries and because it could be construed as giving Russia a veto not only over the behavior of such countries but also over NATO itself.[27]

PFP acquired a following both in and out of governments by seeming to offer something for everyone: countries that were judged able and willing to meet the criteria—political, military, and economic—for NATO membership at some point could prepare themselves by taking part in PFP; countries that would be unlikely to meet the criteria would nonetheless acquire a useful association with NATO. And PFP, it appeared, would buy time that could be spent defusing the issue with Russia over NATO enlargement.

Why not, asked partisans of PFP, get it up and running before grappling with the array of issues arising from NATO enlargement? The answer is that PFP was and remains a good idea, whether as a bridge to enlargement or as a long step toward extending security arrangements eastward; but enlargement, inevitably, became the main event once NATO pronounced in its favor.

LARGER QUESTIONS LIE ahead: Will the commitment to enlarge NATO be upheld by the parliaments of NATO's members? Will the two enlargement processes eventually merge and go forward together? Almost certainly not.

Next, can western governments maneuver this medley of change without taking parallel steps to enlarge Russia's role in Europe's security system? The answer to this question must be no.

Most Russians are unconcerned about NATO enlargement because they are looking only inward. But a large and significant body of opinion, while accepting that enlargement is not anti-Russian in design, feel strongly that it would have the perverse effect of isolating Russia—of excluding it from European security issues for the first time in three centuries. (Russia's neighbors would say, correctly, that its involvement with their security amounted to a quest for hegemony.) Much of the political class feels as if it is being excluded from the only club that matters greatly. These Russians do not expect to see a "second wave" of NATO enlargement, and they worry about being lumped in with Europe's lesser lights. As for the bloc of avowed Russian nationalists, it sees enlargement as the

Devil's mischief, an idea aimed at not just isolating Russia but keeping it weak and vulnerable.

The nationalists' strong feelings have tended to push more moderate opinion toward a hard line on enlargement. Igor Malashenko, the president of NTV, Russia's major independent television network, says as much. He describes himself as indifferent to NATO enlargement but occasionally obliged by the rhetoric of both Russian nationalists and American boosters of the idea to express himself more negatively than he otherwise would. With communism dead, Malashenko says, many Russians feel the need of an ism to adhere to. "Nationalism is the ism," he says, adding that NATO enlargement is an outlet for it.[28]

Russia could be held responsible, rightly or wrongly, if enlargement falls off the track; there would be talk, advocates warn, of having set a dangerous precedent in the form of allowing a Russian veto of NATO's behavior. Conversely, assuming agreement on some enlargement, NATO members must agree on parallel measures designed to discourage the sort of immoderate Russian reaction that some among them expect and worry about. In short, if this part of Europe is to be part of a zone of stability, Russia will require a role in European security that it feels comfortable with.

Most of the thinking about steps leading in that direction has been done in Washington, far too little of it in Moscow or other European capitals. Yet Russia, as Douglas Hurd wrote some months after resigning as Britain's foreign secretary, "is likely to pose the greatest single problem for European statesmanship in the next decade." And, he continued, "I see no reason of interest or instinct why there should not be an agreed common European policy towards Russia. . . . We would then be a valid partner for the U.S. in tackling what is likely to be our great single joint problem."[29]

Russia should have determined early in 1995, and probably sooner, that NATO enlargement was inevitable and started then to seek an appropriate role for itself. Instead, Moscow continued to complain and sputter.

Russia's leadership doesn't seriously aspire to membership in NATO; it is aware that the country is too vast and varied, its politics too volatile, its direction too uncertain. But neither do Russian leaders, starting with Boris Yeltsin, want to remind their people that, unlike other eastern European countries, Russia cannot join NATO. And some Russians either think they should be invited to join or find the issue a good talking point. Why, they ask, should Russia and only Russia be excluded? The simple answer is that Russia hasn't been formally excluded. The real answer is that member parliaments would be unlikely to approve an agreement that committed them to defend Russia against a threat from China. Also, could Russia's civilian leadership make a convincing case that it exercises reliable control over the country's military establishment, even if it seems to do so? And what about formal Russian acceptance of the borders of various former Soviet republics that are now independent states?

Russia wants mainly to be treated like a great power; it would have liked, for example, to join NATO's key members in a kind of security council for Europe—a decision-making mechanism for which the Bosnia Contact Group could be a crude model. The idea was deeply controversial; members left outside the inner circle would become seriously disgruntled; keeping the alliance on an even keel might have become more difficult. Neither this idea nor any variant that gave Russia a veto on NATO activities would be approved by members. Aspirant members, especially the Poles, would equate any such arrangement with a return of the bad old days of domination by their biggest and strongest neighbor. They would act accordingly.

Still, arranging a soft landing for NATO enlargement has a high priority; NATO's interest lies in helping Russia, as it painfully evolves, to become more of a help than a nuisance or a problem. Russia, after all, could be a help if only because it is as closely associated with real security problems—organized crime, "loose nukes"—as any other country. Granting Russia a meaningful role within the system would respond to the logic of European security as it is most likely to evolve, with Berlin and Moscow becoming the key capitals, along with Washington. And it would serve the deep interests of all members in discouraging prospects, however remote, of Germany and Russia finding themselves alone together again one day.

Next, Washington and other key NATO capitals should make clear to Russians that by folding east-central Europe, a historically unstable region, into a zonal region of like-minded societies, a coalition of the willing and like-minded could work together in trying to deal with various sources of instability that form an arc stretching from the Caucasus westward across the Mediterranean. The alliance's main concern is likely to be a more volatile environment and outbreaks of violence outside its territory. Briefly, if Russians want to be part of the effort to deal with threats to Europe's stability, they must meet NATO at least halfway on measures aimed at helping some of their former client states help themselves by joining the western system.

In turn, NATO members could make life easier on Moscow and on themselves by taking a more subdued line on NATO enlargement. Too much of the talk has been simplistic and shrill, and too little of it devoted to related but less contentious steps. Enlargement would present a smaller target in Moscow, as Malashenko says, if it were discussed more dispassionately. The ratification process will generate discord enough, and there is a serious risk of the debate polarizing views not just between Washington and Moscow but within the U.S. Senate; some members will accuse the administration of isolating Russia's moderates and undermining democracy there; others will accuse it of having bought off Russia with too many concessions.

In the end, maneuvering Russia's acquiescence may prove to have been far less difficult than obtaining approval of enlargement in parliamentary bodies. The costs of bringing in new members could agitate debate in the U.S. Senate and also in European parliaments, especially if EMU was discouraging projects that required serious financial outlays. The issue of EU enlargement could find a place in the Senate debate: EU members may stand accused of hiding behind NATO enlargement in order to avoid opening their club and their markets to their eastern neighbors. Briefly, enlarging the alliance may become a more involuted project than either advocates or critics had expected it to be.

GIVEN RUSSIA'S SINGULAR role as a Eurasian power, other steps should be considered, especially where some of its fundamental interests overlap with America's. America and Russia could, for example, initiate a process that would include, besides themselves, Japan, China, Canada, and the two Koreas. (An empty chair could be left for a presumably reluctant North Korea.) The immediate goal would be creation of a consultative forum called the "Northeast Asia Security Organization" or "North Pacific Security Organization." A move in this direction has been worth considering for several years—perhaps since the later years of Gorbachev's tenure. A still-coherent Russia ought to be involved in a process that deals with real political-security problems, as distinct from misplaced, if predictable, concerns about NATO.

Obviously, any move in this direction would first have to stand on its own—be judged worth doing on its own terms. Still, if it were so judged, there could also be a useful, if indirect, effect on Russia's westward perceptions. After all, NATO involves a relatively small and generally stable area, whereas Russia, like America, has fundamental interests in the northern Pacific.

Moscow and Washington both have to worry about the complex relationships among Russia, Japan, and China, which constitute a serious source of potential instability. China must share their concern, as must Japan, which feels threatened, or potentially threatened, by three countries; China, Russia, and North Korea. The first two are nuclear powers, and North Korea may still try to become one, in which case Japan could be expected to move in the same direction—an act, or series of acts, that would destabilize the region.

As seen from Tokyo, once the Soviet threat vanished, Washington would make trade its first priority and put its political interests with Japan onto the back burner. Yet many Asian and other governments equate stability in the region with strong American-Japanese ties.

In Europe, Russia may be seen as the potential problem, whereas most East Asians see China as constituting the now or future problem, with Russia more or less ignored. But Russia is, of course, an Asian power, too, and one with regional interests. Canada aside, relations among the seven parties noted here are flawed by adversarial pasts of one kind or another and by continuing mistrust. Each of them tends to misread, or is suspicious of, the actions and stated intentions of most of the others.

Organizing a security process built around these countries would be arduous; it would be a case of tiny steps for tiny feet. The sensitivities of North Korea and possibly China could for a time discourage a regional approach. China would be certain to say no if either it or North Korea were identified as "the problem." Tensions between China and other members of the group, notably the United States and Japan, might deepen Chinese reluctance to take part.

Not long ago, Japan and China each regarded its American connection as a buffer against the other. That has changed; China seems now to see the link between the United States and Japan as directly threatening, whereas most Asians rely on that tie to maintain regional stability. But Beijing sees America as engaged in a China-containment policy. Its security specialists expect to see Russia regain a big-power mentality and become once again a force for China to reckon with.

Tokyo, Moscow, and perhaps other regional capitals have roughly similar views about China, including these: China must be involved in multilateral and bilateral dialogues on regional security; China will seek new sources of energy and land; the number of Chinese coming into far eastern Russia will increase steadily, and Russia will be unable to curb the inflow; China is key to solving most of the issues that could threaten regional stability.

Japan might be reluctant to take part, given the dispute over the Kurile Islands; chances are, however, that Japan would want to be part of any exercise that involves the United States in direct talks with Russia, China, and perhaps South Korea. South Korea could be cool to the idea of talks on security with Japan, even though both parties recognize their need to consult on problems that confront them impartially. The point is that some or most of these countries would probably find it easier to discuss some problems in a small regional framework than to do so bilaterally. Canada could help, since it has probably given more serious thought to security in this region than any of the other parties has and might be able to soften rough edges and mediate differences. And almost certainly, the direct involvement of the various defense and foreign ministries would enhance the prospects for making something happen.

This idea is suited to a time of multipolar diplomacy—one in which scattered security problems may defy immediate comprehension and the agenda is crowded with large trade and financial issues. And we see the limits on older institutions, some of them, notably the United Nations, overburdened, underfinanced, and politically vulnerable. Regionalism, in whatever form, is becoming a steadily more important force, politically as well as economically.

WHETHER AN EXTENDED zone of stability comes about will be largely determined by two variables: how Germany manages the space between itself and Russia, and how Washington exercises its leadership. Will Germany succeed in arranging to exercise its influence in this region through the EU, or will it have to do so in the more familiar way, a possibility mentioned in the Lamers-Schauble paper cited in Chapter 4? Germany is the only member country that strongly favors expanding the EU eastward. Germany, Kohl has said flatly, "cannot remain indefinitely Europe's eastern boundary."[30]

Communication between EU members and potential members isn't good. Some aspirants, including the Poles, tend to see the process as one in which current members ought to adapt the institution, starting with its agricultural policy, to assist the cause of newcomers. These candidates have not fully accepted their own need to change some of their ways so as to be able to conform to the more rigorous culture of the EU.

Poles, for example, have tended to regard EU enlargement as more symbolic than NATO enlargement, which seems very real to them. And it's unfortunate that EU enlargement has not received the same attention in Warsaw. Poland needs the discipline of the EU's body of rules and regulations, toward which the attitude of Polish officials is often described as cavalier. Some of these officials are said to be unnerved by the prospect of having to adapt to a customs union and the free movement of labor and capital.

Hungary has more of an EU focus than Poland and has taken a more realistic approach to the membership criteria. Unlike Poland, Hungary tends to see Germany as more of a patron than a threat. Hungary's burden of debt is a problem, however, and too much of its financial base is absorbed by debt servicing.

The Czech Republic and Slovenia are the best candiates for EU membership, since meeting the criteria, whether economic or political, is not a major problem for either of them. Slovenia has no social problems and is very rich; it is a net importer of agricultural products, and half of its trade has been redirected to EU members.

The Czechs are a close second. Their per capita wealth is nearly as great as Slovenia's. They don't have much agriculture. And they say they neither need nor want the regional aid that the EU's southern-tier members, notably Portugal, Greece, and Spain, have required. (These countries regard the EU's further enlargement as a threat to their claim on this largesse, at least in the amounts they are accustomed to receiving.)

The three Baltic states are eager to have EU membership, less for economic advantage than because they know that their chances of gaining entry to NATO are small and that the next best refuge would be the EU. All three should be encouraged to apply, and Estonia deserves to be considered, along with the Czechs, in the first wave of negotiations, whenever that may be.

Both clubs always intended to limit the initial rounds of negotiations to a very few candidates, starting with those who came closest to meeting the political and economic criteria for membership. Some combination of Poland, the Czech Republic, Hungary, and Slovenia were expected to lead the way. France pushed hard but unsuccessfully to squeeze Romania into the NATO enlargement; besides providing some geographic balance, Romania would lean closer to France than to Germany. There is, of course, Russia to consider. Restricting the enlargement of each institution—in strict accordance with criteria—might help to persuade the Russians that these moves are not directed against them. And since enlargement in either or both cases could be more protracted as well as methodical than one might assume, Russia should and probably will reconcile itself to a creeping, nonthreatening zone of stability. But with NATO being enlarged, EU members, starting with France, will feel less willing, or pressured, to expand the other club, in which case all of Eastern Europe, including Russia, will look upon the U.S. and Germany as the sole patrons of regional stability. Most of Western Europe's relevance should then further decline. Also, NATO enlargement could run into heavy weather. EU members might stand accused in the U.S. Congress of hiding behind it in order to avoid opening their markets to neighbors farther east.

BOSNIA PREEMPTED THE time and energy of major western capitals, including, of course, Washington. And the situation in the larger part of what was Yugoslavia remains volatile. Yet Bosnia not only called into being a coalition of the willing but may have provided an opportunity to build on; the presence there of American troops suggests as much. The participation of German combat troops in an operation outside the NATO area offers a possibly important precedent. The NATO command structure is being renovated. Briefly, the alliance is shaky, but less so than it was when the crisis in the Balkans was building up.

Still, Europe's decline of confidence and its current weaknesses reinforce the need for American leadership. Because the United States' role is so critical, many Europeans are driven to shrill comment and worst-case assumptions about what they think is going on in America; the concern about American neoisolationism and retreat from the world is unavoidable, if only because Europeans see the signs and hear the voices. They may hear members of Congress asking why the United States is deploying 100,000 troops at a high state of readiness in Europe, whereas its allies there have in many, if not most, cases reduced their combat readiness and defense capacity.

Americans can also see that as the EU expands by taking in neutrals, such as Sweden, Finland, and Austria, not to mention the east-central Europeans standing in line, it is likely to become less rather than more coherent politically. Add to that uncertainty a redistribution of power between capitals, Brussels, and regional entities, as described in Chapter II. Eastern-based organized crime is spreading its wings and may or may not succeed in forcing closer cooperation among hard-pressed national governments. It will probably sharpen the competition between national police organizations and their regional counterparts.

Although national security in the familiar sense has become the least of Europe's current concerns, it could become a problem unless the pattern of weak, otiose governments unwilling to take steps jointly that they can't take alone changes. It isn't likely to change in the near future. If it doesn't, a contagion of angry ethnicity and bilateral maneuver of the traditional sort—insecure societies in central and eastern Europe refashioning alliances with past patrons—could begin to afflict central and eastern Europe.

Although unthreatened militarily, European members are insecure. Their insecurity is fed by the welfare state's increasing vulnerability; by the weakness of leadership; by immigration and the threat of more to come; by overly regulated economies and a sense that wealth-creating dynamics lie elsewhere in the world, in America first and foremost. Insecurity and self-doubt may be deepened by the effects of the drive for a single currency; these might also affect prospects in Europe for ratifying NATO expansion, if the costs of the project become an issue.

But NATO will change; it has even begun to do so. In this new and different environment, the treaty's pivotal Article V, which provides that an attack against one member "shall be considered an attack against them all," is of declining relevance. And as members, some of them anyway, are obliged to focus on genuine threats to stability, most of which lie south and southeast of the NATO perimeter, the alliance will change that much more. The one constant will be the American role; it will remain dominant because a more European alternative won't emerge. In making and fine-tuning European policy, Washington must take account of changes, especially those that may widen differences between the key players, Germany and France. With a great deal at stake, Washington will have to try to influence the changes while accepting, first, that America's leverage and options do have limits;

Britain, under Blair, should help by adopting a less complacent approach to European policy and (*pace* Paris), just as important, building a strong partnership with Germany, France just might develop a pivotal role; the question is whether Paris can allow itself to draw closer to Washington. France badly needs more structure, starting with a stable and productive transatlantic relationship. On NATO matters, Chirac may one day move at least halfway in Washington's direction, even if Franco-American tensions, sometimes accompanied by shrill comment, blur France's larger interests.

A coherent policy of parts is essential. For now and the foreseeable future, any such policy design will have to come from Washington and will have to bridge contesting interests in central and eastern Europe. Germany must be made to feel secure and protected from the forces of history, including its own. The American interest is, or should be, clear.

CHAPTER VII

THE TROUBLED
MEDITERRANEAN

In the Mediterranean—fountainhead of primal cultures, enduring myths, and enduring conflicts—the prospects usually range
from dim to dark, with here and there a gleam of hope. Spain
has interred the troubled past and become a functional, multiparty
democracy. Also, in 1996, the political right came to power demo-
cratically, a first for Spain. In Italy, the government of Romano
Prodi, like its fifty-three postwar predecessors, may not last very
long but will be remembered as having begun the process of making over the country; if the effort is sustained, Italy in the end
could at long last become a real country, as distinct from an assortment of regions with different economies, outlooks, dialects, and
various other cultural contrasts.

In the larger sense, however, the Mediterranean—west, central,
and east—is as volatile as ever—a series of accidents waiting to

happen. Little if any effort has been made in western capitals to treat them within a coherent strategy or framework, mainly because that has defied doing. The area extending from North Africa's Maghreb in the west through the Levant and Turkey is a jumble of disconnected issues and problems; some of these, as in Cyprus, the Aegean, and the Adriatic have deep and tangled roots. A few, as in Algeria, are of recent origin. Most have a pathology that mixes political, economic, and social ills. All harbor violent tendencies that are potentially explosive. Together, they form a rather porous frontier that separates the less troubled societies farther north from multiple threats to continental stability. Streams of unwanted refugees have provoked a backlash and extremist political sentiments in various regions and entire countries, notably France and Italy.

Washington and allied capitals are mainly concerned with the peace processes in the former Yugoslavia and the Middle East. They also share an abiding concern with the intractable Cyprus problem. A long file of special envoys is usually hovering around the island, trying to budge the unbudgeable. In 1996, for example, Washington, Paris, London, and the United Nations all had special negotiators beavering away on Cyprus. However, the French, like the Italians, see the chief threat to their own security as lying due south, in the Maghreb. Washington worries a good deal more about Turkey's difficulties and would like to see its allies treat these with more sensitivity and accord them more importance. What befalls Turkey and its problems, after all, would seem to bear more directly on EU members than on the United States. As a member of the EU, however, Greece can often skew the policies of other members regarding Turkey; but that is only part of the explanation for what, on balance, is the oddly erratic approach of most EU members. They tend to see Turkey as neither this nor that—in any case, as not really part of Europe.

Yet only Turkey lies either close to or at the center of most of the gravest threats to Europe's peace and well-being. Indeed, Turkey is actually enclosed by them. Turkey can be compared to Russia—big and raw, insecure and divided, high-maintenance but very important. Curiously, the degree of public discussion of Turkey, especially in the media, falls well short of its heavy bearing on the interests of its neighbors and a variety of other nations. One hears and reads far more about the other key actors—Israel, Syria, Cyprus, Iraq, the belligerent tribes of the Balkans. Turkey is directly involved with them all, as well as with the newly independent states of Central Asia and the Caucasus and the competition with Russia and Iran for influence in some of them. Besides all that, there is a more immediate focus of Turkish anger and anxiety—the civil war waged since 1984 with Kurdish separatists in its southeastern provinces that periodically spills over into Iraq. Briefly, Turkey is the arena for a persistent clash of diverse forces.

War between Turkey and Greece is one of the accidents in waiting. It almost arrived in January 1996. The issue was control of Imea, a tiny, uninhabited islet just off the Turkish coast in the Aegean. Had the oncoming collision not been turned aside by American diplomacy—conducted literally overnight—the eastern Mediterranean might have become a war zone for a long time to come. Of course, it may yet become one. Nineteen ninety-six was the year in which outside parties, starting with the United States, France, and Britain, were determined to settle the Cyprus issue or at least to set it on the path to closure. But as in the past, their reach exceeded their grasp, not to mention far exceeding the willingness to settle on the part of the Greek and Turkish Cypriots. The year ended with passions in Cyprus running measurably higher than at the start and the pace of an irrational arms buildup accelerating.

The Aegean looked even more menacing. Through the Law of the Sea convention, Greece had acquired a legal right to extend its territorial waters in the Aegean from six to twelve miles. Doing so would deny Turkey's major ports, Istanbul and Izmir, unimpeded access to the rest of the world. The Aegean would become "a

Greek lake," the Turks said. Tansu Ciller, who was then the Turkish prime minister, warned Greece that to exercise its right would be "a cause of war."[1] And her government pointed up the warning by disputing Greece's claim to various islets in the Aegean.

Turks regard the Aegean as a river running between a country of 65 million and one of only 10 million. For Greeks, it's not a river but an archipelago of three thousand islands. Only three hundred of these, including Crete, are populated, but close to one third of all Greeks live on them. Greece is prepared to go to war to protect its interests in the Aegean—interests that include sovereignty over the islands as granted by a complex set of international agreements dating as far back as the Lausanne Treaty in 1923.

Greece was ready to fight for Imea but has no interest in an armed conflict over Cyprus and, if possible, would avoid involvement in one, despite the continuing arms buildup there. A glance at the map partially explains why; Cyprus lies well away from Greece and close to Turkey. Moreover, Greeks worry that Turkey, the larger and more powerful entity, is seeking a casus belli, a concern that puts any Greek government under pressure to be no less militant—to avoid any appearance of appeasing the Turks.

A settlement that meets the major concerns of both sides isn't difficult to work up; the outline of one is fairly clear. Turkey must have assurances that the Aegean won't become a Greek lake. That would require Greece to shelve its claim to twelve-mile rights there and accept the status quo. In theory, the Creeks should have little difficulty in conceding that point, since they are a maritime people and believe strongly in freedom of navigation. In turn, however, they would have to be formally assured that Turkey won't try to turn the Aegean and islands controlled by Greece into a Turkish sphere of influence. Each party should agree to forgo exhuming international agreements affecting the issue. In theory, that shouldn't be so difficult; Greece and Turkey have lived with the status quo for quite a long time and ought to be able to freeze it. Parallel progress on other contentious issues, starting with Cyprus, would help. So would a nonaggression pact perhaps guaranteed by NATO.

Cyprus is more complicated; optional paths to a settlement there are more numerous but harder to envisage, first because the leaders on both sides are unable and/or unwilling to bend their positions. Just about any settlement, they know, would have to be built around a bicommunal, bizonal federation, one that would uphold the political parity of the two communities. However, the parties are far apart on how to define the terms "bicommunal" and "bizonal." The Greek Cypriots want the authority of the central government to cover the entire island. They exclude the idea of a separate Turkish–Cypriot state in the north, which is the part of the status quo that the Turks seem unwilling to give up even when they talk about accepting a federal approach to a comprehensive settlement.[2]

Officials and diplomats in other capitals differ on whether to concentrate on solving Cyprus first or the Aegean, or to put the two disputes onto parallel tracks. The Aegean issue is less complicated but more explosive, the level of concern in Ankara and Athens more intense. Still, while some officials and experts, bearing painful memories of failed efforts to settle Cyprus in the past, would prefer to try something else, many of their colleagues argue for a Cyprus-first approach. Cutting the knot there, they argue, would enable Greece and Turkey to settle other divisive matters more easily. And not having to worry so much about Greeks and Greek Cypriots would allow Turkey to deal more effectively with the long list of other problems, internal and external, that are crippling the country. As for peacemakers and harried leaders elsewhere, clearing the agenda of Cyprus would mean interring a problem that has beset some of them and all of their predecessors for nearly four decades.

Why not, then, get on with it and put Cyprus onto diplomacy's fast track? The answer lies not just in the stubborn resistance to reason by aging Cypriot leaders. It is partly a case of their patrons in Athens and Ankara, especially the latter, wearying of Cyprus and seeing certain other problems as more pressing. The continuing arms buildup might seem to suggest the contrary, but that is only a manifestation of the inherent madness of the problem. Cyprus is of no real strategic importance to Greece (despite a new common defense doctrine), and its people are less self-consciously Greek than are, say, the island dwellers in the Aegean.

Turkey's army would like to end the military buildup on Cyprus and begin a drawdown, the better to focus on what it sees as more serious threats to security, starting with the civil war with Kurdish separatists. Moreover, Cyprus, unlike the Aegean or the Kurdish problem, is not a big issue in Turkey, and there is no sense of urgency about it. Sympathy at home for the Turkish community on Cyprus is declining. Many Turks see it as an albatross costing the country perhaps as much as a billion dollars per year. Finally, in recent years Turkey has been ruled by coalition governments, all of them unstable and incapable of fresh initiatives on an issue as difficult as Cyprus; Turkey has had six foreign ministers in little more than two years.

Instead, however, European politics may accidentally maneuver this entire muddle onto the fast track. The Greek part, known as the Republic of Cyprus and comprising about two thirds of the land and four fifths of the people, is on a roll—experiencing what could be called an economic miracle. More remarkable, the EU got itself committed to open talks on the republic's accession to membership within six months of the conclusion of the IGC— meaning that negotiations should begin around the start of 1998. This odd development was the price exacted by Greece in return for lifting its veto on Turkey's membership not in the EU per se but in a key segment of it—the customs union. Turkey, of course, has sought full EU membership, but there is little, if any, support for that bid among members. And even the partial step would not have been agreed to but for strenuous behind-the-scenes American pressure on behalf of Turkey.

Within the EU, Greece is judged the EU's greatest nuisance, even though in recent years Britain has competed hard for that distinction. In holding a gun to members' heads on Cyprus's accession, Greece embarrassed the EU and probably damaged its credibility in various places. In principle, most members are opposed to admitting Cyprus, especially just one part of the divided island. An intriguing question is whether the EU will use the leverage it appears to have been handed by Greece to insist that only a unified Cyprus would be eligible for membership. All sorts of other questions arise, starting with whether Greece would veto other candidates for membership if a divided Cyprus was excluded. The Greeks have already threatened to delay enlargement if other EU members tried to involve the Turkish Cypriots in talks on admitting Cyprus. Another question is whether any such arrangement would appeal to Turkish Cypriots. Obviously, it should appeal to them *faute de mieux*. But in Cyprus the thinking rarely takes a sensible direction. On current form, Turkish Cypriots would reject involvement with the EU because Greece is a member. Moreover, they have dark suspicions that the Greek Cypriots, once inside the EU, would use their influence there to recapture control of the entire island.

Rauf Denktash, the Turkish Cypriot president, is a changeless, seventy-three-year-old hard-liner. Predictably, he is strongly opposed to the prospect of the Greek community joining the EU. He said it would "destroy equality between us, and then we would be finished here."[3]

It's not as if Denktash and the Turkish Cypriot community had a menu of good options. Integration with mainland Turkey doesn't hold much appeal for either side. In short, Turkish Cypriots are unable to see beyond a status quo that gives them sovereignty over their patch of ground, even as the economic gap between them and the larger Greek Cypriot community widens dramatically. But insistence on full sovereignty would be a deal breaker in any negotiation aimed at unifying the island. Greek Cypriots are playing an increasingly strong hand and would insist on a single sovereignty.

About the only point of agreement between the two Cypriot communities is the importance of America's role. Greek Cypriots feel that only Washington can influence Ankara. Turkish Cypriots feel that the United States is the only power with influence in both Athens and Ankara. Thus far, however, the United States' role hasn't narrowed the gap appreciably between two parties that seem to feel, or like to feel, as if destiny intended them to hate each other.

Early in 1997, the Greek Cypriots elected to buy a large quantity of Russian antiaircraft missiles of sufficient range to bring down aircraft over Turkey as well as Turkish Cyprus. Predictably, the announced move caused Ankara to warn of dire consequences if the weapons were deployed. "The missiles have increased tensions," said Gustave Feissel, the U.N. Secretary General's special representative to Cyprus. "And the message that they drive home is that the status quo here is unstable, untenable—and unless it is fixed . . . is going to get worse."[4]

American diplomacy seems to have maneuvered the missile deal onto the shelf; and it may not come off the shelf, first because the Greek Cypriots, if they pressed for it, would be seriously undercutting their chances to gain entry into the EU. Chancellor Kohl said privately, after the deal was announced, that a divided Cyprus wouldn't be allowed into the EU. Whether he had felt that way before the announcement is unclear.

As two experienced scholars—one of Turkish Cypriot, the other of Greek descent—jointly argue, it may be that if Cyprus is to have peace "the two ethnic communities on the island must, *largely on their own,* resolve their differences."[5] In any case, whatever deal the communities make would have to be approved by Greece and Turkey.

Some outsiders envisage the EU allowing the present Republic of Cyprus to become a member while keeping an empty chair for the Turkish community. The notion is seen as somewhat analogous to the two Germanys during the Cold War; with unification, all Germany, of course, became part of the EU. Progressive thinkers such as Konstantinos Karamanlis, who was Greek prime minister and president and the most prestigious of postwar Athenian political figures, have felt that a unified, unpartitioned Cyprus should be a member of both the EU and NATO. Movement in that direction would be the best way to settle other issues, they feel, especially the Aegean, where the parties have gone to the brink of war three times—in 1976, 1987, and 1996.

Outside diplomacy may not be enough to keep them from going over the brink during another flare-up. Some small military step, possibly inadvertent, could spill over to the dry tinder of the Balkans and create a contagion of violence—a third Balkan war. Or a renewal of serious fighting in the Balkans, especially if it involved Macedonia, could draw in Greece, Bulgaria, and Albania, as in the past. Whether Turkey would stand aloof, especially if atrocities were being committed against Muslims, might depend on the state of play with Greece in the Aegean and perhaps elsewhere, and who was in charge in Athens and Ankara.

Turkey's Muddle

In 1996, Greece and Turkey each got a new leader who was very different from his predecessor. In Greece, Costas Simitis, the new prime minister, was seen on all sides as being the best and most sensible of the current crop of Greek leaders. "Mr. Simitis," said *The Economist,* "brings a whiff of fresh air . . . carries no taint of corruption . . . [and] is keen to undo Greece's reputation as the delinquent of the European Union."[6] Simitis is well regarded in Brussels and other EU capitals. He studied in England and Germany and discusses problems with Helmut Kohl in German. He is said to have made dealing calmly with Turkey his top foreign policy priority, although that has proved even harder to do than banishing corruption and modernizing the economy. In November 1996, Simitis announced that $17 billion would be spent to "combat the Turkish menace" through the purchase of improved weapons.[7] On security matters, he is judged to have little flexibility and cannot oppose the party hawks.

Simitis had a brutal introduction to the heaviest of his new responsibilities; the near disaster in Imea occurred on his second day in office. The incident was a wake-up call for Greece, according to one of its senior diplomats, who thinks it may have alerted both sides to the danger of leaving things as they are. Simitis, he says, intends to banish these Furies so that he can get on with the job of improving Greece's competitive trade position and opening a new chapter. Unlike some of his fellow Greek moderates, including a few who preceded him, Simitis is described as actually wanting to negotiate a solution with Turkey, as distinct from just maintaining, or slightly improving, the status quo—that is, not allowing the conflict to tilt to the other side's favor on his watch. He wants to move quickly, but among the difficulties he faces is the absence of a senior figure in Ankara for him to deal with. Conceivably, the Turkish military could supply one.

Calming relations with Ankara wasn't made easier by the Turkish elections that brought to power Necmettin Erbekan, the country's first Muslim prime minister in its seventy-four-year history as a republic. Erbekan has taken hawkish views on most issues, not least those affecting Greece, and this has jarred the Greeks. Like most western capitals, Athens has hoped that Erbekan's tenure would be a short one and that Turkey's secular parties could regroup and recapture control. Actually, Erbekan has run a coalition government; his partner Tansu Ciller is the leader of the secular True Path Party, and she has tended to be even tougher on the Cyprus issue than Erbekan. It is an unnatural and fragile coalition. Ciller had opposed the inclusion of Islamists in government, a stand she abandoned when it appeared that her only chance of escaping prosecution for corruption charges was forming a coalition with Erbekan's Refah Party. Within Turkey, this dubious collaboration quickly became known as "the government of secrets."

No one knows much about Refah. Stylistically, it's a blur of disparate elements, some more militantly Islamic than others. Simply put, their goal is to reinvent the state. They are patient. They openly state their intention to capture the state from within—to transform it from a republic built upon the secular principles laid down by Mustafa Kemal Atatürk, the father of modern Turkey, into an Islamic state with Islamic principles and goals.

"Few countries honor their gods the way Turkey reveres . . . Atatürk," wrote Celestine Bohlen in *The New York Times.* His

> military skills and authoritarian hand reassembled parts of the crumbling Ottoman empire and fashioned them into the modern Turkish state. Fifty-eight years after his death, Ataturk's cool blue eyes stare down from the walls of every public building in Turkey, and statues of him dominate thousands of central squares. Here in Ankara, the capital, his mausoleum displays a sublime arrogance that even Lenin, the founder of the Soviet state, never achieved. . . . His philosophy of statehood, Kemalism, is required reading in schools, universities and military academies.
>
> . . . But Atatürk's plans for creating a new Turkish man—a Westernized creature with a new identity, new clothes, a new alphabet and a language purged of alien elements did not succeed, any more than the Homo Sovieticus of Lenin's imagination did.[8]

Refah is different from the two main secular parties—True Path and Motherland—in the sense that unlike them it operates as a political party should. It works the grass roots tirelessly. It has built an extensive organization, whereas True Path and Motherland are both elitist. They are accused, correctly, of being indifferent to the poor and disadvantaged.

Among the immediate questions is whether Erbekan can manage the factions within Refah. It's not likely to break up; it is the best-organized and also the fastest-growing Turkish party. However, the leadership, starting with Erbekan, is ready to continue doing business of the kind that Refah's rank and file doesn't like but that the secular parties and, more important, the Turkish military insist on: continued involvement with NATO and its works, support for Turkey's prospering private sector and its dealings with counterparts to the west, the best possible relations with Washington. Refah reached power with just 21.3 percent of the vote, not enough to permit trifling with Atatürk's legacy of secularism and a unitary state. But Erbekan has a problem. While in opposition over the years, he said things that went against the grain. Now in power he can't stray very far from the political mainstream.

Erbekan, who is seventy-one, has been a major player in Turkish politics at various times and is, in short, a known quantity. Far less well known are the younger colleagues who will sooner or later succeed him as leader. They are more radical and see politics as a means to an end—no more.

Erbekan upset the establishment, not to mention Washington, with a few bold moves, and then was warned not to overreach or go too far. Turkey's military sees itself as the guardian of the republic. It is secular, western in orientation, and fully committed to keeping the memory and spirit of Atatürk alive. The forces it deploys in NATO are second in size only to America's. Moreover, among Turkish institutions, only the military has broad public support. By and large, the public doubts the capacity of politicians of whatever stripe to manage the country's affairs.

There is an elite general staff, a group of about 1,900 officers, who do not take part in decision making down the line and are not subordinate to the Ministry of Defense. They have seized power three times since 1960. They imprisoned Erbekan once and banned him from politics during much of the 1980s. Early in 1997, the mayor of Sincan, a suburban town outside Ankara, laid on a boisterous celebration of "Jerusalem Day" (a day of protest against Israel decreed by Iran). Iran's ambassador came and made a fiery speech, telling the audience not to be afraid of calling themselves fundamentalists. Portraits of leaders of extremist Palestinian movements, such as Hamas and Islamic Jihad, were on display. Tensions between the country's secularist majority and Muslim fundamentalists had been rising sharply; the fête at Sincan was only one of what the military saw as a series of provocations, and it elected to draw the line as clearly as possible. A column of thirty-five tanks and personnel carriers rolled into Sincan. After trying to hide, the mayor was detained briefly. Next and more important, the National Security Council formally handed Erbekan an ultimatum: either halt the anti-secularist activity or face "sanctions." "No steps away from contemporary values of the Turkish Republic would be tolerated . . . in Turkey, secularism is not only a form of government but a way of life and the guarantee of democracy and social peace."[9]

These gestures by the military amounted to a warning and were not intended to be seen as step one in a coup. Whatever their feelings about Refah, these senior officers had decided against unseating Erbekan unless he miscalculated and forced their hand. The incompetence of Refah's predecessor—the True Path–Motherland coalition—horrified the military. It always wanted to see Erbekan's fall too, but strictly on its own, and felt that Refah's mishandling of the deeply troubled economy would accomplish that. By early summer 1997, however, increasing pressure from the military obliged Erbekan to resign in what was widely seen as a "soft coup."

In the past, Refah trimmed on the question of the Kurdish separatists. In power, it had to pursue the civil war no less vigorously than its predecessors did. And Refah, whether in or out of power, has challenged the conventional view of the EU being a good thing for Turkey. For that and other reasons, Refah strengthens the hand of EU members who oppose eventual membership for Turkey on the grounds that Turks are not real Europeans, their country not really part of Europe.

Erbekan's talk of an Islamic NATO and an Islamic common market played to this argument, as did his first foreign visit—to fundamentalist Iran, where he agreed to buy $23 billion of natural gas. His next such visit, to Libya in October 1996, was a fiasco, with Colonel Muammar al-Qaddafi biting the hand that Erbekan had extended in friendship. At a joint news conference, Qaddafi denounced Turkey for having forgotten Islam and putting itself "under occupation" by western powers, an obvious allusion to NATO. He also denounced Turkey's campaign against the Kurdish separatists and called for an independent Kurdish state. (Qaddafi also described Libya as a victim of terrorism, although it is all but universally regarded as a sponsor.) Erbekan, apparently stunned by the tirade, did not challenge any of it, and some politicians in Ankara called for him to resign.[10] The coalition government's foreign minister, Tansu Ciller, herself threatened to resign.

Qaddafi also teed off on a military cooperation agreement that Erbekan's predecessors had made with Israel. The question was whether Erbekan would respect it and, indeed, would approve a provision of the agreement that would be coming up for renewal on his watch. He did approve it, doubtless because he knew he had to. For the same reason—general staff priorities—he agreed to sustain Turkish participation in an operation that allows NATO aircraft based in Turkey to patrol northern Iraq in order to protect the Kurdish population there; not surprisingly, Refah had always opposed this operation, which it continues to regard as directed against a fellow Islamic state, Iraq.

Although Turks see themselves, correctly, as encircled by enemies, real or potential, the corrosive, unresolved Kurdish problem is their dominant concern. And because the struggle weakens Turkey and adds to its vulnerability, neighboring states, starting with Syria, have treated it opportunistically; the relations between Damascus and Ankara are poisonous, with Turks accusing Syria of providing aid and comfort to Kurdish terrorists. Syria sees Turkey's policies, especially its agreement with Israel, as a betrayal of the Arab/Islamic world. Here again, Turks are seen as vulnerable, as having too little understanding of how societies beyond their borders remember the Ottoman Empire. And it is true that a great many Turks see Atatürk's creation as a clean break with the past.

What they don't see is how, when they assert their interests, others do recall the past.

The collapse of the Soviet Union, another break with the past, seemed to offer Turks the chance to expand their influence in newly independent republics in the Caucasus and Central Asia. In 1993, Suleyman Demirel, upon being elected president, said, "In Central Asia, we are the emissaries of Europe. We are Europeans who are taking European values to Central Asia."[11] Although Turkey does offer some of these societies a channel to the West, its efforts to gain political influence, notably in the transcaucasus, have lagged well behind Russia's. It is, or was, a competition in which Russia cleaned Turkey's clock. Moreover, in their bilateral relations Russia has treated Turkey shabbily. Indeed, the most acute source of tension between Russia and NATO lies not in the enlargement issue but in Turko-Russian relations.

Now Turks are beginning to see themselves through the eyes of others, which adds to the ambient pessimism. Greece impresses them as having little incentive to make equitable deals with an adversary that is oppressed by its problems and weakly governed. On becoming prime minister, Erbekan acquired partial control of foreign and security policy; he conceded the larger part of it to the general staff and Ciller, his predecessor and foreign minister. Within the National Security Council, which is composed of the five senior military leaders and five senior political figures, Erbekan became the only "nonsecularist." But continuing to bend to the will of the military on security issues only increased Erbekan's problems with the advanced Islamists within his party. In his instinct and thinking about foreign policy, Erbekan relates to the Ottomans and the glory days. Turkey, he believes, should not be critical of other Islamic countries and should have no dealings with Israel. Nonetheless, he is identified beyond Turkey with policies that run in another direction. Finally, each party to the Erbekan–Ciller marriage of convenience, waited for the other to stumble and each maneuvered from the start to portray the other in a bad light.

For a few western capitals, especially Washington, Turkey is more worrisome than Russia, the society's tolerances closer to being overstretched. The Turkish establishment, which looks resolutely westward, has shared the concern of Turkey's major allies about Refah's priorities and its rising strength and its ability to create a broadly based political organization. Also, with the mainstream parties having made a major mess of Turkey's affairs, Refah got a bit of a mandate and some room for maneuver. Let's see what they can do, said the slice of the electorate that voted for the Islamists.

But with all their weaknesses and vulnerabilities, Erbekan and Refah are in closer contact with the electorate than their rivals are. Unlike them, they don't believe, or pretend to believe, that Turkey is well on the way to becoming a modern western state. They see that the huge efforts that have been undertaken to transform the country haven't yet altered the lives of most people, at least not in ways they approve of. There is massive population growth in the rural areas, but huge numbers of people there are moving to the cities; a half million per year are resettling in Istanbul. The economic reforms of the 1980s, which produced impressive statistics, haven't had much of a trickle-down effect.

Erbekan and Refah are also benefiting from a religious revival, which is hardly surprising. The elite that has governed since the time of Atatürk has made little effort to represent the interests of the country's diverse groups. The crucial question isn't whether or when the military will take control, which it does not want to do. The question is whether this still largely secular society can recover its political balance. It won't unless the the big center parties emulate Refah by working the grass roots and creating broad-based constituencies. The 21.3 percent that Refah got in the elections is probably more than its real strength. What is missing now in Turkish political life is an alternative to Refah. The process of creating one—of modernizing secular politics—must start with pressure from the private sector, according to some Turkey watchers. The private sector is strong and prosperous, but it's also concentrated in the western part of the country; it may be incapable of providing political direction—of transforming elitist institutions.

In any case, the private sector may be denied a political voice. The country's chief business federation has already drawn one sharp rebuff from the military by issuing a report urging swifter progress toward a more democratic society. Although elections are free, Turkey is widely seen as having traveled only part way toward democracy. The business group's report, which appeared early in 1997, offered a number of suggestions, one of which called for abolishing the national Security Council, the military's main instrument for affecting government policy. It also proposed giving Kurds who live in southwestern Turkey the right to educate children in their own language. The reaction to the report from Turkish political figures, as well as military leaders, was described in the *New York Times* as "explosive." The military summoned Halis Komili, the head of the group, and warned him that the report was ill-timed and potentially destabilizing.[12]

Also, the back-of-the-hand and altogether cavalier treatment of Turkish interests by most of the EU membership has disillusioned key figures in the country's private sector. It may also lessen their incentive to play a more active role in political life.

More obvious and hence more important is the EU's silly but worrisome tendency to embarrass, even humble Turkey when the issue of joining the club arises. Turkey, said Tansu Ciller in January, 1997, "could not be excluded from the expanding map of Europe." A few weeks later, on March 4, Chancellor Kohl and five fellow leaders delivered what the *Financial Times* called "an unequivocal rebuff to Turkey's renewed bid to join the European Union." Their spokesman, Wilfred Martens, president of the European People's Party, characterized Turkish membership as "not acceptable." "We are creating a European Union," he said. "This is a European project."[13]

It's not as if Turkey is a plausible candidate for near term membership, not with its human rights record, its sheer size, and its uncertain political direction. But for the EU to slap down Turkey's quest for a more European role and identity is gratuitous and may harm all sides.

Turkey's domestic muddle adds to the pressure already felt by a few western capitals, especially Washington: how to persuade a Turkish leader to take the risks required to bring his military establishment into serious bargaining with Greece's (assuming you could persuade the Greeks). Washington has had trouble developing a coherent policy toward Turkey in the post–Cold-War environment. Turkey's problems bear on U.S. interests, and Washington requires a working relationship with Ankara, even if it's sometimes hard to remember who is in charge there at a given moment and even if that person is the front man for a a crowd of anti-West Islamists.

Ankara has an Israeli card to play in Washington, thanks to Turkey's defense agreement with Israel, but it doesn't know how to play it. Meanwhile, Turkey is demonized on Capitol Hill for its treatment of Kurdish prisoners, human rights in general, the chip-on-the-shoulder approach to Aegean problems, and so on. Moreover, when it comes to defending their interests politically, the Turks are incompetent. Adversary lobbies such as the Armenian-Americans and the Greek-Americans are among the most effective in Washington. The Kurds, too, work Capitol Hill very well and also operate in concert with the Greek and Armenian lobbies. The Turks' paid lobbyists, on the other hand, are regarded as ineffective. The Turks appear to think that the State and Defense Departments, along with defense contractors doing business with Turkey, can and should look after their interests but somehow fail to do so. The Turkish Embassy is less active on Capitol Hill than most of the others and is described as disdaining contact there.

American policy makers must strive to find the right balance between Turkish interests and competing interests. With Refah on what seems a rising political curve, getting that balance right may become a consuming task.

Algeria's Torment, France's Chagrin

None of the problems in the western Mediterranean is yet as demanding as some farther east, including most of those that involve Turkey in one way or another. Still, it should be clear to Europe's leaders that the chief sources of serious future instability not only lie in the Mediterranean but may span it. The savage conflict in Algeria that is believed to have claimed at least 60,000 lives could spread to other parts of the Maghreb and to Egypt, where the tinder is dry and the pathology similar: people cut off from their cultural roots and seeking an identity, especially the young; a future that offers little or nothing—least of all gainful employment—to educated and noneducated youths, many of whom are turning to the principles of Islam as laid down by militants and terrorists; the decline, if not the absence, of peaceful means of political expression.

France, too, is being victimized by the conflict. After 132 years of ruling Algeria, France lost this last of its colonial wars. Most of its *colon* are back in France, but roughly 3 million Muslims, perhaps two thirds of them Algerian, are there as well. For the impoverished and unemployed young, the future can be a boat ride. The greatest fear is that the civil war may provoke a mass exodus, with the largest number of refugees heading to France, a more homogeneous and insular society than many and one whose tendencies toward bigotry are being manipulated by small-minded but resourceful political figures. Immigration is now a major issue in French politics and in hard times could bring down, or contribute to bringing down, a French government.

In Algeria, society is a hostage, trapped between random, indiscriminate violence and the preplanned, targeted variety. Its government cannot cope with either kind. Nor can it create an environment that will deny recruits to terrorist groups. Algeria's recruitment pool is huge. Seventy percent of the population is under thirty, with a median age of seventeen or eighteen, and 70 percent of these fifteen- to thirty-year-olds are unemployed and without prospects. They live ten to fifteen to a room and are unable to marry.

As an independent state, Algeria hasn't always been an unstable place given to violence. Not until 1988 did small groups of militants—"soldiers of God"—present a serious challenge to their secular one-party government, which reacted in a sensible way by authorizing new political parties and agreeing to constitutional reform and a free press. From mid-1989 to mid-1991, as two authoritative figures, William Quandt and Andrew Pierre, have written, "Algeria was probably the freest country in the Arab world. Political parties were formed with abandon."[14]

The most successful of the new parties was the Islamic Salvation Front (FIS), which claimed to be the sole representative of the people. It obtained a clear majority in the first round of elections in December 1991. At that point, the military stepped in to prevent the FIS from taking power. The reactions were predictable, with some Algerians relieved to have been spared being governed by an Islamic party, others feeling victimized by this flouting of the agreed-upon rules that all sides had played by. The military imposed a new president, an experienced and, it seems, well-intentioned nationalist named Mohamed Boudiaf, who didn't last long; he was assassinated by a member of his guard for reasons never made clear. The military then ran the show with their own people, in early 1995 finally settling on an officer named Liamine Zéroual. He was designated to serve as president for an indefinite period.[15]

Even before Boudiaf's death, the FIS had begun a struggle, both violent and nonviolent, against a regime that stood accused of reneging on its promises to open the political process and allow a multiparty state. FIS leaders were imprisoned, and the struggle deepened and spread. The regime insisted that the FIS renounce and condemn the use of violence by its own and other armed groups. The FIS refused to issue any such call until its leaders were released.

Elections were actually called in November 1995, but most of the major opposition parties refused to participate. In any case, only four people, including Zéroual, could meet the conditions for becoming candidates.[16] In a larger-than-expected turnout, Zéroual won handily, drawing 75 percent of the votes, according to the tally.

At first this decisive outcome was seen as good news, since the government was the only stable institution; its opposition was split into numerous groups, some more violent than others. It then appeared that the terror hadn't diminished; the government's ability to protect society from throat-slitting bandits, marauders, and terrorist groups was no greater than before. In fact, the government, once mandated, fanned the flame by issuing a memorandum on constitutional reform whose precise intent was unclear but was widely interpreted as a step back; its thrust seemed intended to outlaw all or most religious parties, barely distinguishing between the extremist and moderate, including the Islamic party that had supported Zéroual in the election. The FIS remained on the list of proscribed groups.

The best-informed Algeria watchers probably belong to the Order of Sant' Egidio, a highly competent Catholic lay organization with special interests in conflict resolution and religious ecumenism. Both these interests drew Sant' Egidio, which is based in Rome, to the Algerian crisis. After examining it, the order convened two meetings of the various groups in Rome over the winter of 1994–1995. The affair was notable for producing a declaration of "values and principles" in which representatives of eight groups, including the FIS, committed themelves to a "rejection of violence" and "consecration of political pluralism." Zéroual's government, which wasn't represented, elected to ignore Sant' Egidio's disinterested, clear-eyed efforts to bridge the gap.

In mid-1996, over a long meeting in the garden of their church in Rome's Trastevere quarter, Sant' Egidio's leadership observed that the people who rule in Algiers still don't understand that the terrorists' chief strength lies in the denial of political expression to Islamists. Zéroual's memorandum, they said, gave terrorists an object to rally around. "Algeria has a lively and mature society," said one of the leaders. "But it needs a peaceful environment in which to express itself." The FIS, he added, must be part of the process of getting there, even under another name, if necessary. Otherwise, we see this moving into "an endemic state of terrorism." The government needs opposition parties, but it doesn't want to negotiate.[17]

The related problem, according to Sant' Egidio and foreign diplomats, is the army; it doesn't recognize the government's need for opposition parties. It is the dominant political force—exercising what some call undue influence and others call control—over Zéroual. And within the army there are contesting factions. Whether its resolute hard liners hold the balance of power is unclear but probable. What is clear is that influential groups within the army and secret services are well known to and in close touch with their counterparts in France.

Algeria's importance to France, politically and culturally, is hard to measure but hard to exaggerate. The economic tie is also strong. About half of the Marseilles economy is tied to Algeria. And the idea of an Islamic regime in Algiers, just two hours from Paris, is simply not acceptable to France. Not long ago, there were about eighty flights per week between Paris and Algiers. But in 1995, after an Air France flight was hijacked, air service was suspended.

Apart from not rocking the regime's boat, the French authorities don't know what to do about Algeria; they are not even sure of how to think about the problem. They see the army, correctly, as the stable element and worry that if it is removed, the entire structure will collapse and give way to chaos and mass migration. But neither do they want to alienate the FIS or some successor, since it may constitute the power structure of tomorrow. Former prime minister Juppé, when he was foreign minister, criticized what he called the regime's "all-out repression" and called for dialogue among nonviolent groups. Opposed to such thinking is Charles Pasqua, who, because he is perceived to be telling it like it is, has made himself one of France's most popular political figures.

Sant' Egidio makes the following points: the French are inhibited by being unable to see beyond their colonial ties; they fear being displaced as the key external power, notably by the United States. But none of the other closely involved European parties—that is, Italy and Spain—is willing, or perhaps able, to take on the Algerian problem frontally.

France does appear to have little leverage with the Zéroual government, which instead may have a perverse kind of leverage with the French. If France tried to pressure Zéroual to take the step he ought to take—opening the political process to nonviolent Islamic groups—he could threaten to reject French economic aid and let Paris contemplate the risk of being blamed if the government in Algiers fell and chaos ensued. In any case, the French refuse to rock Zéroual's boat, if only out of fear that bringing Islamic parties into the government could provoke a new exodus.

In May 1996, the bodies of seven French monks, murdered by Algerian terrorists, were found very close to where they had been abducted—about four miles away. The episode pointed up the weakness of the Zéroual government; it can provide some security, but only where and when it chooses to provide it. Also pointed up was the state of relations between Paris and Algiers—neither close nor productive. France made little effort to find the missing monks because the regime in Algiers couldn't help—or wouldn't.

One French civil servant has broken ranks and attacked her government's policy in a book called *La seconde guerre d'Algerie* and written under the pen-name Lucile Provost. By uncritically backing a feckless regime in Algiers, she wrote, France will pay a stiff price.[18]

The regime persists in highlighting the surreal aspect: toward the end of 1996, it held a referendum asking voters to aprove a constitutional amendment expanding the powers of the president and banning political parties tied to religions. The Interior Ministry reported a turnout of nearly 80 percent, more than 85 percent of which was claimed as a "yes" vote. Opposition parties claimed fraud and reported a "no" vote in big cities and the center of the country of at least 50 percent. "The point of the constitutional changes," editorialized *The Economist*, "is to exclude the FIS, to prevent it or anything like it from having influence, let alone from taking power. The paradox is that this exclusion, intended to bring about peace, may help to keep Algeria at war."[19]

A good model for reforming the political process, according to Sant' Egidio, would be Jordan, where the king did some gerrymandering of voting districts to obtain a pattern he needed for stability. Sant' Egidio also feels that Italy would be better able to effect change in Algeria than any of its EU partners, partly because of France's inhibitions. Italy imports a fourth of its oil from Algeria, although it could buy it more cheaply from Russia. Rightly or wrongly, Sant' Egidio believes that Italy could use this commercial tie to leverage a more moderate attitude in Algiers to Islamists' participation in the political process.

The Italian Foreign Ministry is not as overtly pessimistic as Sant' Egidio, although both feel strongly that Zéroual must fulfill his commitment to open the political process or confront a situation that can only worsen. But Italian experts observe that Zéroual's influence with what one of them calls "the inner core of the army" is limited. Perhaps predictably, the Italians see the United States as the only external power capable of influencing Zéroual's regime. "The French have no policy and refuse to act," says an Italian official who deals with Algeria. And Sant' Egidio, also despairing of the French, thinks the United States could and should say to the Italians, "If you push directly on this with Algiers, we will back you up." Franco-Italian relations on Mediterranean matters are rarely warm; given France's proprietary approach to Algeria, Italy won't go forward on its own. The United States is not likely to either; Algeria's torment doesn't bear on any primary American interests, not yet at least.

Some say the EU is best positioned to play a role, politically as well as economically, since it supposedly carries no political baggage in Algeria and has more flexibility than the World Bank and the International Monetary Fund. In fact, Algeria's insurgents see the EU as a French surrogate; given Paris's insistence on being the dominant, if not the only, external influence, they are probably more right than wrong. Also, according to a senior German official, "some members" have concern (probably misplaced or exaggerated) that France's goal is a Mediterranean bloc, protectionist and French-led, with North Africa bought off and stabilized by infusions of money provided by rich northern Europeans.

None of the terrorist groups is strong, but they are strong enough to impede Algeria's economic development; they could in fact block it altogether, according to Sant' Egidio. For now, neither side will overcome the other; government forces can't control the countryside, and the opposition groups, even if they were less divided, couldn't prevail against the government forces. Sant' Egidio's leaders feel that the government's policy, if unchanged, will lead to what some call "a soft Somaliazation" of Algeria. "As the violence worsens," one of them suggested, "individual leaders will begin fighting among themselves for power. The situation will devolve into independent clans or groups along religious and ethnic lines competing for power with no solution in sight."

This scenario, if played out, would also produce a realization of the worst of French expectations about an exodus from Algeria.

Italy Redux?

Italy, too, feels theatened by a persistent, potentially large migratory flow from from the Maghreb. And Italy's interest in calming the demons of the Mediterranean is as great as that of France or any other member of the EU's southern tier, including Spain. But Italy, curiously, exercises relatively little influence in Mediter-

ranean affairs. Spain plays a larger role in the western Mediterranean, larger probably than France, which sees itself as Europe's
natural leader there, especially in Algerian affairs, but operates independently rather than within the EU. "France and Spain are behind much of what happens in the Mediterranean, Italy less so,"
says a retired Italian ambassador.

Unlike the French, Italians are not depressed, and do not feel as
if they have slipped into a decline. They do feel frustrated by the
tendency elsewhere to see them as belonging to the Mediterranean
instead of to northern Europe where they do, of course, have
strong ties.

"France and Germany see Italy as a Mediterranean country,"
says Luca Caracciolo, editor of *Limes,* an influential Italian quarterly. "We are there geographically but see ourselves first as westerners, second as Europeans, third as Mediterraneans."[20]

Northern Italians care about northern Europe. They are interested in the Mediterranean only as the route of a migration that
they see as excessive and threatening. Various foreign policy buffs
in Italy do think about the Mediterranean—the problems of Islamic fundmentalism, the threat from a spread of weapons of mass
destruction. They see the range of Super Scud missiles based
around Benghazi in Libya as limited to Italian cities. For security,
however, Italy has relied on the United States for fifty years without ever having to spend more than 2 percent of its GDP on defense; along with the rest of NATO, Italy sheltered under the
American nuclear umbrella during the Cold War; now it is the U.S.
Sixth Fleet, based in the Mediterranean, that is seen as the country's source of security.

France, and to a lesser extent Germany, want to create a European defense capacity, if only as a hedge against American disengagement. Not so Italy, which doesn't look beyond America's
commitment and the presence of its fleet. Quite simply, Italy, with
its long and vulnerable coastline, doesn't want to be left alone in
the Mediterranean; its ties to Spain are weak, and France is judged

disdainful of Italian interests. But defense aside, there is no more keenly "European" member of the EU than Italy, which largely explains why the country's outlook is less Mediterranean than its situation. What explains the depth of the Italian commitment to the EU is a more complex question, the answer to which seems to lie in a mix of negatives:

- The sense of nationhood that had grown up between the Risorgimento and the outbreak of World War II began to decline midway through the war
- The impermanence of governments; the average Italian government in the postwar period has lasted ten months
- The reluctance and/or inability of the political structure and the press to grapple with serious issues
- The strong affinity of the prosperous northern part of the country with Mitteleuropa, a sentiment that is linked to the region's increasing hostility toward the central government in Rome and the heavy drain on resources created by the poorer south
- Subsurface frustration within a society that could be described as more inward looking than its neighbors but that yearns to be a big European power rather than the biggest of the middleweights
- A society that has come to rely on the EU as an instrument for imposing on its members beneficial rules, regulations, and habits that Italy would be unable to adopt if left to itself
- A political class that sees the EU, of which Italy was a founding member, as providing its country with a place at Europe's top table—as giving it parity, at least formally, with France and Germany

Italy and the European movement seemed at first to be a mismatch. All or most of Italy's major business figures, including Fiat's Gianni Agnelli, who was to become a true believer, opposed the creation of a European customs union. Italian business and industry, they felt strongly, required protection. But after some experience, Italian business learned that it could compete; in time, one could hear some Italians, notably northerners, deplore the quality of governance in Rome by saying that Italy, if cut off from Brussels and its discipline, would float off to Africa.

Rome and Milan have developed different priorities. As the seat of government, Rome seeks to promote the country's political fortunes but encounters more indifference than sympathy in the EU capitals that matter most—Bonn and Paris. Milan sees the EU as obliging Italy to take its medicine, thereby enabling it to take steps that would otherwise be impossible. Rome assigns equal weight to three priorities: the EU, NATO, and the tie with the United States. Politically, no group—left or right—challenges the central importance of any of them. The EU, as noted, is seen as enabling Italy to take steps that would otherwise be impossible, as well as providing status.

As for the United States, apart from providing security, it is seen in Rome and elsewhere as the best, or only, external advocate of Italian interests. The chief venues for Italian foreign policy are NATO and the G7, the club consisting of the major hard currency countries. The United States dominates the first and got Italy into the second. Back in the late 1980s, Italians were struggling to gain admittance to the G7. No one within the EU was helping, and Washington, concerned that Italy, if excluded, would become demoralized and unstable, had to overcome French and British objections to arrange membership. Italy's press contains the least anti-Americanism of any in western Europe.

In Rome, the struggle to enlarge Italy's role continues; it is mostly uphill and disappointing, whether the issue is aligning Italy with Germany and Japan as a candidate for permanent membership in the U.N. Security Council or placing an Italian in the role of president of the EU or as secretary-general of NATO.

Milan is a lot less interested in Italy's status than in the amount of business that can be done with Germany, other EU members, and potential members such as Poland. From Bologna in the center to the region north of the Po River, people are more inclined to ask whether Italy is capable of functioning as a unitary state. And if not, they wonder, does the solution lie in a separatist movement? Listen to Piero Bassetti, a former president of the Lombardy region, a former member of parliament, and a member of the Trilateral Commission. Bassetti is a product of an old and rich Milanese manufacturing family; he is currently serving as president of Milan's Chamber of Commerce. "Rome can complain about being insulted," he says. "But Milan's elite cannot and does not. Milan is accepted [in northern Europe]. People here used to say, 'We can do without the state.' Now they say, 'We can survive only if we get rid of the state or radically change it.' "[21]

Germany is as lively a topic of conversation as there is in Milan. The elite of northern Italy, one is told repeatedly, feels itself as belonging to Mitteleuropa. Some Milanese political figures accuse Rome of trying to discourage special links between northern Italy and Germany—of wanting to tie all of the country to the Mediterranean.

The talk about Germany in northern Italy, including its supposed coming dominance, is more open than in other parts of Europe where the actual concern is probably higher. An American may be asked by a northern Italian what Washington will do to head off German hegemony in Europe. In the next breath, however, the person asking may suggest that none of that really matters and what does are the economic ties between northern Italy and Germany. A propos northern Italians are relaxed and concede no advantage to their German neighbors. We work harder than Germans, they observe correctly, noting, again correctly, that Germans are well aware of the difference.

Germans are especially sensitive to Italy as a competitor, partly because both are competing for a large part of the same market; it could be described as the area that once formed the Austro-Hungarian Empire and other parts of east-central Europe. The stakes are enormous. And the Germans know—probably better than any of the other big traders—just how good the Italian competition is.

"We are exporting investment capital, not just goods and services," said a senior government official. "We are the number one investor in Poland. Eastern Europe is our best area of economic expansion. We are Japan without MITI [a reference to Japan's famously aggressive Ministry of International Trade and Industry]."[22] His comment reflects a sentiment shared by various entrepreneurial figures in the north that their future lies more in central and eastern Europe than in the markets of France, Spain, and other EU members.

Japan and Germany are competitors but also constitute major markets for the innumerable small and medium-sized exporters that carpet northern Italy. The region's strengths (hence the country's, many would say) lie in machine tools, textiles, fashion, and an array of niche products, many of them highly innovative and specialized. Some of these products have long been used in both the car and aircraft industries in Germany and Japan. Many, if not most, of the components of various German cars, including the BMW and Mercedes-Benz, are supplied by Italian firms, partly because they are cheaper and partly because they are better designed. The companies that specialize in these products are typically small and run by a family, some member of which is likely to be a brilliant innovator. (In a typical transaction, the company receives design specifications from a German car company by fax. The Italian supplier may modify the specs and adapt his design for somewhat broader consumption; stated simply, the supplier may be able to sell a new carburetor that is being designed for BMW to Volkswagen or Daimler-Benz.) Briefly, there is a complex interaction, or symbiosis, between these big German companies, which are less innovative and less able to control their costs, and their smaller, more entrepreneurial Italian supplier/competitors.

Italian and German companies share the same seemingly odd

lack of interest in exploiting the knowledge-intensive sector of industry. As in Germany, serious corporate figures in northern Italy remain doubtful that competing in the global market requires investing heavily in the leading edge of technology.

Companies in central and northern Italy are famous for their flexibility and versatility. Natuzzi, a leather furniture maker, may have as many as one hundred and twenty new models each year; according to one report, it "can produce any of more than one million combinations of color and design on a single assembly line." Again according to this report, a company in Bergamo called Brembo, "whose brakes are used by two-thirds of the teams in Formula 1 motor racing, can introduce one hundred new products each year; seven hundred different parts go into its braking systems."[23]

What the Italian companies, virtually all of which are family-owned, find difficult is translating their skills in product and process innovation into high-quality management and organization on a large scale. But that doesn't seem to matter. Smaller seems to work better in this region, as illustrated by its prosperity—more concentrated than elsewhere in the EU—and its unemployment rate—lower. The area around Treviso in the Veneto—a boom district for the past thirty years—is home base not only for the Benetton Group but also for about 56,000 small firms, one for every eight families.[24] Some wealthy pockets in the north are made up of little villages called "industrial districts." Typically, they specialize in a single niche product, such as eyeglass frames, home security devices, or stockings. Another technique is the so-called no-factory enterprise, in which an entrepreneur sees a demand for a product and produces it by assembling networks of small industrial boutiques, each of which may specialize in one segment of the production process. The entrepreneur may operate on a global scale, either traveling the world or, more typically now, running his worldwide business by computer.

These are people who prosper in the German market and seem

indifferent to the heavy German presence. "Germany is again becoming imperial," said an unconcerned Bassetti. "The Wall had
been a border and forced Germany to become a nation-state, a status it was never comfortable with. Now German influence is radi-
ating." He observes that Italian banking is strongly influenced by
German banking; that the modern Italian banking system was
founded by Germans.

Deutsche Bank's presence is highly visible. In the fall of 1994,
the signs on Milan's Banca d'America e d'Italia were changed to
read "Deutsche Bank." In fact, this subsidiary of BankAmerica had
been sold to Deutsche Bank seven years earlier. The signs were
changed because the D-mark was perceived in Milan as a stronger
and more stable currency than the dollar. The bank's new name
drew in new clients.[25]

Today's Milanese feel more comfortable with Germany than
with France. They see Germans as strongly attracted to Italian culture and also to British culture, but not to French. "Germany is
culturally dependent on Italy as in the past," says Bassetti. "French
culture is brilliant but lacks a Dante, Goethe, or Shakespeare. Germans are the best Danteists."[26]

German unification was unsettling to many northern Italians,
mainly because it pointed up their country's serious disunity and,
conversely, the appeal of regionalism. There was Germany, united
at the federal level but granting a large measure of authority to
competent *Land* governments that would surely claim more. During the summer of 1995, Milan's German Cultural Institute invited
Italian scholars to participate in a discussion of the current mood.
The scholars chose the title of the discussion: "Germany United,
Italy Divided."[27]

Divided Italy

Italy is often described as three countries: the colonial south; the
Church state in the center; and the culturally independent, indus-

trialized north. Like many another commonplace, this one is clearer than the truth. First, the Emilia-Romagna region and its capital city, Bologna, in the center of the country, are as "northern" by most measures, including wealth and productivity, as Lombardy and the Piedmont. Second, the Church has lost much of its influence. By and large, Italians still consider themselves Catholics, but fewer and fewer are attending Mass. As in Spain, Italy's birthrate is in a sharp decline and is ranked among the world's lowest. A majority of Italians are Christian Democrats, and they used to belong to one party, the Christian Democratic Union. That's changed. After the elections of March 1994, the CDU metaphormosed into seven fragments. The Communists, who had been the second largest party, also split into a weaker gathering.

Actually, these elections completed the demolition of the deeply encrusted party system that had gotten under way two years earlier. Party chiefs who had prospered throughout the Cold War, both politically and financially, were driven from the scene. This time, the leadership wasn't delivered by the "House Without Windows," a popular reference to a Parliament that appeared to see nothing of what went on within the country. Instead, the country rejected the past and anointed Silvio Berlusconi, a broadcasting magnate who controlled a family-run empire estimated to be worth $8 billion. Berlusconi had no connection with Italy's political culture; he had never been a party figure, had never spent his time splitting the difference between the preferences of various factions and avoiding hard choices.

Stylistically, Berlusconi seemed more American than Italian—a wheeler-dealer of the new right. It didn't seem to matter that his ties to the ingrained corruption of the country's politics resembled those of the various officials whom his company allegedly was accustomed to bribing. As Alexander Stille, a writer who follows Italy closely, has written,

Berlusconi had decided to enter politics when the powerful Christian Democrat and Socialist politicians who had helped

him create a virtual monopoly of private television were impli-
cated in the Milan corruption scandal that broke in February,
1992. The Socialist leader, Bettino Craxi, who backed legisla-
tion allowing Berlusconi to own three television stations, was
accused and convicted of collecting millions of dollars in bribes
and was getting ready to flee the country for Tunisia. Berlusconi's own company, Fininvest, was under the scrutiny of prosecutors who had discovered a 300,000 dollar payment to the
government official who drafted the law regulating Italian television—money that Berlusconi insists was a consulting fee but
which prosecutors consider a bribe.[28]

Ironically, it was the left, sensing victory, that had pushed for
the 1994 elections. In defeat, the left saw that a better outcome
next time would require a long step toward the center. The step
was taken by Massimo D'Alema, a former Communist and leader
of a left-wing party, who formed a new coalition called "L'Ulivo"
(The Olive Tree). As candidate for prime minister in the 1996 elections, D'Alema selected Romano Prodi, who was even more atypi-
cal than Berlusconi: first, unlike Berlusconi, he wasn't tainted by
troublesome ties that bind; second, he was a Catholic intellectual—an economics professor from Bologna who had also compe-
tently managed IRI, Italy's largest state-owned holding company.
He has been described as wanting to make "a normal country of
Italy."

Prodi started well, getting good notices in European capitals, including Paris, where the comment on Italian leadership normally
ranges between derisive and harsh. A dozen of Prodi's ministers,
three of them women, were new to government. Major jobs were
given to the former prime minister, Lamberto Dini, and Carlo
Ciampi, both former central bankers and both heavyweights. Anto-
nio Di Pietro, the Milan magistrate who had led the "clean hands"
investigation that wiped out the old order, agreed to take charge of
public works, known widely as the "suitcase ministry."[29] (He later
resigned.)

Prodi formed his government with record dispatch—within seventeen hours of being formally designated prime minister. The financial markets responded favorably. The new government watched the lira gain ground against the D-mark and become stronger than it had been in more than a year.

Still, at this point, Italy was a tough hand to play, as Prodi well knew. The country was even more confused and down on itself. Its stable core—a strong economy, a strong and vital people—no longer seemed capable of redressing the past and heading off decline. In his campaign, part of which was conducted by touring the country in an old bus, and in his initial period as prime minister, Prodi promised a sharp break with the past. Italy had been run by a collection of cliques—political guilds—that relied upon a passive government that wouldn't interfere. No one rocked anyone else's boat. The corruption was pervasive, the natural product of a system in which there were no sanctions against misbehavior.

"The Italian way of life solves no problems," Luigi Barzini wrote in *The Italians*, his surpassingly revealing book on the country.[30] "It makes them worse," he went on. "It would be a success of sorts if it made Italians happy. But it does not." Barzini's words, written more than thirty years ago, still ring true.

Prodi saw the need to dissolve the link between the economy and the state. However, breaking sharply with past practice is an arduous and protracted project wherever it is tried. In Italy, it may be even harder, Sisyphean perhaps. Prodi, or some like-minded successor, must impose his will on a system in which deal making is an art form—a system in which no one faction is an outright winner or total loser on any given issue. The deal must benefit all sides. It goes beyond compromise of the sort that oils the wheels in other parliamentary governments; compromise of that sort is normally open—openly accommodating divergent viewpoints when necessary. In Italy, all interest groups are supposed to be in the game and the idea is to make each of them as comfortable as possible; it's been called cross-bribing, not necessarily in the financial sense but in making sure that all sides benefit. Most of the system's oligarchs have gone, along with their parties, but the style and the old habits die harder. Clearly, it is harder to govern a society in which the government is expected to avoid playing for full advantage.

How, for example, to cope with the unions? In most other western democracies, they have lost power. In Italy, thanks mainly to political anemia, the power of the unions has grown.

An Italian bureaucrat tried pointing out how Italy, France, and Germany diverge in their approaches to helping citizens help themselves. He cited the major floods of 1995 as an example. France and Germany provided no relief to victims, who should have carried flood insurance, according to the official position. But in Italy, he said, the government, under pressure, did provide financial relief, which was seen by experts as bad practice, because it discouraged the practice of buying flood insurance.

Prodi had for some time favored weakening the state apparatus and granting more authority to regions and cities. His model was Germany's federal system. Prodi would like to see a federal Italy as part of a federal Europe or some near equivalent. But as noted in Chapter III, the state apparatus is deeply entrenched. Moreover, the not-so-desirable effects of devolving power on Italy's regions must be understood and planned for. A serious move toward a federal system would highlight the differences among regions. People from the Mezzogiorno, fearing the worst, would flock to the north, where public services would be more reliable and prospects for an easier life brighter. With more autonomy, the northern regions would be even less disposed to share their wealth with the south. " 'The idea of two Italys was not invented by Bossi.' said Mariano Lombardi, the chief anti-Mafia prosecutor for the province of Crotone in the south. 'It is a reality. In the north you see one factory per kilometer. Here you can travel for 100 kilometers and not see one chimney stack.' "[31]

In early 1997, d'Alema, the chief of the center-left, began the arduous process of trying to overhaul the wornout institutions of the Italian government. The effort was partly directed toward strengthening the powers of the prime minister and his direct election. Parliament had agreed some months earlier to allow a commission to draw up proposals to reform and modernize the state. Berlusconi, who had opposed the commission, withdrew his objections and seemed to be working in harness with d'Alema, his major political adversary. Discussions and negotiations got under way and were certain to last for several months, at least.[32]

Around this same time, Prodi seemed to be staking not just his design for Italy but his very survival as leader on monetary union. As theater, the drama played well, and the convergence of EMU with Italy's struggle to change direction may have been inevitable. According to a few serious people, northerners, Italy will split if it fails to gain admittance to the EMU club.

Prodi's first budget, unveiled in the fall of 1996, surprised all sides by its daring; the key proposal—to cut the deficit by more than $41 billion—was clearly aimed at allowing Italy to meet the Maastricht criteria and ride into EMU on the first wave. Predictably, the financial markets greeted the budget gleefully. Otherwise, the reaction ranged from guarded to skeptical. It would be a hard sell. But Prodi was determined and stayed on course. He would not be the prime minister, he said, "to take Italy out of Europe." And four days after the budget submission, Prodi told the *Financial Times'* correspondent, "Slowly, and with some slips, Italy is acquiring a government able to govern—and that is new."[33]

The rationale for the heavy cuts was largely political. Italy's own institutions are weak, the argument runs, and it must remain part of the EU's basic structure. Still, getting the country's finances from where they were in late 1996 to where they would have to be at the end of 1997 to qualify for EMU would be onerous and painful.

The most sensitive areas for cuts were pensions and health care, the two largest budgetary items (aside from interest on Italy's huge debt). As of early 1997, no move had been made to cut pensions or to make other than a cosmetic cut in health care. Italians are cosseted by a health care system that is second to none in its munificence. A piece in *The New York Times* in May 1995 described in detail the scope of maternity benefits alone. It showed that a woman who had been on the job for eighteen months could draw her salary for nearly five years by taking full advantage of the maternity leave package. The piece noted that whereas some EU countries are beginning (or trying) to cut health care benefits, "in Italy, challenging maternity benefits is still regarded as political death—even though the Italian state bears more of a direct burden than most other countries do." Some of the benefits haven't been legislated, as the piece says, "but are simply sanctioned by tradition." For instance, "women with risky pregnancies are entitled with the appropriate doctor's certificate to take all nine months of pregnancy off." Many women, it appears, simply claim the risky pregnancies from the first trimester.[34] Whether this cat can be belled is far from clear.

Another of Prodi's bolder measures was a "Eurotax"—a onetime levy on incomes that is expected to produce about $8.5 billion in revenue. It provoked a blast from Berlusconi, who said the levy would provoke a recession.[35] Otherwise, the reaction seems to have been mixed. In the north, where the outcry against taxation is strongest and tax-evasion widespread, the Eurotax has been manageable; the label must have helped. But the north also feels strongly that the spending cuts proposed by Prodi do not go nearly far enough.

Prodi's *pièce de théâtre* is long on suspense, starting with whether Italy can reach the Maastricht targets—the infamous criteria—by the end of 1997. Chances are that even with a supplemental budget and creative accounting, it will fall short. The next question is whether Italy's partners, abetted by indulgent number crunchers in Brussels, will decide that Rome's submission may still lie outside the benchmarks but nonetheless has come far enough in the right direction to justify cutting Italy some slack. The Germans, notably the Bundesbank, would be deeply unhappy to see Italy slide into EMU in this fashion. The betting in early 1997 was that the Germans could and would prevent that.

Italians, especially northerners, feel strongly as if their country should be a founding member of EMU, just as it was one of the six founding members of the European movement and its institutions. Italy, they point out, is one of the world's major trading nations; it possesses the fifth largest economy and one of the two or three highest savings rates.

Europe needs Italy inside and close to the center of what goes on, say a great many Italians, who seem convinced of what they are saying. Outside EMU, some of them say, we would be seen as an independent economic force, like Taiwan.

Yes, and Italy has about as much political reach as Taiwan, according to critics—European and American, diplomats and nondiplomats alike—who deplore the striking indifference of Italians to what goes on around them. Italians could reply that other societies are also a lot more inward- than outward-looking. That's true, but Italy's indifference is greater and does the country serious self-injury, according to friendly but reproachful Italy watchers. "Italy has punched under its weight in international affairs for most of the post-war period," writes John W. Holmes, a retired American diplomat who served eleven years in Italy over three tours of duty and remains highly respected there. "Italy's foreign policy," he continues, "has been characterized not just by its muted tones, but also by a lack of the traditional instruments of power: Italy's military capability has been derisory; its foreign policy apparatus small; its foreign assistance program . . . both small and ineffective. Foreign policy has not engaged the interest of Italians, in or out of politics."[36]

Italy is one country, not two. It doesn't belong to northern Europe. It has strong interests there, but its largest market is still the southern part of the country, which, by the way, isn't one great depressed area and does contain pockets of growth and prosperity.

Italy's interests in the Mediterranean are clearly as important as those farther north. And they are much tougher to defend and promote, especially if the government in Rome persists in talking about them in hopeful generalities, as distinct from actually trying to do something about them.

AFTERWORD

Europe today has broken with the past more completely than at any time since the end of the Thirty Years' War and the Peace of Westphalia in 1648. That transitional moment marked the beginning of the system of nation-states in Europe, and the recurrent threat that one of them—Spain, France, Germany— would upset the balance of power.

Between 1914 and 1945, Europeans endured another, even more destructive thirty years of conflict and then nearly half a century of Cold War, during which the greatest concentration of military force ever seen was deployed in central Europe. Out of this most turbulent of centuries, a new and different order is emerging in Europe, its contours barely visible. "What happened in 1989 was not just the end of the Cold War but also the end of the balance of power system in Europe," writes Robert Cooper, a British diplomat. "This change is less obvious and less dramatic than the lifting of the Iron Curtain or the fall of the Berlin Wall, but it is no less important. What is now emerging into the daylight is not a re-arrangement of the old system but a new system."[1]

It's a different kind of system because it lacks an organizing principle, like coping with the threat from a superpower. Waging the Cold War did provide a focus and an organizing principle. After the Cold War ended in the fall of 1989, it took time for western governments to accept victory or, more precisely, to recognize that the other side really had been routed, if largely by its own hand. Although the end had been in sight for some time, governments hadn't planned for it. It was soon borne in on them that political life had actually become more complicated and more demanding.

In 1989, as in 1945, Europe stood on the threshold of an era—a time when the restless energies of states would be released in ways that defied easy comprehension, let alone prediction. And in 1989, as before, there was talk, much of it sensible, of devising a new European architecture. But this time it was mostly that—talk. Events, not governments, had taken charge. At first, they were being shaped by the interplay of the former Soviet Union spinning out of control and a Germany that, besides being rich, might sooner or later be unified; a unified Germany would eventually revert to behaving like a fully sovereign nation-state, as distinct from a more or less compliant, guilt-ridden loser of the last great hot war. European governments would begin to behave as they had when there was no rallying point or organizing principle. Some of the tendencies that had put Europe onto its self-destructive path early in this century would reappear.

During the Cold War, Western Europeans did lay claim to another organizing principle: making a federation, or some close approximation, out of their economic community. France and Germany would be tied together in an integrated bloc, with Britain brought in to impart balance and moderation. But the community's fortunes crested with the creation of its single market. Subsequent efforts at Maastricht and in the recent IGC to take a great leap toward political union were not successful. It's unlikely that Europe, or any large part of it, will become a political entity capable of joint decision-making. Trying to go beyond the political tolerances of its societies is unrealistic and unpopular.

The Maastricht Accord called for creating "an ever closer union among the peoples of Europe." However, the EU's own opinion polls have shown that not many of its 370 million or so citizens think of themselves as Europeans first. Only one tenth of Belgians and Luxembourgers feel as if they will see themselves as purely European anytime soon. If one also defines as "European" those who think of themselves as European first and their nationalities second, roughly a quarter of Belgians, Germans, French, and Luxembourgers become "European."[2]

Many EU officials demur and counsel patience; they like to equate their problems with America's prolonged growing pains. Acceptance of union itself, they note, required a civil war more than a half century after the United States had launched itself. Europe, they say, is trying to overcome centuries of strife and disunity, not to mention two civil wars in this century, and has made a good deal of progress toward unity that won't be undone. The effort to build Europe has been compared by some to the creation of a Gothic cathedral. But the Church of Rome sustained that kind of effort, skeptics reply.

The progress already made by the EU probably won't be undone. European countries can prosper economically only on the scale provided by the single market. Nonetheless, some are arguing, the organization must move forward or it will regress, with its foundation, that is, the Franco-German partnership, losing strength.

Moving forward should mean enlargement. If west Europeans are to recapture the larger part of their former strength and influence, they must expand their club eastward. They need the energy and drive of these other Europeans to avoid becoming more demoralized and less capable of holding their own, politically and economically, in a rapidly changing world.

In the early 1990s, EU members were consumed by the argument over whether to deepen or widen the organization. Which would it be—more integration or more enlargement? The Germans, as noted, argued for both. It appears that they were right. Taking in more countries would require some streamlining of the EU's institutions, starting with decision making. Rules that were adopted forty years ago by a club of six are working far less well in a club with fifteen members, any one of which can paralyze the institution by using its veto power to block measures requiring consensus. Decisions in the less sensitive areas may be taken by weighted majority voting. Where that applies, a measure can be adopted only if supported by about 70 percent of the votes, meaning sixty-two votes. But vote allocation is weighted in favor of small members. For example, Germany, Britain, and the Netherlands, which together make up two fifths of the EU's population, cannot form a "blocking minority." But Ireland, Luxembourg, Sweden, Greece, Austria, Belgium, and Finland—with only 12.5 percent of the EU's population—could become an effective minority bloc.[3]

Various members would like to change the rules. Some of them want to expand the number of topics that can be dealt with by majority voting instead of consensus. In the past, Britain could always be relied on to veto movement in that direction, but the Blair government may take a broader, more flexible approach, if not at once. France and Britain have also opposed transferring more power to the EU's institutions, and at an EU summit meeting in mid-1997 Kohl, to the gallery's considerable surprise, bowed to pressure from his *Länder* and took the same position. Yet all sides are keenly aware that an even bigger club would require institutional reform of the kind that has been, and may continue to be, out of reach.

Nor is it clear that enlargement itself is within reach, despite comforting rhetoric from various EU leaders. During visits to Poland and Hungary, French President Jacques Chirac announced

that they could become EU members by the year 2000. He knows
that cannot happen, partly because those countries will not be
ready. Poland's deputy prime minister, Grzegorz Kolodko, has said
that his country would be unable to meet the criteria for entry by
then; he cited the year 2002 as the earliest it could. The Czechs
have talked, overoptimistically in all likelihood, about 2002 or 2003
as being a realistic date for joining the EU.[4]

Of course, Chirac's hosts were aware that France, while acqui-
escent, dislikes the idea of enlarging the EU further. That is also
true of most of the other EU members. A senior Italian official,
commenting acidly on the last enlargement cycle, said, "The EU
Commission now resembles Amnesty International, with Swedes
and Finns joining the other moralists, the Dutch and the Danes."[5]
He expressed support for NATO enlargement because it would
recommit the United States to European security. But on EU enlargement, he was as negative as most of his counterparts in the
EU's southern tier.

As 1996 ended, the European Parliament, the EU's legislative
arm, issued a report warning against "hasty enlargement," bluntly
noting that the costs of enlargement had not yet been worked
out and that estimates varied widely. Candidates for membership
would have to commit themselves to EMU, the report further
warned. Thus, they would have to "commit themselves to pursuing
an economic policy consistent with that objective."[6]

The tone and language of the report are closer to the actual feelings of EU officialdom than the reassurances uttered by people
such as Chirac and Kohl when they visit Warsaw, Prague, or Budapest. Briefly, the talk is about why enlargement is so difficult, not
about why it should be done. EU members convey an impression
of being skeptical about enlargement, the project that should be
priority one, while being ready to risk all on EMU, a project that
may end in tears, whether it goes forward on schedule or is postponed. Their skepticism is breeding cynicism farther east.

The societies of central and eastern Europe diverge in various ways, but most of them are becoming steadily more enmeshed in parliamentary democracy and the free market. The former Communists are no less committed to western ways than their opposition. All sides are looking westward, with central Europeans feeling as if they are again part of the West, even if the key institutional ties haven't been made. There is, of course, a line between central and eastern Europe, as shown by a survey in *The Economist*:

> Today's Central Europeans are very precise about where the boundaries lie. They object to the title 'East Europeans' which they bore during the cold war. Eastern Europe, they say, lies to their east. It is Russia, Ukraine, Romania and Bulgaria that look to the Black Sea. The Central Europeans look to the Mediterranean or to northern waters, at a pinch to the Atlantic. Some talk, rather less precisely, of the 'vodka line,' separating beer and wine drinkers in Central Europe from those who prefer harder stuff further east; or of the 'secret police line,' separating those who fully dismantled their old security services when communism collapsed in 1990 from those who did rather less.[7]

Enlargement, if it actually happens, will draw a sharper line between central and eastern Europeans, since the first in will be those who can play by the rules and create minimal ripples in making the transition; that means all or most of the central Europeans and none of the eastern Europeans. They, too, can enter, says the EU, when they are able to meet the political and economic criteria.

In the end, none may make it in, a prospect Munich's *Süddeutsche Zeitung* warned against in a strong editorial in March 1996: "If the new democracies of east-central Europe do not receive a home with all possible speed, they will fall back into all the insecurities that gave the late nineteenth century its ugly face: rivalries, fears and conflicts . . . the nineteenth century might well be coming back; thus, the order of the hour is to extend the 'sphere of influence' of democracy and stability as widely and as quickly as possible."

A more recent analogy might be the 1930s, when western Europeans, to their heavy cost, stood aside as central Europe was overwhelmed by totalitarian aggression and the Great Depression. The issues and the context then were wholly different, but it was nonetheless a case of western Europe letting down the side, the European side.

It could happen again. The single-minded campaign to create a single currency could sidetrack serious negotiations about enlargement. The economic effects of the campaign could retard, if not block, progress, because the Maastricht criteria impose stringent limits on what governments can spend. Those limits then become additional barriers to enlargement. Monetary union may in the end vindicate its patrons, Kohl and Chirac. More likely it will not, in which case EMU may cause serious injury to all or most of Europe by dividing France and Germany.

Signs of impending trouble emerged more strongly over the winter of 1996–1997 as Chirac began calling for prospective members of EMU to act as a political counterweight to the proposed European central bank. France wants to have what its officials call a *pouvoir politique* over the sweeping authority of any European central bank, and it has talked about giving the bank its "general orientations." Conversely, Germany has insisted on maintaining fiscal discipline through a self-enforcing mechanism administered by a fully independent European central bank. In making this point, Kohl usually disavows Germany's interest in acquiring more influence than any other member state and adds his intention to make European integration "irreversible."

Some German officials are showing nervousness. It's one thing to talk about using a single currency to give the EU a big political boost. It's quite another, as these officials are discovering, to manage not just the domestic but the intra-European politics of the enterprise. Telling the Italians, for example, that they won't be in the first wave is hard, especially when their leaders insist that they must be there.

The patrons of monetary union and a single currency may yet discover—if not decide—that Europeans aren't ready; that they lack the degree of cultural unity required by a project so far-reaching and full of pitfalls. Those who don't see the risks they have taken on have drifted into denial.

EUROPEAN GOVERNMENTS ARE no more capable of deterring, containing, or neutralizing threats to peace and stability than they were during the Cold War or the pre–World War II years. Security, although no longer the dominant issue, continues to be threatened. Localized internal disputes can erupt into savage violence; regional frontiers within states tend to follow rivers and mountain ridges, not ethnic boundaries; and as the former Yugoslavia has shown, institutions such as NATO and the United Nations were not set up to deal with conflicts *within* national borders. Since the fall of the Berlin Wall, ninety-six conflicts have erupted, of which ninety-one have been within nations. Ninety percent of the dead and wounded have been civilians.[8] Streams of unwanted refugees have provoked a backlash and political extremism in various regions. The influx of darker-skinned people is putting pressure on France, Italy, and Spain. Moreover, as noted in Chapter 2, organized crime is a rising threat to European security; the mix of porous borders and weakened national governments and police forces has complicated efforts to combat illegal drugs and hot money.

Controlling the spread of arms outside the NATO perimeter is a major problem. The lesson of the Gulf War for many regimes was their need to acquire more, better, and more destructive weapons. The rogue states are striving to acquire so-called weapons of mass destruction, although the next wave of proliferation could involve pro-Western countries like Egypt and Saudi Arabia. Israel is already a full-fledged nuclear weapons state. Egypt, a country beset by problems and latent instabilities, is trying to acquire long-range ballistic missiles, and is reported to be expanding its efforts to develop chemical and biological weapons. Then the immense problem of controlling and reducing strategic arms still confronts Washington and Moscow. During the Cold War, taking a look at the closely held list of American strategic weapons assigned to cover targets in the East Bloc was like taking a drink of water from a fire hose. Yet the prudent men who ran the Soviet Union would not have contemplated an attack with nuclear weapons. Now there is a concern about loose nukes—a fear that Russia's leadership may at some point not be in full control of its weapons. The two most worrisome variables of the Cold War were the spread of nuclear weapons and the vulnerability and unwieldiness of the command and control structures. They are at least as worrisome now, and there is no easy, let alone obvious, solution to either problem. In various ways, the world is now a more dangerous place than it was during the Cold War.

An immediate question confronting Moscow and NATO capitals quite impartially is what to do about short-range nuclear weapons. The United States has somewhere between five hundred and six hundred of them in Europe. All or most are bombs and are in storage. They have no military utility. NATO has announced that no such weapons will be deployed on the territory of new members. Depending on what Russia would be willing to do about dismantling its own tactical nuclear arsenal, the United States should consider taking all such weapons home and retiring them.

If one issue has created more passion and controversy than any other in the post–Cold War era, it is NATO enlargement. When talk of enlarging NATO first began, various Washington luminaries—people with voices that carry—pushed the idea as a way of preemptively containing, or stifling, Russia's imperial impulses. While Russia was still weak, the argument ran, NATO's reach should be extended eastward in order to deny Moscow the chance to extend its own reach westward yet again. It was the wrong argument, but Russian political elites were listening.

The so-called stability argument is more persuasive; the incentive of countries to join NATO and the obligation to behave once inside may help maintain stability. It's too soon to say what will befall NATO enlargement as it nears the stage of ratification by parliaments, including the U.S. Senate, where there could be a struggle. The financial costs are still somewhat speculative. At times, Washington is a one-subject town; if NATO enlargement took full possession of center stage, it might be accused of distracting attention from threats to stability in the Mediterranean or the North Pacific or elsewhere.

Public support may also be an imponderable, especially in some of the candidate countries. There is little doubt about Poland. Public support there for joining NATO is on the high side. As an institution, the military is more respected by Poles than the Catholic Church. And Poland has done more than other countries about assessing the costs of becoming a member of NATO.

Public support in Hungary for the move may be weaker than elsewhere. There the military ranks low in public opinion. And Hungary has the region's lowest defense budget as a percentage of national output.

The Czechs fall somewhere between the Poles and Hungarians. Support for joining NATO is soft, although stronger than in Hungary. There is also more of a commitment to defense than in Hungary but less than in Poland. Although Czechs do worry about the financial cost of joining NATO, there isn't much doubt that the Czech government, and Hungary's too, will be able to manage the issue politically. Moreover, if enlargement was postponed or rejected by, say, the U.S. Senate, the outcry in Warsaw, Prague, and elsewhere in the region would be loud and angry; Russia would be seen to have acquired control of NATO's behavior, at least in its former dominions; epithets like "sellout," "Yalta," and even "Munich" would be heard everywhere.

Farther west, one wonders whether enlargement will satisfy hawkish elements and contain their hostility to Russia. Or could it work the other way? Would parallel moves to give Russia a role in

European security provoke such elements? Russia's elites, although aware that joining NATO is not an option, crave membership in the Euro-American family; they won't stop pressing for a role in Europe's security system that is consistent with their country's size, history, and political significance.

As GERMANY GOES, so goes Europe. This bears repeating. Germans don't like to hear that geography positioned them between east and west. They say instead that Germany is the center of an increasingly cohesive Europe. Hans-Dietrich Genscher often made that point. But Germany itself isn't even close to being unified; it still resembles two divided societies. The Cold War's Iron Curtain shielded West Germans from the crises and problems to the east. However, Germany is now vulnerable to the troublesome forces arising in eastern Europe even as it becomes the region's dominant political and economic influence.

Germany is, of course, the most important member of the EU and seems destined to bear out statements by Presidents Bush and Clinton by becoming America's senior partner in Europe. Within German business and some political circles, however, an attitude has developed that, when expressed, doesn't augur well for Kohl's vision of a united Europe—a Europeanized Germany. It goes like this: We Germans are good Europeans, and we have proved it. No country has done more in the name of European integration. Indeed, not many have done as much, let alone contributed as much to the EU budget. We like the single market, and it is working. But maybe that's enough. We are a big player in the global market, and that is where we must be able to compete. Maybe these institutions in Brussels should remain as they are, not be allowed to exercise more control over what we do than they already have. Our interests—German interests—must come first.

Just how these interests are to be advanced is far from clear. Little effort is being made in Germany, or in most of Europe, to enlarge the service sector of the economy, to find ways to expand the availability of venture capital, or to close the gap with America in knowledge-intensive pursuits. "My biggest concern for Europe is that its companies operate like oldline U.S. companies did ten years ago," said Andy Grove, chief executive of Intel, in a speech at the World Economic Forum in Davos, Switzerland, in February 1997. Europeans, he said, lag in adapting Internet applications such as e-mail. "Those applications let you react in minutes and hours instead of days. In that sense, Europe is way behind." In the same week, the EU's Council of Ministers was given a report that warned of a "disturbing" competitiveness gap between Europe's information technology industry and those of the United States and Japan.[9]

Information technology and the global economy have formed an imperious tandem that is reshaping much of what is fundamental to modern societies. As a force, the tandem is being closely examined. And the degree to which its effects, on balance, are positive, negative, or neutral is a contentious question. So far the pluses seem to outweigh minuses, but the answer, such as it may be, lies ahead. Writing in *Foreign Affairs,* Jessica Mathews, a senior fellow at the Council on Foreign Relations, says,

> These technologies have the potential to divide society along new lines, separating ordinary people from elites with the wealth and education to command technology's power. . . . Above all, the information technologies disrupt hierarchies, spreading power among more people and groups. . . . In a network, individuals or groups link for joint action without building a physical or formal institutional presence. Networks have no person at the top and no center. Instead, they have multiple nodes where collections of individuals or groups interact for different purposes. Businesses, citizens organizations, ethnic groups, and crime cartels have all readily adopted the network model. Governments, on the other hand, are quintessential hi-

erarchies, wedded to an organizational form incompatible with all that the new technologies make possible.[10]

For various reasons, most of them obvious, the United States has been and remains better able to adapt to the changing environment; the essential steps seem to include corporate restructuring, wholesale layoffs in traditional business sectors, relocation of production and jobs, and finally—and perhaps most important—an approach to new technologies that combines massive investment with rapid commercial exploitation.

All of the above come harder for countries such as Germany and France, where social peace has relied on highly developed social security systems and where deregulation and liberalization of business in general are countercultural. The globalized economy increases pressure on the social safety net as capital moves out of the EU toward lower-wage societies in other parts of the world. Most German investment is going abroad—to the United States and Asia.

For as long as most people can remember, Europeans have lived within the terms of a social compact that obliged governments to deliver jobs and security. The compact appears to be breaking down. And as they wrestle the global dynamic, governments must consider its Darwinian possibilities. They talk about and may take comfort in the downside of the new American experience: the widening gap between rich and poor and the large numbers of "working poor."

It's not as if France and Germany have been slow to develop Information Age technologies. The Germans, as noted in Chapter 4, were among the pioneers. And in 1982 France began selling a system called Minitel; it offered video terminals that were connected electronically to a phone line, allowing the transmission of text and images. The system gave France an edge in the global information market, but like some other French products that were ahead of their time, it wasn't marketed effectively or modernized and adapted to accommodate the rapidly moving changes of the basic technologies.

According to a detailed and closely informed *New York Times* piece, France "tends to identify with the critics of globalization. Indeed, it increasingly seems to equate its welfare state with its very identity . . . fewer than fifteen percent of homes have personal computers, and fewer than one percent are connected to the Internet, figures well below not only the United States but also France's European neighbors." The article goes on to say that President Chirac "has spoken dismissively of the Internet as 'an Anglo-Saxon network.' "[11] It is resisted by France because of the U.S. content that is transmitted.

One wonders what the French, Germans, and other Europeans make of comments such as that made by Robert Reich when he was President Clinton's secretary of labor: "Transnational companies have grown faster than world trade in the last twenty years. In future, there will be no more national products, national technologies or national corporations. There will not even be national economies."

Europe's former imperial powers left no legatees, but as the Information Age proceeds, we see that British Telecom, Deutsche Telekom, France Télécom, and Spain's Telefónica become as aggressive in their own way and prone to shifting allegiances. With Europe's airlines being privatized, some of these big telecommunications companies represent all but the last vestiges of outreach by states. Distance isn't a factor in their business; they are "distance-insensitive."

The telecoms, as they are called, are seen by some Europeans as an instrument for moving EU members from manufacturing-based to service-based economies. When facing serious competition, telecoms create jobs at a more rapid rate than most other industries and pay higher wages than most. The annual growth in international telecom traffic is 17 percent but even higher in the trans-Atlantic sector. Within a few years, telecoms should replace the automotive industry as the world's dominant industry. Estimates show sales of service in the European telecom market alone as reaching $267 billion by the year 2003.[12] In November 1996, Vimpel, Russia's chief mobile phone provider, became the first Russian company to be listed on the New York Stock Exchange.

Martin Bangemann, the EU's minister of telecommunications and a former telecom minister in Germany, has urged members to liberalize their telecom markets. He wants them to begin competing vigorously. He and others worry about Europe being well behind America in multimedia and missing their chance to seize major shares of this exuberant market. His efforts yielded a ruling by the EU that members must open their domestic markets to telecom competititon by January 1, 1998.

There is some hope that a major deal reached by the World Trade Organization (WTO) in Geneva in February 1997 will allow the big American and European telecoms to enter each other's markets as well as invading Third World markets. The agreement *may* put a bit more pressure on countries, especially in Europe, that are trying to protect semimonopolies at home while being more aggressive abroad. The mix of monopoly pricing and high overhead costs in Europe accounts for the excessive cost of overseas phone calls. Long-distance rates in the United States average ten cents to fifteen cents a minute, according to the FCC. From the United States to Europe, they average about one dollar per minute because the lower American rates are blended with the higher rates in other countries. But satellite and fiber optic transmission costs between New York and Los Angeles are about the same as between New York and London.[13]

Experience shows, first, that telecoms in a protected market fare much better when that market is opened to competition and, second, that when a telecom monopoly is broken up, all market players, including the former monopolist, may gain as much as a 30 percent expansion in business volume. Still, compliance with the EU ruling is far from certain. Some members will implement it slowly and devise ways in which to maintain quasiofficial control. In much of Europe, the habit and tradition of government control of telecoms won't surrender easily to privatization or the free market ethos.

Italy has sold off pieces of Stet—a huge state-owned company that controls Telecom Italia. Privatizing Stet would be a major event in Italy and a signal that Italy's government is serious about privatization. Elsewhere, France's Socialist Party said during the campaign that it couldn't privatize France Télécom after regaining power. Deutsche Telekom has taken a few steps, but the company and the government are reluctant to confront the winds of competition. In November, Deutsche Telekom issued the largest initial public offering of stock ever, and the company is planning two more—one in 1998, the other possibly in 2000. However, these large public distributions won't affect the government's majority ownership and control. The company has convinced the government—if it needed convincing—that any more competition for the German market would be bad all around. Other telecoms, both domestic and foreign, say openly that the German agreement is waging preventive war against would-be competitors of Deutsche Telekom.

Deutsche Telekom could and should be the bellwether. It is Europe's largest phone operator. It deploys one of the best high-speed telephone networks in the world. But among the world's corporate entities, it is second only to Tokyo Power in the load of debt it carries—110 billion marks ($67 billion).[14]

Technological innovation has brought down the cost of delivering an ordinary phone call to about one-thousandth of what it was in the late 1950s, while prices to consumers have fallen much more slowly.[15] Profits are huge, and any company that feels capable of providing the service craves a piece of the action. With volume soaring and no end in sight, U.S. telecom companies, besides facing robust competition at home, are being stretched financially, thus providing a still broader opening in the global market for their European competitors.

Deutsche Telekom is slowly spreading its wings, mainly into a natural sphere, Mitteleuropa. It has made deals in Hungary, Poland, Ukraine, and the Czech Republic. It is trying to pin down a share of the Russian market. Looking beyond the region, Deutsche Telekom has bought a piece of a Malaysian telephone company.

Spain's company, Telefónica, is the most aggressive of Europe's monopoly telecoms, mainly in the Hispanic sphere. It paid $2 billion, three times more than its closest competitor, to gain a major market share in Peru. Telefónica also operates in Argentina, Brazil, Chile, Colombia, Puerto Rico, and Venezuela.

The model for the continental Europeans should be British Telecom, which began to flourish after being fully privatized in 1984. Britain is determined to be Europe's information hub, as well its banking hub. The company is doing its part, showing its heels to the other European telecoms by becoming steadily more productive. In 1996, in the biggest merger in U.S. history, British Telecom reached agreement to take over MCI (assuming the deal is granted federal approval).

The other European telecoms are not emulating the British Telecom experience. Neither are they keeping pace with developments within their own industry. In Germany, Mannesmann, a producer of pipe fitting and tool and die, started a small mobile phone business in the early 1990s. This subsidiary now accounts for half of Mannesmann's profits, even though it is only a small piece of the whole. A battle is now being waged over the company's corporate culture, with the traditionalists pitted against the telecom people.

According to *The Economist,* Germany "is unique among big industrial countries in that only about five percent of its population hold shares. (In Britain, for instance, the figure is nearer twenty-five percent.) This is partly a function of history: having lost their savings twice this century in post-war currency reforms, Germans are notably risk-averse. But it also reflects the poor performance of shares in most of Germany's biggest companies, which have offered miserable returns compared with those of government bonds and mortgage-backed securities."[16]

What Germany and France do with their telecoms will test their adaptability. It will show whether they can create an equity culture and whether they can compete with the major players in the mainstream of the global economy as it changes course.

GERMANY, EUROPE'S NOMINAL leader, is providing little direction, political or entrepreneurial. Britain is divided and hard to predict. France is weak, its mood pessimistic; a spirit of alienation is beginning to afflict much of French society.

Europe's enigmatic new order, as it slowly develops behind the façade of institutions, will be essentially benign. It may also be regressive, though not necessarily; the regressive tendencies could be offset by events or by new and creative leadership.

What Europe makes of itself, however, is crucial. In a world of dynamic change and shifting power centers, Europe can and should remain the citadel of civilized values, a center of peace and stability. If societies elsewhere begin to think of Europe as becoming less stable and more volatile, the reaction will probably breed greater instability. Others would be troubled and probably confused, partly because they wouldn't know whether America would be drawn into and weakened by Europe's troubles.

Neither Europeans nor Americans are clear about where events have maneuvered them and how best to advance what appear to be their larger interests. One of those interests lies in their political and economic cohesion. Thanks to shared adversaries, the transatlantic tie became a continuity, an abnormality in international life. But without a hostile force threatening all sides, the tie can no longer be taken for granted.

For now, there remains some sense on both sides of being joined together in the same civilization and confronting the same latent threats. Both sides of the Atlantic are committed to the rule of law. As weapons of mass destruction reach the desperate and the irreconcilable, the rule of law will become increasingly attractive to Europe and America.

Europe and America do, of course, diverge culturally, but it's not clear that Europe itself has sufficient cultural unity to develop any approximation of political unity. Probably it hasn't. Language and localism sustain cultural divides in most of Europe. The revival of regional cultures may point up the limits of the "European" idea. Also, regions within countries may become the natural political constituencies, rather than nations themselves. That, too, is unclear. Europeans have yet to define themselves as belonging to a country, a region, or a community. Being European may be no more than a state of mind. Everyone talks about being European, including, say, Azerbaijanis; and most do have a claim, including those who see themselves first as belonging to a region, second to Europe. Spanish diplomat philosopher Salvador de Madariaga said it as well as anyone: "Born of a mixture of bloods, carrying in his veins several collective memories, the European is a living debate, a permanent and never settled argument."[17]

NOTES

I. Europe Redefining Itself

1. Václav Havel, "How Europe Could Fail," Address to the General Assembly of the Council of Europe, Vienna, Nov. 9, 1993. Quoted in Václav Havel, *The New York Review of Books,* Nov. 18, 1993, p. 3.

II. European Subnational Regionalism

1. Author's conversation with Helmut Becker, Munich, Sept. 7, 1994.
2. Author's conversation with Jordi Pujol, Barcelona, May 31, 1995.
3. Author's conversation with Kurt Biedenkopf, Dresden, Sept. 14, 1994.
4. Author's conversation with German diplomat, Bonn, Nov. 9, 1995.

5. Author's conversation with official of European Commission, Brussels, Oct. 26, 1995.

6. Author's conversation with Dietrich Pause, Munich, Sept. 8, 1994.

7. Author's conversation in Brussels, Nov. 10, 1995.

8. Author's conversation with Hans-Peter Mengele, Stuttgart, Sept. 12, 1994.

9. Author's conversation with officials from the Foreign Economics Office, Stuttgart, Sept. 13, 1994.

10. *Financial Times,* May 9, 1996, p. 1.

11. Uwe Thaysen, "The Bundesrat, the German *Länder* and German Federalism" (German Issues), American Institute for Contemporary German Studies, The Johns Hopkins University, Baltimore, Md., 1994.

12. Dana Milbank, *The Wall Street Journal,* Feb. 24, 1995.

13. Author's conversation with Herbert A. Henzler, Munich, Sept. 12, 1995.

14. Author's conversation, Munich, Sept. 8, 1994. Background.

15. Author's conversation with Dietrich Pause, Sept. 8, 1994.

16. Author's conversation in Munich, Sept. 8, 1994.

17. Author's conversation with Herbertus Desloch, Munich, Sept. 7, 1994.

18. Ibid.

19. Author's conversation with Manfred Rommel, Stuttgart, Sept. 11, 1994.

20. Author's conversation with Kurt Biedenkopf, Dresden, Sept. 14, 1994.

21. Author's conversation in Dresden, Sept. 14, 1994.

22. Author's conversation with Kurt Biedenkopf, Dresden, Sept. 14, 1994.

23. John Hale, *The Civilization of Europe in the Renaissance* (New York: Atheneum, 1994), pp. 89–90.

24. Author's conversation with Joaquim Llimona, Barcelona, May 30, 1995.

25. Author's conversation with Carlos A. Gasoliba, Barcelona, June 1, 1996.

26. *The New York Times,* May 5, 1996, p. 10.

27. Author's conversation with Aleix Vidal-Quadros, Barcelona, May 30, 1995.

28. Robert Hughes, *Barcelona* (New York: Vintage Books, 1993), p. 34.

29. Ibid., p. 20.

30. Marlisle Simons, "A Reborn Provençal Heralds Revival of Regional Tongues," *The New York Times International,* May 3, 1996, pp. 1, 8.

31. Hughes, *Barcelona,* p. 35.

32. William Drozdiak, "Regions on the Rise," *The Washington Post,* Oct. 22, 1995, p. 22.

33. Author's conversation with Pasqual Maragall, Barcelona, May 31, 1995.

34. Author's conversation with Aleix Vidal-Quadros, Barcelona, May 30, 1995.

35. Author's conversation in Barcelona, June 1, 1995.

36. Author's conversation with Jordi Pujol, June 2, 1995.

37. *Financial Times,* June 12, 1995, p. 17.

38. Hughes, *Barcelona,* p. 19.

39. Ibid., p. 32.

40. Author's conversation in Barcelona, June 2, 1995.

41. *Financial Times,* June 12, 1995, p. 17.

42. Ibid.

43. Author's conversation with Pasqual Maragall, Barcelona, May 31, 1995.

44. Ibid.

45. John Ardagh, "Toulouse," *A Tale of Five Cities* (New York: Harper & Row, 1979), p. 290.

46. Drozdiak, "Regions on the Rise."

47. Christopher Harvie, *The Rise of Regional Europe* (London: Routledge, 1994), p. 58.

48. "France's Regionalist Awakening" (series), *Le Monde,* May 18, 20, 22, 23, 27, and 31, 1996.

49. *Financial Times,* July 3, 1996, p. 14.

50. Author's conversation with Jacques Moulinier, Lyon, June 6, 1996.

51. Author's conversation Alain Mérieux, Lyon, June 7, 1996.

52. Author's conversation with Robert Maury, Lyon, June 6, 1996.

53. Author's conversation with Michel Foucher, Lyon, June 6, 1996.

54. Drozdiak, "Regions on the Rise."

55. Ibid.

56. Unsigned, "L'Arc Sud Européen Région Rhône-Alpes, Région Piémont," April 1996.

57. Drozdiak, "Regions on the Rise."

58. Michel Destot, quoted in Les Cahiers du Conseil International de Lyon, Nov. 14, 1995, p. 51.

59. *Financial Times,* May 31, 1996, p. 6.

60. Author's conversation with Piero Bassetti, Milan, May 27, 1995.

61. *The New York Times,* Mar. 11, 1994, p. 14.

62. *The Economist,* May 25, 1996, p. 35.

63. Celestine Bohlen, *The New York Times,* June 11, 1996, p. 1.

64. Ibid.

65. Author's conversation with Northern League officials, Milan, May 27, 1996.

66. Author's conversation with Luca Caracciolo, Rome, June 2, 1996.

67. *The Economist,* July 20, 1996, p. 46.

68. Ibid.

69. *The Economist,* Mar. 23, 1996, p. 47.

70. *The Wall Street Journal,* Apr. 30, 1996, p. 13.

III. A Collective Nervous Breakdown

1. John Newhouse, "The New Europe," *The New Yorker,* Aug. 27, 1990, p. 81.

2. Quoted in "A Union Blessed But Not Yet Consummated," *The Economist,* Jan. 13, 1996, p. 47.

3. Ibid.

4. David Marsh, *Financial Times,* Jan. 17, 1996.

5. *Financial Times,* Mar. 11–12, 1995.

6. *The Wall Street Journal,* Jan. 17, 1996, pp. 1, 9.

7. Douglas Hurd, *Financial Times,* Jan. 31, 1996, p. 13.

8. *The Economist,* Feb. 17, 1996, p. 50.

9. Ibid.

10. *The New York Times,* Dec. 9, 1993, p. 13.

11. Tony Judt, "Europe: The Grand Illusion," *The New York Review of Books,* July 11, 1996, p. 6.

12. Robert Samuelson, *Newsweek,* Mar. 14, 1994, p. 53.

13. Hurd, *Financial Times,* Jan. 31, 1996, p. 13.

14. Quoted in Martin Wolfe, *Financial Times,* Apr. 9, 1996, p. 16.

15. Ibid.

16. Lord Tebbitt, *The Sun.*

17. Hurd.

18. *The Week in Germany,* Jan. 12, 1996, p. 5.

19. *Financial Times,* Jan. 29, 1996, p. 19.

20. Steven Philip Kramer and Irene Kyriakopoulos, *Trouble in Paradise? Europe in the 21st Century* (Washington, D.C.: Institute for National Strategic Studies, National Defense University, 1996), p. 28.

21. John Kampfner, "Labour will not join in EMU before 2,002," *Financial Times,* Apr. 7, 1997, p. 18.

22. Author's conversation with Kurt Lauck, Düsseldorf, Nov. 8, 1985.

23. *Financial Times,* Aug. 9, 1995, p. 2.

24. *Financial Times,* Mar. 22, 1996, p. 12.

25. *The New York Times,* Jan. 17, 1996, p. D1.

26. *The Wall Street Journal,* July 28, 1995, p. 10.

27. *Financial Times,* Apr. 19, 1996.

28. *Financial Times,* Aug. 9, 1996, p. 10.

29. *The Economist,* Jan. 27, 1996, p. 44.

30. *The Economist,* Mar. 23, 1996, p. 52.

31. *Financial Times*

32. *Financial Times,* July 19, 1996, p. 1.

33. "Figure it in," *The Economist,* Apr. 26, 1997, p. 47.

34. Thomas Kamm and Greg Steinmate, "Europeans See March to One Currency Hit New Stumbling Blocks," *Wall Street Journal,* June 1, 1997, pp. 1–12.

35. David Owen and Andrew Jack, "Jospin Cool on Maastricht," *Financial Times,* June 3, 1997, p. 1.

36. Wolfgang Munchau, "Delay Worries Give Way to Other Concerns," *Financial Times,* June 3, 1997, p. 2.

37. *The Economist,* Aug. 3, 1996, p. 41.

38. *The Economist,* Nov. 16, 1996, p. 36.
39. Noel Malcolm, *Foreign Affairs,* Mar./Apr. 1995, pp. 57–58.
40. *The Economist,* July 29, 1995, p. 36.
41. *Financial Times,* Nov. 8.

IV. Germany Adrift

1. Martin Walker, "Overstretching Teutonia—Making the Best of the Fourth Reich," *World Policy Journal,* Spring 1995, p. 7.

2. *The Economist,* Dec. 3, 1994, p. 62.

3. Author's conversation in Bonn, Nov. 5, 1995.

4. Author's conversation in Bonn, Sept. 19, 1994.

5. "Reflections on European Policy," policy paper prepared by the CDU/CSU Parliamentary Group, Bundestag, Bonn, Sept. 1, 1994.

6. Author's conversation with Jean-François Poncet, Paris, Nov. 26, 1994.

7. *Le Monde,* Nov. 30, 1994, p. 1.

8. Author's conversation with Lászlo Kovács, Budapest, Nov. 18, 1994.

9. Author's conversation with Giuliano Amato, Rome, May 26, 1995.

10. Author's conversation with Karl Lamers, Bonn, Nov. 9, 1995.

11. John Newhouse, "The Diplomatic Round: European Turmoil," *The New Yorker,* Sept. 2, 1991, p. 95.

12. Author's conversation with Herbert A. Henzler, Munich, Sept. 12, 1995.

13. Michael Mertes, "Germany's Social and Political Culture," *Daedalus,* Winter 1994, p. 13.

14. William Drozdiak, "German Economy Flagging in Race to Stay Competitive," *The Washington Post,* May 7, 1997, pp. 23, 27.

15. Kurt Lauck, "Germany at the Crossroads," *Daedalus,* p. 59.

16. Rick Atkinson, "Germany Forced to Re-examine Key Elements of Economy," *The Washington Post,* Aug. 9, 1994, p. 12.

17. Nathaniel C. Nash, "Germany Shuns Biotechnology," *The New York Times,* Dec. 21, 1994, p. D5.

18. Ibid.

19. "Those German Banks and Their Industrial Treasures," *The Economist,* Jan. 21, 1995, p. 71.

20. Ibid.

21. Atkinson, "Germany Forced to Re-examine Key Elements of Economy."

22. Ibid.

23. A. J. P. Taylor, *Bismarck: The Man and the Statesman* (New York: Vintage Books), p. 63.

24. Otto, Prince von Bismarck, *The Memoirs,* vol. 1 (trans. under the supervision of A. J. Butler) (Howard Fertig, 1996), p. 321.

25. Timothy Garton-Ash, "Germany's Choice," *Foreign Affairs,* July–August 1994, p. 75.

26. Ibid., p. 69.

27. Jürgen Kocka, "Crisis of Unification: How Germany Changes," *Daedalus,* Winter 1994, p. 185.

28. Ibid.

29. Author's conversation with Anne-Marie Le Gloannec, Paris, Nov. 10, 1996.

30. *Financial Times,* Oct. 4, 1995, p. 15.

31. Author's conversation with Kurt Biedenkopf, Dresden, Sept. 14, 1994, and Washington, Sept. 22, 1995.

32. Author's conversation in Dresden, Sept. 14, 1994.

33. "Helmut Kohl's One Man Band," *The Economist,* Sept. 7, 1996, p. 45.

34. Paul Goldberger, "Re-imagining Berlin," *The New York Times Magazine,* Feb. 5, 1995, pp. 45–53.

35. Mertes, "Germany's Social and Political Culture": Michael Mertes, "Germany in Transition," *Daedalus,* Winter 1994, pp. 15, 17–18, 27.

36. Garton-Ash, "Germany's Choice." *Foreign Affairs,* July–Aug. 1994, p. 67.

37. Author's conversation with Kurt Biedenkopf, Dresden, Sept. 14, 1994.

38. Mertes, "Germany in Transition," pp. 18–19.

39. Rick Atkinson, "Haunted by History," *The Washington Post,* Jan. 27, 1996, p. 14.

40. Klaus J. Bade, "Immigration and Social Peace in United Germany," *Daedalus,* Winter 1994, pp. 91–92.

41. Walker, "Overstretching Teutonia—Making the Best of the Fourth Reich," pp. 2–3.

V. France and Britain: *L'Entente Ambigue*

1. Reginald Dale, "Europe's Odd Couple," *France,* Summer 1995, p. 4.

2. Dominique Moisi, "An Awkward Time for France to Take Over," *Financial Times,* Nov. 20, 1995, p. 16. In that sense, France has remained a Gaullist state.

3. Stanley Hoffmann, "The New France?," *The New York Review of Books,* p. 50.

4. Author's conversation in Paris, Nov. 12, 1995.

5. "Reflections on European Policy," policy paper prepared by the CDU/CSU Parliamentary Group, Bundestag, Bonn, Sept. 1, 1994.

6. Author's conversation in Paris, Nov. 23, 1996.

7. Dominique Bocquet, "A German Proposal Still in Need of a French Answer," *Promethée,* Jan. 1995, p. 25.

8. Author's conversation in Paris, Nov. 22, 1994.

9. *Financial Times,* June 12, 1995, p. 14.

10. Ibid.

11. Author's conversation in London, Dec. 4, 1995.

12. Author's conversation in Paris, Nov. 13, 1995.

13. Dale, "Europe's Odd Couple."

14. *The Economist,* Apr. 16, 1966, p. 52.

15. Ibid.

16. *News from France,* Dec. 23, 1994, p. 2.

17. *The Economist,* Apr. 8, 1995, p. 43.

18. *The Economist,* Oct. 26, 1996, p. 61.

19. Philip Gourevitch, "The Unthinkable," *The New Yorker,* Apr. 28/May 5, 1997, p. iii.

20. Roger Cohen, "For France, Sagging Self-Image and Esprit," *The New York Times,* Feb. 11, 1997, pp. 1, 8.

21. "Immigration Study Yields Surprising Results," *News from France,* Apr. 10, 1995, p. 1.

22. Ibid.

23. *Le Monde,* Oct. 13, 1994.

24. Hoffmann, "The New France?"

25. *The Economist,* Jan. 6, 1996, p. 38.

26. "Retire early, bust the state," *The Economist,* Feb. 15, 1997, p. 47.

27. Ibid.

28. *The Economist,* Sept. 21, 1996, p. 50.

29. David Owen and Andrew Jack, "Downturn Increases French Gloom," *Financial Times,* Sept. 5, 1996, p. 11.

30. Ibid.

31. "Crossed Fingers in France," *The Economist,* Apr. 26, 1997, p. 45.

32. Philip Stephens, "Message from Messina," *Financial Times,* May 19, 1995, p. 13.

33. Hugh Thomas, *Suez* (New York: Harper & Row, 1967), p. 154.

34. "No More Mr. Nice Guy," cited by Anthony Lewis, *The New York Times,* Apr. 18, 1997, p. 33.

35. *Financial Times,* May 23, 1996, p. 15.

36. *Financial Times,* Jan. 30, 1995, p. 1.

37. John Newhouse, "The Gamefish," *The New Yorker,* Feb. 10, 1986, p. 90.

38. Author's conversation in London, July 17, 1993.

39. *The Economist,* May 25, 1996, p. 15.

40. *Financial Times,* May 23, 1996.

41. *The Economist,* May 25, 1996, pp. 33–34.

42. Ibid.

43. *The Economist,* Dec. 3, 1994, p. 73.

44. Reuters World Service, May 25, 1994.

45. Sir Robin Renwick, *Fighting with Allies* (New York: Times Books, 1996), p. 394.

VI. Unthreatened Yet Insecure

1. Christophe Bertram, *Europe in the Balance* (Carnegie Endowment for International Peace, 1995), p. 33.

2. "Russia's Market Kicks Off '97 as Top Performer, Earning 60%," *The Wall Street Journal,* Feb. 28, 1997, pp. C i–12.

3. Frederick Starr, "The Paradox of Yeltsin's Russia," *Wilson Quarterly* 2 (1995), pp. 66–73.

4. Interview with Sergey Rogov on *America's Defense Monitor* (television program), Oct. 7, 1995.

5. *The New York Times,* Feb. 15, 1997, p. 3.

6. Clifford Gaddy, "Deepening Russia's Tax Woes," *The Journal of Commerce,* Nov. 6, 1996.

7. *The Economist,* Oct. 26, 1996.

8. *Arms Control and the U.S–Russian Relationship,* Report of an Independent Task Force Sponsored by the Council on Foreign Relations and the Nixon Center for Peace and Freedom, p. 17.

9. Ibid., p. 14.

10. *The New York Times,* Feb. 15, 1997, p. 3.

11. Komsomolskaya Pravda, Mar. 15, 1997, translated by *Daily Review,* Mar. 20, 1997.

12. Conversation with Bruce Blair, Washington, Mar. 20, 1997.

13. Bruce Blair, "Who's Got the Button?," *The Washington Post,* Sept. 29, 1996, pp. C1–4.

14. John Newhouse, *War and Peace in the Nuclear Age* (New York: Alfred A. Knopf, 1989), p. 425.

15. William Drozdiak, *The Washington Post,* Dec. 14, 1996, pp. 1, 24.

16. *The Economist,* Sept. 7, 1996, p. 46.

17. *The Military Balance* (Tables and Analyses: International Institute for Strategic Studies, 1996–97), p. 306.

18. David Buchan, *Financial Times,* June 12, 1995, p. 14.

19. *International Herald Tribune,* July 7, 1996, p. 11.

20. *This Week in Germany,* June 7, 1996, p. 1.

21. Philip Gordon, "'Europeanization' of NATO: A Convenient Myth," *International Herald Tribune,* June 7, 1996, p. 11.

22. *The Economist,* Mar. 30, 1996, p. 50.

23. Bill Clinton, address, Warsaw, July 1994.

24. Sam Nunn, "The Future of NATO in an Uncertain World," address to SACCLANT (Supreme Allied Command Atlantic), Seminar '95, Norfolk, Va., June 21, 1995.

25. Sergei Karganov, "Where Is Russia Going? Foreign and Defense Policies in a New Era," *PRIF Report* 34, Apr. 1, 1994.

26. Catherine McArdle Kelleher, *The Future of European Security: An Interim Assessment* (Washington, D.C.: Brookings Institution, 1995), p. 82.

27. Ibid.

28. Igor Malashenko, *Russia Roundtable*, Carnegie Endowment for International Peace, 1996.

29. Douglas Hurd, *Financial Times*, Jan. 31, 1996, p. 14.

30. Richard Holbrooke, "America, A European Power," *Foreign Affairs*, Mar.–Apr. 1995, pp. 63–64.

VII. The Troubled Mediterranean

1. D. G. Kousoulas, "The Aegean as 'A Greek Lake,'" *The Washington Post*, July 16, 1996, p. 15.

2. Tozun Bahcheli and Nicholas X. Rizopoulos, "The Cyprus Impasse: What Next?" *World Policy Journal* 13:4 (Winter 1996–97), pp. 27–39.

3. *The New York Times*, Jan. 18, 1997, p. 2.

4. Ibid.

5. Bahcheli and Rizopoulos, "The Cypress Impasse."

6. "A Bloom of Hope in Greece," *The Economist*, Feb. 24, 1996, p. 53.

7. *The Economist*, Jan. 11, 1997, p. 48.

8. Celestine Bohlen, "In Search for 'Turkishness,' Turks Reveal Their Destiny," *The New York Times*, May 18, 1996, pp. 16–17.

9. Stephen Kinzer, "In Defense of Secularism, Turkish Army Warns Rulers," *The New York Times*, Mar. 2, 1997, p. 9.

10. Stephen Kinzer, "Tirade by Qaddafi Stuns Turkey's Premier," *The New York Times*, Oct. 9, 1996, p. 6.

11. Anthony Hyman, "Central Asia and the Middle East," in *Central Asia and the Caucasus after the Soviet Union* (Melbourne: University of Florida Press, 1994), p. 258.

12. Stephen Kinzer, "Businesses Urge Turkey to Broaden Democracy," *The New York Times,* Mar. 23, 1997, p. 4.

13. Lionel Barber, "EU Group Rebuffs Turkish Entry Bid," *Financial Times,* Mar. 5, 1997, p. 2.

14. Andrew J. Pierre and William B. Quandt, *The Algerian Crisis: Policy Options for the West* (Carnegie Endowment, 1996), p. 7.

15. Ibid, p. 9.

16. Ibid., p. 10.

17. Author's conversation with Sant'Egidio leaders, Rome, June 4, 1996.

18. "Wanted, an Algerian Policy," *The Economist,* Mar. 22, 1997, p. 47.

19. *The Economist,* Dec. 7, 1996, p. 16.

20. Author's conversation with Luca Caracciolo, Rome, June 4, 1996.

21. Author's conversation with Piero Bassetti, Milan, May 29, 1995.

22. Author's conversation in Rome, May 26, 1995.

23. *The Economist,* Mar. 22, 1996, p. 57.

24. *The Economist,* May 25, 1996, p. 35.

25. John Tagliabue, *The New York Times,* Aug. 6, 1995.

26. Author's conversation with Piero Bassetti, Milan, May 29, 1995.

27. John Tagliabue.

28. Alexander Stille, "Italy: The Convulsions of Normalcy," *The New York Review of Books,* June 6, 1996, p. 42.

29. *The Economist,* May 25, 1996, p. 25.

30. Luigi Barzini, "Conclusions," *The Italians* (New York: Atheneum, 1964), p. 339.

31. Celestine Bohlen, *The New York Times International,* Nov. 15, 1996, pp. 1, 7.

32. Robert Graham, "Talks Start on Reform of Italian State," *Financial Times,* Feb. 12, 1997, p. 3.

33. Robert Graham, "Italy's Road to Maastricht," *Financial Times,* Oct. 2, 1996, p. 12.

34. Celestine Bohlen, "Where Every Day Is Mother's Day," *The New York Times,* May 6, 1996, sec. 4, pp. 1, 5.

35. *Financial Times,* Nov. 20, 1996, p. 17.

36. John W. Holmes, "Italy: In the Mediterranean, but of It?," *Frank Cass Journals* (London: Newbury House), p. 176.

Afterword

1. Robert Cooper, *The Post-Modern State and the World Order* (London: Demos, 1996), p. 7.

2. *The Economist,* Aug. 26, 1995.

3. *The Economist,* Mar. 30, 1996, p. 47.

4. *Financial Times,* Feb. 4, 1997, p. 17.

5. Author's conversation in Rome, May 28, 1995.

6. *Financial Times,* Dec. 11, 1996, p. 2.

7. "Central Europe Survey," *The Economist,* Nov. 18, 1995, p. 5.

8. Pierre Schori, Swedish Minister for International Development Corporation. "From Marshall to Post-Communism. A New Deal for Internationalism." Lecture celebrating the fiftieth anniversary of the Marshall Plan.

9. Nicholas Denton, "Drive to Plug the Gap," *Financial Times,* Feb. 3, 1997, p. 13.

10. Jessica T. Mathews, "Power Shift," *Foreign Affairs,* Jan.–Feb. 1997, p. 52.

11. Roger Cohen, "For France, Sagging Self-Image and Esprit," *The New York Times,* Feb. 11, 1997, pp. 1, 8.

12. Quoted in Wilfried Guth, keynote address at the Symposium on Germany, Japan, and the United States, May 30, 1996.

13. *The Economist,* Oct. 26, 1996, p. 73.

14. Robert J. Samuelson, "Global Phone Power," *The Washington Post,* Feb. 26, 1997, p. 19.

15. *The Economist,* Nov. 9, 1996, p. 20.

16. *The Economist,* Oct. 26, 1996, p. 73.

17. Salvador de Madariaga, *Portrait of Europe* (University of Alabama Press, 1967), p. 35.

BIBLIOGRAPHY

Ardagh, John. *A Tale of Five Cities*. New York: Harper & Row, 1979.

Barzini, Luigi. "Conclusions." *The Italians*. New York: Atheneum, 1964.

Beales, Derek. *From Castlereagh to Gladstone, 1815–1885*. New York: W. W. Norton & Co., 1969.

Bertram, Christoph. *Europe in the Balance: Securing the Peace Won in the Cold War*. Washington, D.C.: Carnegie Endowment, 1995.

Boniface, Pascal, and François Heisbourg. *La Puce les Hommes et la Bombe: l'Europe Face aux Nouveaux Défis Technologique et Militaire*. Hachette, 1986.

Buchan, David. *Europe: The Strange Superpower*. Aldershot, Eng.: Dartmouth Publishing Co., Ltd., 1993.

Buruma, Ian. *The Wages of Guilt*. New York: Farrar, Straus & Giroux, 1994.

Cassa, Ralph A. *The Major Powers in Northeast Asia*. Washington, D.C.: National Defense University, 1996.

Craig, Gordon A. *The Germans.* New York: G. P. Putnam Sons, 1982.

Delmas, Philippe. *le Bel Avenir de la Guerre.* Gallimard, 1995.

De Madariaga, Salvador. *Portrait of Europe.* University of Alabama, 1967.

Duchene, François. *Jean Monnet: The First Statesman of Interdependence.* New York and London: W. W. Norton & Co., 1994.

Frei, Matt. *Getting the Boot: Italy's Unfinished Revolution.* New York: Times Books, 1995.

Garton-Ash, Timothy. *In Europe's Name: Germany and the Divided Continent.* New York: Random House, 1993.

Glenny, Misha. *The Fall of Yugoslavia: The Third Balkan War.* New York: Penguin, 1992.

Grant, Charles. *Delors: Inside the House That Jacques Built.* London: Nicholas Brealey Publishing, 1994.

Greider, William. *One World, Ready or Not.* New York: Simon & Schuster, 1997.

Hale, John. *The Civilization of Europe in the Renaissance.* New York: Atheneum, 1994.

Hamilton, Daniel S. *Beyond Bonn: America and the Berlin Republic.* Washington, D.C.: Carnegie Endowment, 1994.

Harvie, Christopher. *The Rise of Regional Europe.* London: Routledge, 1994.

Henzler, Herbert A. *Europreneurs: The Men Who Are Shaping Europe.* New York: Bantam, 1994.

Holmes, John W., ed. *Maelstrom: The United States, Southern Europe and the Challenges of the Mediterranean.* Cambridge, Mass.: The World Peace Foundation, 1995.

Hughes, Robert. *Barcelona.* New York: Vintage Books, 1993.

Hyman, Anthony. "Central Asia and the Middle East" in *Central Asia and the Caucasus after the Soviet Union.* University of Florida Press, 1994.

Kahler, Miles. *Regional Futures and Transatlantic Economic Relations.* New York: Council on Foreign Relations Press, 1995.

Kelleher, Catharine Mcardle. *The Future of Security: An Interim Assessment.* Washington, D.C.: The Brookings Institution, 1995.

Kennan, George F. *The Marquis de Custine and His "Russia in 1839."* Princeton: Princeton University Press, 1971.

Kissinger, Henry A. *Diplomacy.* New York: Simon & Schuster, 1994.

Kinross, Lord. *The Ottoman Centuries: The Rise and Fall of the Turkish Empire.* New York: Morrow, Quill Paperbacks, 1977.

Kramer, Steven Philip, and Irene Kyriakopoulos. *Trouble in Paradise? Europe in the 21st Century.* Washington, D.C.: National Defense University, 1996.

McCarthy, Patrick. *The Crisis of the Italian State.* New York: St. Martin's Press, 1995.

Mandelbaum, Michael, ed. *The Strategic Quadrangle: Russia, China, Japan, and the United States in East Asia.* Contributions by Michael Mandelbaum, Robert Legvold, David M. Lampton, Mike M. Mochizuki, and Richard H. Solomon. New York: Council on Foreign Relations Press, 1995.

Marr, Andrew. *Ruling Britannia: The Failure and Future of British Democracy.* London: Michael Joseph, 1995.

Newhouse, John. *War and Peace in the Nuclear Age.* New York: Alfred A. Knopf, 1989.

Ohmae, Keniche. *The End of the Nation State: The Rise of Regional Economics.* New York: McKinsey & Co., Inc., 1995.

Pierre, Andrew J., and William B. Quandt. *The Algerian Crisis: Policy Options for the West.* Washington, D.C.: Carnegie Endowment, 1996.

Pond, Elizabeth. *Beyond the Wall: Germany's Road to Unification.* A Twentieth Century Fund Book. Washington, D.C.: The Brookings Institution, 1993.

Porter, Michael E. *The Competitive Advantage of Nations.* New York: The Free Press, 1990.

Putnam, Robert D. *Making Democracy Work: Civic Traditions in Modern Italy.* Princeton: Princeton University Press, 1993.

Reinicke, Wolfgang H. *Deepening the Atlantic: Toward a New Transatlantic Marketplace.* Gutersloh: Bertelsmann Foundation Publishers, 1996.

Renwick, Sir Robin. *Fighting with Allies.* New York: Times Books, 1996.

Rosenberg, Tina. *The Haunted Land: Europe's Ghosts After Communism.* New York: Random House, 1995.

Schmidt, Bernadotte E., and Harold C. Vedeler. *The World in the Crucible: The Rise of Modern Europe.* New York: Harper & Row, 1984.

Schroeder, Paul W. *The Transformation of European Politics, 1763–1848.* Oxford History of Modern Europe. New York: Oxford University Press, 1994.

Stern, Fritz. *Dreams and Delusions: The Drama of German History.* New York: Alfred A. Knopf, 1987.

Taylor, A. J. P. *Bismarck: The Man and the Statesman.* New York: Vintage Books, 1967.

Thomas, Hugh. *Suez.* New York: Harper & Row, 1974.

von Bismarck, Prince Otto. *The Memoirs,* vol. 1 (translated under the supervision of A. J. Butler). Howard Fertig, 1996.

Woodward, Susan L. *Balkan Tragedy.* Washington, D.C.: The Brookings Institution, 1995.

Zimmerman, Warren. *Origins of a Catastrophe.* New York: Times Books, 1996.

INDEX

Index

3 3 9

John Newhouse is the author of six previous books, including *War and Peace in the Nuclear Age* and *The Sporty Game.* Formerly a staff writer for *The New Yorker,* where he covered mainly foreign policy, he is currently a guest scholar at The Brookings Institution and a consultant to the State Department. He lives in Washington, D.C.